Little Girl in Big Pictures

Autobiography of Marilyn Knowlden

Marilyn Knowlden

To my father, Robert E. Knowlden,
for teaching me to keep at it.

To my mother, Bretta McKenzie Knowlden,
for giving me life—and a way of looking at it.

Published in the USA by:
BearManor Media
P O Box 71426
Albany, Georgia 31708
www.bearmanormedia.com

ISBN 978-1-59393-638-9

Printed in the United States of America.

Book and cover design by Darlene Swanson of Van-garde Imagery, Inc.
Copy Editor: David W. Menefee

Contents

Preface

I've had a wonderfully rich life, beginning with my years as a child actress in the1930s, when I performed under outstanding directors, alongside famous stars, and in great motion pictures. In 1993, when I wrote my musical "I'm Gonna Get You in the Movies!" I assured everyone that the show was not based on my life, but only what I'd learned firsthand about Hollywood. However, as I began writing this autobiography, the lyrics to many of my songs just seemed to fit. You'll find them scattered throughout.

—Marilyn Knowlden 2011

Acknowledgements

To my daughter Carolyn, for all her help.

To Richard Goates for his stories and poems.

To my family and friends for moral support.

To film studios Paramount, Fox, RKO, MGM, Warner Bros., Universal, and Monogram for their photographs, all rights reserved.

Part One:

1 Beginnings

How did it all begin? How did I become the little girl in so many movies of the 1930s, including six that were nominated by the Academy of Motion Picture Arts & Sciences for Best Production of the Year? How did my life mirror the early history of the "talkies" themselves? How was my later life affected by my childhood experiences?

Long ago, before there were DVDs, computers, or even television, every Saturday afternoon in America:

> *Let's go to the Movies, see a Saturday matinee.*
> *Let's go to the Movies.*
> *Gee, I wonder what picture's playing*
> *At our favorite theater down the way.*
> *Let's go to the Movies today!*

In the beginning, they were all just *silent* "movies"—pictures that moved—often accompanied by live organ or piano music, but without recorded sound. Then in 1926, Warner Bros. produced *Don Juan*, complete with sound effects and the music of the New York Philharmonic on an accompanying disk. On May 12 of that same year, in an Oakland, California hospital, my mother produced *me*, complete with sound effects and music!

Into loving arms, I arrived!

By 1927, movies with recorded sound were one year old, and so was I. Seeing the lighted candle on my birthday cake, I uttered my favorite phrase, "Oh, Boy!"

Soon after, a strangely dressed woman climbed aboard the streetcar on which my mother and I were riding. The woman's extraordinary outfit included a hat with a tall feather and a straggly mink fur-piece complete with real heads and tails! "Oh Boy!" I exclaimed, to everyone's amusement and my mother's embarrassment.

I loved jumping up and down in my crib to the strong rhythmic beat of "Valencia," played on our tall mahogany Victrola. My mother soon bought several Al Jolson songs to play on that record player,

My cake with one candle.

My favorite expression—
"Oh, Boy!"

for 1927 was the year Warner Bros. released *The Jazz Singer*. The film featured sentimental songs such as "Mammy" that were sung by its star. Plus there were a few synchronized lines of Al Jolson's ad lib dialogue that were recorded on a separate phonograph record, such as "Wait a minute. Wait a minute! You ain't heard nothing yet, folks. Listen to this!"

Me in my crib,
jumping to the beat.

The movie caused a sensation and long lines at box offices, and Harry M. Warner had to eat his previous words, "Who the hell wants to hear actors talk!" Shortly thereafter, that sound-on-disc was replaced by an optical system that printed sound directly on film. Someone wrote the song, "I Can't Sleep in the Movies Any More!" for the era of the "talkies" had begun!

Before long, the Academy of Motion Picture Arts and Sciences held their very first annual celebration. That was before there was such a thing as an "Oscar," a name later given to that prized statuette by Bette Davis, who said its backside reminded her of one of her husbands!

Soon we will be seeing all our favorite movies stars,
Up there on that giant silver screen.
Makes you feel like they are truly real-life friends of ours,
Not just someone in a magazine.

Headlines, headlines: shortly before the Great Stock Market crash of 1929, my father had noticed that the area Grocers Association was having a "Most Beautiful Baby Contest."

When he suggested they enter me in the contest, my mother would have none of it. "To me, our baby is the most beautiful in the world, and I couldn't stand it if she didn't win." My mother eventually relented. I have an early memory of standing on a raised platform with other small children, while a crowd of people looked on. Yes, I won the contest—and was awarded a fifteen-inch-high silver loving cup. When I called out, "Look, Mommy, they gave me a coffee pot!" the crowd roared with laughter! So it was that I made the newspaper headlines at the tender age of two-and-a-half! They read: "BABY CONTEST WINNER LIKES COFFEE POT."

BABY CONTEST WINNER LIKES 'COFFEE POT'

Girl Takes Loving Cup Given as Award to Best Oakland Child, 3, at Food Show of Grocers' Association

Little Marilyn Knowlden, aged 3, daughter of Mr. and Mrs. A. J. Knowlden, 285 Van Buren avenue, today is the possessor of a silver "coffee pot" as the prize three-year-old child of Oakland.

She won the trophy, which really is a loving cup, at the annual food show of the Retail Grocers' association of Alameda county now in progress at the Municipal auditorium by outclassing a score of other children in a baby show competition sponsored by the show management.

"Coffee pot" is her own name for the first prize award, given to her by a committee of judges consisting of Mrs. Grace Coleman, Mrs. H. R. Mathieson and Mrs. Alva McBroom.

Headlines at the age of two-and-one-half!
(Clipping from the *San Francisco Examiner.*)

"Look, Mommy, they gave me a coffee pot!"

To say that my parents welcomed my arrival is an understatement. They had been married five years and had already lost one baby. What's more, my mother lost her own mother when she was only two years old and had no memory of her whatsoever.

Her father, William Alma McKenzie, was on the road a great deal of the time, building the railroad for the Central Pacific in Utah, so my mother and her brother were first sent to live with their aunt and uncle, then their grandparents. When little Bretta was five years old, she and her brother moved back home, for her widowed father had remarried, to a woman who already had one child. My mother was excited about, at long last, having a mother of her own, but before long, the new wife gave birth to five other children, making my mother the oldest girl in a family of ten!

Clothes were washed by being boiled in a copper boiler on top of a wood-burning stove, then scrubbed, rinsed by hand, and hung to dry. Even diapers were ironed! In that era of horse-drawn carriages, cows to be milked, and butter to be churned, the work was endless. My mother's stepmother had a hard time understanding her artistic step-daughter, Bertha (my mother's given name, which she hated with a passion and eventually changed to Bretta). Her freshly ironed blouse and handkerchief were considered a bunch of foolishness out there in rustic pioneer territory. Unintentionally her father never invited my mother on excursions to the bustling railroad camps where he'd taken all his other children. (Perhaps she reminded him too much of the wife he'd lost.) With a wistful look, she would sometimes tell me, "I never knew a mother's love!" I'm sure that my arrival helped to fill that emptiness!

My very special, dear mother spent hours teaching me to sing all kinds of nursery rhymes and reading me stories. My favorites were her improvised "makeup stories," and to her dismay, when she finished telling one, I often pleaded, "Please . . . tell it again!" Because I loved music so, though I was only three, my parents enrolled me in Elsa Gilson's Dancing School. I participated in several recitals, where I danced or did readings.

To this day, I remember the lines to a little skit I was in: "Fairy Queen, under the sun, will you open the door to a woman of one? (It can't be done!)

Fairy Queen under sky of blue, will you open the door to a woman of two? (It's not for you.)

Fairy Queen, under the tree, will you open the door to a woman of three? (It cannot be!)

Fairy Queen, I ask once more, will you open the door to a woman of four??"

And then the door opened!

My dancing teacher, Mrs. Gilson, was always announcing to my family, "Someday I'm going to take Marilyn to Hollywood and get her in the movies!" I never had seen a motion picture, so I wasn't sure what she was talking about, but it sounded nice.

I'm gonna get you in the Movies. It's clear to me that you'll go far.
I'm gonna get you in the Movies – and make you a star!
That little way you tip your chin up, that kind of crinkly way you smile:
People will wait in line to see you – and stand in the aisle! *

(* All the little poems in italics are actually song lyrics with words and music by this memoir's author—Marilyn Knowlden.)

2 Journey to Hollywood

In 1931, my father made a business trip to Hollywood at the wheel of our box-shaped Oldsmobile, and to my great delight, my mother and I went along. My father had apparently been listening closely to Mrs. Gilson, for on the second day he said, "Just for fun, I'm going to call some of the studios."

Already a successful attorney, my father was a very good talker. Without connections of any kind, he managed to speak on the phone to Fred Datig, the Head Casting Director of Paramount Studios, and arranged an appointment for us for that very day. (Considering that said Casting Director had five or six assistants, just being able to meet with him and give him my photograph was something of a triumph.)

Mr. Datig told my father he had a very nice daughter and that it was really too bad I was only four years old.

"We do need an eight-year-old for a large part in a film we're making."

"Well, what's wrong with a four-year-old?"

"Oh, she couldn't memorize all the lines."

"But my little girl is very good at memorizing!" proclaimed my father, handing him a picture of me reciting one of my monologues.

In the Chinese costume I wore in one of my skits.

"Well, I think not, but good luck to you," said Mr. Datig.

And we returned to the friend's place where we were staying.

The next day, there was a phone call from Paramount: "Would it be too much trouble to bring Marilyn in for a screen test tomorrow?" In the early 1930s, glamour and motherhood did not seem to go together, and having a four-year-old daughter, instead of the eight-year-old they'd tentatively cast, sounded much better to Eleanor Boardman, the chosen leading lady for *Women Love Once*. The question was: would a four-year-old be able to memorize the 500 words of dialogue the part called for?

To this day, I remember sitting on one of the grip's black suitcases while my mother taught me my lines for the screen test, just as she'd previously taught me little poems to recite. They told me I would be doing the scene in bed, but when I began taking off my shoes, the director said, "Oh, don't bother taking off your shoes!"

"But my Mommy doesn't let me get in bed with my shoes on!"

Finally, I climbed into bed, shoes and all, and got my first realization that Hollywood was a very weird place!

Not just a town, but more of a dream: that's Hollywood!
Everything more than a little extreme: that's Hollywood!
We know that dreams don't always come true,
But we hang on, for sometimes they do!

Little did my family realize how unusual our Hollywood experience had been so far! I'm not sure that I understood what a screen test was all about. In this case, they wanted to know if I was right for the part and if I could memorize lines and take direction. I must have done okay, for I got the role as Eleanor Boardman and Paul Lukas' daughter. At the request of Paramount, we drove to the Child Welfare Office to get my work permit. They weighed me, tested my eyes, etc., and then gave their approval. We drove off to the studio to deliver it.

On the way to Paramount, disaster struck; the car in which we were riding was smashed into by another automobile! The accident occurred in front of Warner Bros. Vitaphone Studios, where Dolores Costello was shooting a street scene for an early talking picture being shot in front of the studio. (Known as "The Goddess of the Silent Screen, she can also be remembered as the future grandmother of Drew Barrymore.) That beautiful lady was truly my "angel of mercy," taking me inside her dressing room, giving me first aid, and placing soothing cold cloths over my right eye.

My father had a gash on his leg, but my uncomplaining mother had a broken collarbone and three broken ribs, and she had to be taken to the hospital by ambulance. As for me, I had a bump on my cheek and a bruise near my forehead that threatened to turn into a black eye.

So, my mother was in the hospital, my father had to return to Oakland for important legal business, and there was I, with bumps and bruises on my face. Like a movie "cliff-hanger," those moments in a serial where the horse-and-rider fall over a cliff, only to be saved by an overhanging branch — as revealed in the next week's episode—everyone wondered if I would be able to show up the next day for my part!

3 "Lights! Camera! Action!"

Those who work in show biz have just one rule that's certain:
The one excuse for absence is death ringing down the final curtain!
If a case of chicken pox keeps you up 'till dawn,
Dab some makeup on those spots! The show must go on!

The studio makeup man actually did dab some makeup on my spots, when I showed up the next day for work in the company of "Aunt" Cora Bird. She was my mother's lifelong best friend with whom we had been staying. With her beautiful singing voice, Cora had moved to Hollywood herself to get in pictures, had done choral work in a few films, and seemed pleased to take me to the studio. Less than a week after we'd arrived, my life as a Hollywood actress had begun. I know all this sounds like the fanciful plot of a B movie, but this was the way it happened.

Even in 1931, Hollywood was overflowing with children whose mothers had moved there to try to get them in the movies. Paramount was the very first real movie studio, with handsome filigreed wrought-iron gates that would some day be immortalized in the film and musical versions of *Sunset Boulevard*. As we drove through those gates, I was totally unaware how unusual my Hollywood experience had been so far.

STARTS FILM CAREER YOUNG

Marilyn Knowlden

BABE'S 'CAREER' SURVIVES CRASH

Oakland Girl, 4, Chosen for Film Despite Hurts

A bruised cheek and a discolored eye, the result of an automobile accident, almost cost Marilyn Knowlden, 4, blonde Oakland girl, her chance to star in a Hollywood motion picture production.

The story of the child's unexpected selection to play a juvenile lead and of her injury in an automobile accident as she was being taken to the Paramount studios to complete details of her engagement were told yesterday by her father, Robert E. Knowlden, Oakland attorney living at 285 Van Buren street.

Knowlden, his wife and their daughter were visiting friends in Hollywood when the child attracted the attention of Fred Datig, Paramount casting director who was seeking a child to play the part of Janet in the film version of "Daddy's Gone A'Hunting."

As the Knowldens were driving to the studio the automobile in which they were riding collided with another machine. Mrs. Knowlden suffered a fractured collar bone and was removed to a hospital. It was at first believed that Marilyn had escaped uninjured, but when she arrived at the studio a red blotch appeared on her cheek and faint discoloration showed around her right eye. It was not until the day that first "shots" were taken of the production that the youngster recovered sufficiently to assure directors that she could be used for the part.

Clipping from the *San Francisco Chronicle* **about our accident**

I was slated to work in *Women Love Once* (1931). I had no sense of the expertise of director Edward Goodman, the fame of future Oscar-winner Paul Lukas who would play my father, nor of the past experience of the Broadway stage actress, Eleanor Boardman, who would play my mother. All I could think of was my own mother in the hospital and was she going to be all right!

Having a heart-to-heart talk with my screen "mother," Eleanor Boardman.
(Photo courtesy of Paramount Pictures.)

I must have been more upset than anyone realized, for I chose to experiment with a pair of scissors and cut a piece out of the front of my hair! Happily, my black eye failed to materialize, most of the time the hairdressers were able to disguise my hair, with its missing chunk, and my mother soon recovered enough to accompany me to the studio herself. What a relief, to have her back with me and be able to share everything with her. It was also nice to have her there in the evening to teach me my lines just before I went to sleep.

Women Love Once

For me, acting in a movie was sort of like being in one of my dance recital skits, except that the visible audience was Paramount's much smaller film crew. I didn't know that the talkies were something new; yet only a year or so earlier the problem of camera noise had been solved by having the cameraman sit, with his movie camera, inside a too-small and very hot padded box. By 1931, the camera was still padded in something called a "blimp," but the cameraman himself was not inside. Moreover, instead of being hidden onstage in perhaps a flowerpot, microphones were readily movable, thanks to a kind of crane called a "boom."

Film editing is complicated by the fact that the sound runs twenty frames ahead of the picture, and I was fascinated by that black-and-white board with a hinged "clapper" at the top whose snapping sound assists the movie editor in post-production matching of sound and picture. (Of course, today's clapper-boards are usually electronic. And videotaping produces an immediate synchronization of sound and picture.) Certainly, I was unaware that

In a scene with my new "father," Paul Lukas.
(Photo courtesy of Paramount Pictures.)

just three years earlier, Paramount Studios had moved to brand-new quarters and switched exclusively to movies with sound.

I not only had 500 words of dialogue in *Women Love Once,* I also was in thirty different scenes. (My father counted every one.) As a little four-year-old girl, I was an "Alice" dropped into a giant Wonderland with incredibly thick soundproofed walls, huge tall doors, and a loud bell that sounded when things were about to happen. There were the strange rooms without ceilings, but with overhead walkways where mysterious figures endlessly adjusted and put what looked like colored cellophane in front of lights of all shapes and sizes. There was the gentleman who liked to thrust a measuring tape next to my face, as well as the strange creature with circles over his ears, who turned impressive looking dials on a box in front of him, always assisted by the man who held a long pole with a round thing at the end of it over our heads.

Supervising all this was the Big Boss, as powerful as any Queen of Hearts, who sometimes placed next to my face a small box with a moving needle, which he wore on a cord around his neck. In that topsy-turvy world, the scenes we were acting out seemed in no particular order, the last coming first and the first perhaps coming last, and assistants were constantly using combs, powder puffs, and even lipstick on not only the women, but the men.

There were the huge painted backdrops that made indoors look like outdoors. There were artificial flowers, trees, and snowflakes. There was a large steamship prop, sitting on dry land and most of which was actually missing, and then the streets were full of solid looking buildings, but their doorways opened to nowhere. Yes, I was truly an Alice in Movie Wonderland!

Women Love Once was taken from Zoe Akins' play, *Daddy's*

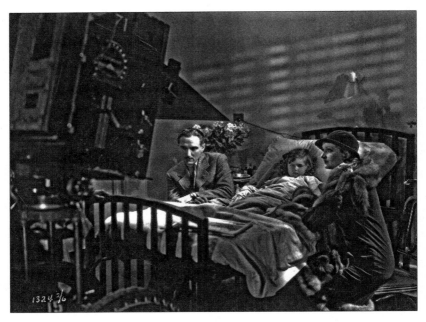

My "deathbed" scene with Paul Lukas and Eleanor Boardman.

Gone A-Hunting. The nursery rhyme goes: "Bye baby bunting. Daddy's gone a hunting, to get a little rabbit-skin to wrap the baby-bunting in!" In the story, the wife of a commercial artist offers to support the family as a seamstress while her husband studies art in Europe, courtesy of an attractive female mentor, all of this resulting in the breakup of the marriage. Toward the end of the film, I run down the street after my "mother" and am supposedly hit by an automobile, after which my estranged "parents" are reunited in the hospital at my "deathbed." (As part of the plot, I had to trip myself for that scene, but the prop man placed a nice padded quilt for me to fall on—and happily, I never was actually filmed in the same shot with the automobile that supposedly hit me.) It is also the first film I ever remember seeing, and I was certainly moved by my "deathbed" scene with my estranged "parents." Never having had to deal with death before, I left the theater quite disturbed, saying, "But, Mommy, I died!"

Mr. Goodman, a director fresh from Broadway, was extremely nice to me and my mother and invited us several times to his classic Malibu beach-home, where I splashed in the ocean and first tasted its salt water. He also arranged for various people to visit our set to meet me, such as Jackie Searle and Mitzi Green, teenage actors under contract to Paramount.

Monkey Business

The set of *Monkey Business* was even more fun. Mr. Goodman took me and my mother over to the soundstage where the four zany Marx Brothers were shooting *Monkey Business*. Formerly filming in New York, this was their very first Hollywood movie—and the last one that would include their rather bland brother, Zeppo.

Wearing his signature glasses, fake eyebrows, and painted-on mustache, Groucho Marx seemed much like W. C. Fields who, when asked how he liked children, answered *"Parboiled!"* Harpo, wearing his curly-haired blond wig and honking his bicycle horn, silently clowned around with me. Then, he performed an exciting glissando on his harp, (a glide from one musical pitch to another) making a beautiful swirling sound as he dragged his fingers along the full length of his harp. However, I particularly loved creative Chico, the pianist of the group, who sat me on the bench beside him and gave me a private performance of his favorite comic piano routine. This included his famous *"Shooting the Keys,"* where he lifted his left hand high in the air, crossed his left hand over his right, and then slammed one of the keys with his index finger. He even showed me a couple of notes to play so that we were able to perform a duet together—such heady stuff for a four-year-old. However, I didn't realize I was meeting famous people; I just enjoyed them!

In one of the movie's scenes, the script called for me to toss a coin to a street organ-grinder's tiny trained monkey, which the monkey then would catch and deliver to his master. My skill as a pitcher was regrettably worse than poor, so for the long shot, property man Lew Asher threw coins from a third story window to the brim of the hat of the organ grinder, successfully landing one out of three. (Heaven knows how many tosses it would have taken me to throw it to the right spot.) Through what was very innovative editing for the time, the final film showed a close-up of me throwing the coin up in the air, followed by a long shot of the coin sailing through the air near the cleverly costumed monkey, and then ending with a close-up of the monkey catching it!

Being in the Movies

On the set, I was only allowed by law to work a few hours a day, and I had to have two people looking out for my welfare—my mother or guardian, plus a welfare worker or tutor. Many of the silent stars, notably John Gilbert, were having big vocal problems switching to the talkies, for beautiful silent stars didn't necessarily have beautiful voices and often fell by the wayside for the lack of a good stage voice. In those early days of recorded sound, Broadway actresses such as Eleanor Boardman were at a premium, for women's voices often sounded squeaky, and children's voices were a special problem. The soundmen told my mother that my unusually low-pitched voice recorded well.

May 12, 1931, the last day of filming, was to be my fifth birthday. A week ahead of time, Mr. Goodman asked me, "Marilyn, what would you like for your birthday?"

Apparently already under the influence of Hollywood, I thought for a moment and answered, "I'd love a swimming pool!"

Mr. Goodman recovered his composure, and then asked me if there was anything else I wanted.

I replied, "Oh, just make it a surprise!"

The day of my birthday, Mr. Goodman told me he was giving me a special birthday party at the commissary (the studio restaurant) and that I could invite anyone I wanted. He also added, "And, Marilyn, I have that swimming pool for you!"

Was I excited! Until my mother finally called a halt, I invited around thirty people, including lots of prop men, cameramen, grips, sound engineers, and electricians (the latter including the crew's "gaffer" and "best boy)." Everyone came, including Mitzi Green and Jackie Searle, who came because they were invited by the studio. Again, I didn't realize they were famous teenage actors.

Mr. Goodman told my mother and me that he would have his chauffeur drive us home in his large black limousine, followed by a truck that would deliver my swimming pool. In that time before plastic, my swimming pool turned out to be a large square rubberized-canvas wading pool supported by a wooden frame. I used it for years, and never saw another one like it. For a while, I even had a pet duck that swam in it.

Right away Paramount Studios arranged for me to go on a personal appearance tour. In that time of the Great Depression, bank failures, unemployment, business closures, and even suicides were

The Birthday party given me by Director Goodman, with guests
Mitzi Green, Jackie Searle, and about twenty others I had invited.
(Photo courtesy of Paramount Pictures.)

all too common. "Talkies" were all the rage, and admission was only
5¢ to 15¢ a ticket. Movies were something to take people's minds off
their troubles in those days before computers, mobile phones, video
games, CDs, television, VCRs, and DVDs. Movies were sometimes
accompanied by live entertainment consisting of dancers, comedi-
ans, or whatever, the final remnants of vaudeville. That was exactly

With the poster in front of the theater, my mother standing nearby.

the case when *Women Love Once* opened in my hometown at the Fox Oakland, and I was part of that live entertainment.

Just five years old, in what would be the very last year of vaudeville acts accompanying a movie, I appeared on stage all by myself in the second largest theater in Northern California. With my hair piled high on my head and wearing an oversize dress and a large lady's hat, I pushed a baby carriage full of dolls while singing a little song and reciting the poem, "My Family." My closing lines were,

With my onstage "family," the one that almost made "my hair turn gray!"

"Sometimes I think that my hair will turn gray. But still I love my family. I wouldn't give one away!"

I wasn't nervous; I had been appearing in public all my short life. My parents also helped by never making the mistake of asking me, "Are you nervous, Marilyn?"

Because I was a "hometown girl making good," the Mayor of Oakland presented me with the Key to the City—a gold-colored cardboard cutout. Yes, I know that Gertrude Stein said of my birthplace, "The trouble with Oakland is that when you get there, there isn't any *there* there!" A few years ago, Oakland proved her wrong by erecting a huge abstract sculpture in the city square entitled "There!"

The trade paper reviewers were critical of our film, but kind to me. The *Hollywood Herald* said, "Marilyn Knowlden, appearing for the first time on the screen, 'stole the picture,' according to comments made after the showing," while the *Hollywood Reporter* stated, "Little Marilyn Knowlden deserves special mention for her appealing portrayal of the child."

They had given me the star's dressing room, and on opening night, in true Hollywood style, I was presented with large baskets full of colorful gladiolus flowers. My parents were afraid I would get conceited from all that, so they drove us around to the back of the theater so I wouldn't see my name in lights—a fact that I only learned a full half-century later. Of course, I couldn't escape the applause of a live audience, but I was just concentrating on the job I had to do.

Billboard promoting our movie and my personal appearance.

My name in lights —at such a tender age.

And so while others toil and labor
In drug stores or at the Five and Dime,
You'll live a life that's full of glamour
And have yourself a wonderful time!

4 One Thing Leads to Another

Cisco Kid

In 1931, while I was appearing onstage at the Fox Oakland, we received an exciting telegram from Fox Studios. They wanted me for a part in *Cisco Kid,* a movie to star Warner Baxter. (The very first Academy Awards ceremony had been held in 1929, just four days after my third birthday, and Warner Baxter had won the Best Actor award for *Old Arizona*, portraying the dashing Cisco Kid.)

Doing my own stunt—at age five! (Photo courtesy of Fox Studios.)

Reconciliation time for Warner Baxter and Edmund Lowe—over my prostrate body. (Photo courtesy of Fox Studios.)

I had been run over by a car in *Women Love Once.* I guess it was type-casting, for I was now scheduled to be run over by a horse! I was to scoot in front of a large gate, trying to stop the Cisco Kid from leaving the ranch, while his horse supposedly jumps over both me and the gate.

In a scene reminiscent of my first movie, enemies Baxter and Edmund Lowe are then reconciled over my prostrate form. To say that my mother was nervous about that gate scene is putting it mildly, but they assured her that the horse running toward me was a non-jumping horse. At the last moment, as that horse screeched to a halt, I was replaced by a cloth dummy, and a jumping horse was substituted for the rest of the scene. In other words, at the tender age of five, I was performing my own stunts!

The *Hollywood Reporter*'s review stated, "There is a clever baby in the cast, essential to the plot, who almost steals the show." (Children and animals are routinely feared by adult fellow actors for their natural scene-stealing abilities.)

My parents had been advised to skip acting lessons for me, probably since most acting teachers of the time taught the exaggerated style of acting favored in silent movies. Besides, acting was natural to me, like dolls or playing house.

At the red-carpet premiere of the picture at Grauman's Chinese Theatre in Hollywood, I was called on stage to receive a full fourteen dozen roses in a little red wheelbarrow. I have to admit, I was the most thrilled by the wheelbarrow—and in the theater's courtyard. I loved putting my hands and feet into the foot and handprints previously left there in wet cement by people like Mary Pickford.

> *My hand fits in this very space.*
> *This footprint could be mine.*
> *I must belong here in this place.*
> *It has to be a sign!*

Husband's Holiday

In no time at all, I was hired for another film at Paramount, *Husband's Holiday*, where I was to play the daughter of Vivienne Osborne and Clive Brook, and the "older" sister of Dickie Moore. Dickie was actually a year older than I, but he looked much younger. Contrary to the usual Hollywood scheme of things, I did *not* look young for my age, and I was just average in height, rather than unusually short.

It was about that time that I decided why some people were

Another movie, another new "mother," Vivienne Osborne, and
new "brother" Dickie Moore. (Photo courtesy of Paramount Pictures.)

telling my parents I was pretty. I knew the secret: my mother put my hair up in doubled kid curlers (a bit of wire topped by cotton padding, covered with kid leather) and skillfully fixed my hair. Also, she sewed most of my dresses, and they were beautiful. No fussy ruffles or anything—just simple and beautiful.

Dickie and I just loved the scene where we "played horsey," the

Fun for Dickie & me. Not much fun for Clive Brook.
(Photo courtesy of Paramount Pictures)

**Another chance to touch a piano. With Dickie and Charles Winninger.
(Photo courtesy of Paramount Pictures)**

two of us riding on Clive Brook's back as he crawled on all fours. I'm afraid by the time we were through filming for the day, the poor man was worn out!

No one bothered to explain to me the plot for *Husband's Holiday*. That was just as well, for I gather the story was about another philandering husband!

Little did I realize the conflicts my budding Hollywood career must have presented to my father, Robert E. Knowlden. He had received his Doctor of Jurisprudence degree from the University of California at Berkeley in 1925 and was the first in his class to open

Vivienne Osborne struggling to protect her two screen children, Dickie Moore and Marilyn Knowlden. (Photo courtesy of Paramount Pictures.)

a law office. Considering the difficulty of conducting his business long distance, he could have insisted we remain in Oakland. Instead, we moved to Hollywood and rented a one-bedroom apartment on Canyon Drive, with a wonderful pull-down Murphy bed in the living room.

> *Hollywood's where there's sun and no snow. It's right for me.*
> *Hollywood's where you stay on the go and feel so free!*
> *So much that seems exciting and new;*
> *So many roads just waiting for you;*
> *So much to see and do, that's Hollywood!*

In 1931, Hollywood was a pleasant little town to live in, one where children could safely walk to school. The three-story Hollywood Hotel was charming, and the imposing Chinese, Egyptian, Warner Bros, and Pantages theaters on Hollywood Boulevard were the setting for many fabulous premieres. Likely to be found on Hollywood Boulevard were my old friends the organ grinder and his monkey that I'd met in *Women Love Once,* plus my friend Angelo, the incredibly small dwarf, who was a perennial newspaper salesman in front of the Warner Bros. Theatre.

Eager souvenir merchants sold miniature replicas of orange crates to visiting tourists, for immediately surrounding Hollywood were acres of sweet-smelling orange trees and fields of mustard and strawberries. On nearby hills was the real estate developers' Hollywoodland sign (later to be shortened to" Hollywood"),

That was a time when visitors just might see movie stars strolling down Hollywood Boulevard—without any paparazzi in sight. Joining the automobiles were the Red Car electric trolleys, complete with tracks and an overhead electrical line. One might also see an occasional ice wagon or milk truck pulled by a horse. Pitchmen hawked maps revealing the locations of movie stars' homes, plus limousines that would take visitors on guided tours. Signs advertised cheap lots in nearby Bel Air and other neighboring suburbs, sold by mercenary con-men who never dreamed of the multi-millions of dollars those properties would one day be worth!

5 Hollywood Education— with Greta Garbo

Susan Lenox

One exceptional teacher I had in 1931 was Greta Garbo, who played my private tutor in *Susan Lenox*. She was the shy, glamorous, reclusive actress famous for not allowing interviews, as well as her favorite catch-phrase, "I *vant* to be alone!" Just the year before, she had made her first talking picture, *Anna Christie*, which MGM advertised with the phrase, "Garbo Talks!" the film earned a million dollars for the studio, a huge amount for those times. Greta Garbo was MGM's top star of the 1930s, appearing in such films as *Anna Karenina* and Academy Award-winning *Grand Hotel*. At her insistence, no visitors were allowed on our set, and when someone knocked on her dressing room door, she just might say, "Not in!"

Susan Lenox gave me the chance to meet Miss Garbo's newcomer co-star, Clark Gable. (I thought he looked a lot like my father, except that he had big ears.) Miss Garbo was probably the first woman I ever saw wearing slacks. Ladies in the 1930s always wore dresses or blouses with skirts. Sad to say, to my dismay, they also wore uncomfortable corsets or ugly garter belts to hold up their silk stockings (no nylons or pantyhose yet, and no jeans for women).

To this day, I can hear her saying in her deep-voiced, Swedish accent, "Italy is shaped like a boot!" That was when I learned that important basic geography lesson. She warned me, "In Hollywood, don't count on anything!" and she was right. *Susan Lenox* must have proven too long for prime time, for when I recently viewed that film, my scene with my exceptional teacher was nowhere to be found!

My other exceptional teacher was my mother. Now that I was five, I begged her to teach me how to read. Before her marriage, my mother had taught first grade in the Manti School System in Utah. Because they paid teachers according to a grading system, she was paid more than many high school teachers of her time. I remember her cutting out letters and words from trade magazines and teaching me in her own expert way, using the phonetic method. When I finally entered school, I was quite a reader. In fact, Miss Howe, my kindergarten teacher, would often divide the class and let me read to half of the students while she read to the other half.

I'll never forget the day I went to see the sensational horror movie, *Frankenstein*. Too scary for me, I ended up seeking the peaceful luxury of the Pantages Theatre basement, its aptly-named "restroom" filled with comfortable overstuffed lounge chairs.

The Conquerors

In 1932, two young children were cast as the children of Richard Dix and Ann Harding for RKO's coming saga, *The Conquerors*. The kids were both blonds, so the little boy's hair was dyed brown to make him look like his screen father. When filming began, Director William Wellman became increasingly irritated with the young girl, who was probably the product of too many elocution lessons—or else perhaps coached to look "cute." He finally told the Assistant Director, "Get me a child who acts like a child!" Shooting stopped for a short time while a replacement was found, and I was that replacement.

Little Wally Albright had already had his blond hair dyed brown to make him resemble his screen father—dark-haired Richard Dix. The studio then insisted that my naturally auburn hair be *bleached*, to make me resemble my screen mother, very blond Ann Harding. One child's hair bleached, the other dyed. Yes, Hollywood can seem a little weird at times!

When the mother of the original young girl learned that her daughter had been replaced, she reacted like a mother lioness. That true "Stage Mother" spread the rumor that the reason for the replacement was that my father had a lawsuit against the studio, which he would agree to drop if I were put in the movie. The powers-that-be did not take kindly to the totally false story, especially the Assistant Director:

I'd rather face a saber-tooth tiger than a child actor's angry mother!
My idea of hell is a place filled with nothing but Stage Mothers!
I do not do well when I dwell in the presence of Stage Mothers.
Don't think my employment is cushy,
Considering I deal with pushy,
Demanding and grating and infuriating Stage Mothers!

In all my bad dreams, I fight off the mad schemes of those Stage Mothers!
In nightmares I dare to pull out all the hair of those Stage Mothers!
Their children don't have half a chance
Unless they can act, sing and dance.
In dreams I discover, then slowly I smother those Stage Mothers!

With my newly bleached hair and new straw hat.

Produced by David O. Selznick of future *Gone With the Wind* fame and directed by William Wellman, *The Conquerors* was an early example of an epic Hollywood talkie, and told the story of the building of the railroad to the West (of which my own Grandfather McKenzie was an important part). Wellman utilized many effective montages, and his skill as a director is evident in the film's dramatic scene of a train hitting a horse-drawn carriage that carries an old man and a little boy—remarkable by any standard.

Some of the outdoor scenes called for an ancient still-operating steam locomotive, surrounded by empty plains, all of which necessitated our shooting "on location" and traveling to Victorville, California. In those long-ago days, there wasn't much of anything in Victorville, and certainly no hotels. Consequently, we not only

A railroad handcar is used as a platform for the camera crew's unusual setup, William Wellman, center, directing. (Photo courtesy of RKO Studios.)

traveled to Victorville by train, we ate our meals in its dining car, and slept in its Pullman cars. Of course, I loved it all, especially the upper berth that folded into the ceiling.

The charming outfits prepared for me by the wardrobe department included an old-fashioned straw hat, a long-waisted dress, and an item I'll never forget—a pair of custom-made, high-topped, very narrow-toed Victorian shoes. But problems arose when it was time for me to get dressed for the first day of shooting. The intense heat of Victorville had swollen my feet to the point that my custom-made shoes no longer fit! My mother was really upset. "Marilyn, what can we do?" There were certainly no shoe repair shops anywhere to be found, in fact, no stores of any kind. My mother

Guy Kibbee hugs Wally Albright and Marilyn Knowlden—with her newly bleached hair and wearing those painful shoes! (Photo courtesy of RKO Studios.)

made a bargain with me: If I could tolerate those too-tight shoes, she'd buy me a beautiful baby-doll upon our return to Hollywood. I accepted the deal, and the show went on.

Two things are true, as sure as the dawn:
The mail must go through, and the show must go on!
If your puppy eats your script and all your lines are gone,
Better plan a few ad-libs. The show must go on.
If you lose your car-keys and they're somewhere in the lawn,
Better plan on walking there! The show must go on!

As soon as we got home, we made a quick trip to the department store to buy me my wonderful baby-doll "Tousle-Head."

Chatting with Bill Boyd, of future Hopalong Cassidy fame.
(Photo courtesy of RKO Studios.)

Helen Mack admiring my new baby doll. (Photo courtesy of RKO Studios.)

(Her hair was real lamb's wool fur.) I returned to RKO to have my hair dyed back to its natural color and enjoyed showing off my new doll to the various actors to whom I was introduced, such as Helen Mack, William Gargan, future TV refrigerator demonstrator Betty Furness, and *Hopalong Cassidy's* Bill Boyd.

My mother often asked me, before I started a film, whether I was sure I wanted to do this. For me, that was like asking if I'd just as soon skip Christmas this year! However, I do remember one horrible experience I had when I was very little. Without telling me what was going on, the director of a screen test asked my mother to leave the set and go to an adjoining soundstage. He then tried to see if he could make me cry by telling me my mother was angry with me and had left me. Of course, I never believed the director, and the whole thing was a disaster! You can bet that, from then on, my mother stayed nearby. All this, of course, was similar to when they tried to make Jackie Cooper cry by telling him his dog was about to be shot.

> *For a little girl in a grownup world,*
> *There're lots of unwritten rules,*
> *And you learn that it is wise to be careful*
> *Of gossips—and phonies—and fools!*

6 My "Daughter" Clara Bow and Other Pioneers

Call Her Savage

Now, the 1930's equivalent of Marilyn Monroe was Clara Bow, a favorite silent screen star, who was popularly advertised as "The It Girl." In the 1932 Fox talkies film, *Call Her Savage,* as a five-year-old, believe it or not, I next played her *mother*—in the role of a pioneer girl crossing the plains. (In retrospect, I think I did look quite a bit like the lady.) In the process of making that movie, I gained a lot of empathy for my very my own ancestors. I soon learned what they had gone through when I discovered how uncomfortable it was, riding in a real covered wagon.

Some of my ancestors not only rode in a covered wagon, some were among the Mormon pioneer groups who *walked* 1,300 miles across the country, pushing their handcarts. My father's relatives were actually in the famous—but unfortunate—Martin Handcart Company that got stranded in an early snowstorm, traveling from Missouri to Salt Lake City in 1856. Of the original 576 in the Martin Company, 145 perished from exposure to the 11° Fahrenheit weather, starvation, or the many other perils of the journey. Sadly, though my father's ancestors, the Twelves Family, had six children (ages 13, 11, 7, 6, 3, and 2) when they began their journey, they had only three when they arrived.

Now coincidently, my *mother's* grandfather was one of "Brigham's Boys," young men who were dispatched by Brigham Young to rescue the stranded pioneers. Amazingly, the family of John Twelves, the eleven-year-old who would become my father's great-grandfather, was rescued by nineteen-year-old George McKenzie, who would become my mother's grandfather! (Just one of many extraordinary coincidences that I marvel at that has affected my life!) I think I must have inherited his genes, for my great-grandfather's hobbies were poetry and song-writing, and his mother was a leading-lady type actress. Some time after 1856, he wrote a poem giving an *eyewitness* account of that rescue:

> . . . *Next the Hand-cart emigration, caught by the wintry storms*
> *Two hundred miles from rescue and our Rocky Mountain home.*
> *They were starving, they were dying, their hope and strength had fled,*
> *And the grey wolves of the mountain standing sentinel over their dead.*

> *Then our Great Chief sent word to rally, that a rescue must be made;*
> *To take all of the best horses and form a light brigade;*
> *Load up with food and raiment, bring shawls and dresses warm;*
> *For to dig through the mountain snow-drifts great trials must be borne.*
> *Then at the call to rescue forth went the light brigade*
> *With courage like those others that filled a soldier's grave.*

They dug through the mountain snow-drifts
And crossed the snow-clad land
To the sorrowful camp at the end of the tramp
Of the starving Hand-cart band.

The scenes of that rescue never can be told
The weak and the weary, the young and the old
Down on their knees; the prayers that were said
To their father in heaven and that grand light brigade
That brought hope, food and raiment, and for all sorrows laid.

Well, we rescued all the living and gave burial to the dead;
Then from home across the mountains that grand retreat was made.
Again we dug the snow-drifts and crossed the snow-clad land.
Then down to Salt Lake City we brought that Hand-cart band.

Then the shouting of the people, as they cheered the light brigade
That had crossed the snowy mountains and the rescue they had made.
Then a hush fell on the people, as our chief stepped forth and said:
"Nobly done! You grand young heroes;
With all honors you shall be paid."

George McKenzie (1836-1915) c1856

In *Little Women*, I'm one of the King children, with my teacher Frances Dee. (Photo courtesy of RKO Studios.)

7 "Little Women" and Other Fascinating Folks

In 1932, George Cukor cast me as Mary King in the RKO film, *Little Women*. It was only a small part, but it was anything but a small picture. I was able to meet several lovely ladies: Frances Dee (my teacher in the film), and the beautiful Joan Bennett. The third "Little Woman" was charismatic Katharine Hepburn, with whom I would later film two other movies.

Most important, this film introduced me to George Cukor, the man who would one day win an Academy Award for Best Director for *My Fair Lady* with Audrey Hepburn. His *Little Women* was the year's top money-maker, and the Motion Picture Academy nominated it for Best Production of the Year. No, it didn't win the big award, (edged out by *Cavalcade)* but in Hollywood, it's considered a real prize to come that close. Of course, at my young age, Academy Awards meant absolutely nothing to me.

I was then attending my public Cherimoya School where, as needed, my regular teacher would suggest what my on-set studio tutor should be teaching me, at the card-table that would serve as my studio "school-room." By state law, I was required to have three hours of school—to be worked in all at once or in-between scenes as convenient, plus one hour of "recreation" (including time for

Touring the RKO lot with Frances Dee. (Photo courtesy of RKO Studios.)

lunch). I was then permitted to work four hours before the camera, all together or spread throughout the day. My schoolwork never seemed to suffer. However, since I only "free-lanced" as an actor, that tutoring arrangement was not a year-round setup for me, unlike those children who were under studio contract and never attended public school. I think that single fact helped keep my life reasonably normal.

Morning Glory

A little later in the year, Director Lowell Sherman cast me in *Morning Glory*, for which Katharine Hepburn would later win an Academy Award for Best Actress. I had a fun part in the film's prologue, where I was a fussily-dressed aspiring child actress in a casting office. (My white fur coat and ermine muff were so soft!)

Unfortunately, somewhere along the line, a balcony scene between Douglas Fairbanks, Jr. and Katharine Hepburn was cut from the show, along with the *entire* prologue. Sadly, I became "the face on the cutting room floor," and *Morning Glory,* which brought Katharine Hepburn an Oscar, became my "Sunset Disappointment."

Once again, I was reminded not to "count your chickens before they're hatched!" Instead of anxiously waiting for the phone to ring, my parents taught me not to talk about—or even think much about—a part for which I was being considered. That way, it was just a nice surprise if I got the part. It was also unwise to broadcast the fact that such a part was available because someone else might go after it!

There followed lots of interviews and quite a few screen tests.

Showing my new fur outfit to *Morning Glory's* Director Lowell Sherman.
(Photo courtesy of RKO Studios.)

Of course, in that time before the invention of videotape, those tests were a very costly way to audition actors, as they involved expensive 35-millimeter film, a director, cameraman, light and sound technicians, and, perhaps, other actors. Mostly, I was cast in a movie because the powers-that-be had seen one of my previous films.

As for acting itself, there were no lessons. Acting seemed natural to me; I just pretended I was someone else. However, film acting can be quite tricky—continuity-wise—since scenes are shot according to the logistics involved, not the storyline. All scenes in the same location or with the same actor are filmed grouped together, and a close-up can be a very isolated affair, with nothing leading up to it to get us in the proper mood. Plus, our cues just might be read by the "script girl," not necessarily spoken by the person actually with us in the scene. Another thing that particularly drives some stage actors crazy is the endless waiting between "takes" that often occurs. Possibly a scene only takes a minute or so to shoot, followed by perhaps an hour for a changed lighting setup. I witnessed several tantrums by former Broadway actors who were new to the movies and thoroughly annoyed by those endless waits between takes.

By then, I was learning many new things, such as not looking directly at the camera, "hitting my mark" (a tape or chalk mark on the floor) without looking at my feet, "cheating" with my eyes (in a profile situation, looking slightly in the direction of the camera, rather than directly at someone), plus resisting my instinct to turn away from light in my eyes—and instead welcoming the warmth of the lights upon my face.

I also was becoming adjusted to the "hurry up and wait" aspect of movie-making, the endless time spent between scenes adjusting the lights, props, sound, costumes, makeup, hairstyles, and camera angles, not to mention the time the director spent working with his actors. There was also the continuity angle, which the director had to cover by consultation with the script girl, so that visual clues would be coordinated from one scene to the next. (No dirty blouse at the beginning of a scene and clean at the end of it.)

We had a particularly merry Christmas at the end of 1932, on December 22 to be exact, when I rode with Santa Claus and Bernice Foley down Hollywood's Santa Claus Lane in the second year the Hollywood Christmas Parade was held. (I remember that I was wearing a bright red snowsuit with a red aviator hat.) Another year, I rode down that same Christmas tree-lined Hollywood Boulevard in the company of Robert Cummings and Santa himself! The Santa Claus float at the end of the Christmas parade was a huge thing consisting of Santa's sleigh plus eight plaster-of-Paris reindeer pulling it. There was no "Rudolph the Red-Nosed Reindeer" because he hadn't yet been added to Santa's team, since the story of Rudolph was yet to be written. Nowadays, Santa has his nine reindeer, but rides alone in his sleigh down Hollywood Boulevard—probably to avoid jealousy among actors— but I was always privileged to ride in his sleigh, right along with Santa.

It was fun meeting all the people who were to ride in the parade. I remember how I enjoyed meeting Leo Carillo, who was riding on horseback (and who would someday play Cisco Kid's sidekick Pancho on television.) When I produced my autograph book, Mr. Carillo enriched it by drawing a fine self-portrait. (In 2009, I visited Carlsbad's Leo Carillo Ranch Historic Park, and I discovered that they had nothing similar on display.)

Santa Claus always did pay a visit to our home, even one with-

Leo Carillo's entry in my autograph book—his own self-portrait.

out a chimney, and even after I was far too "old" for such a visit. Each Christmas, I was asked to figure out the one thing I hoped Santa would bring me. One year, I received a tricycle, another bicycle, and still another Erector Set (with a motor) that was my heart's desire. (Eventually, I built a working Ferris wheel with it, and, oh yes, I still own it!) I can imagine how my parents must have struggled in 1934 when Santa brought me the twenty-volume Book of Knowledge encyclopedia set I passionately desired and which I eventually read, more-or-less, cover-to-cover. (The Book of Knowledge was arranged so that each volume covered a variety of approaches: stories, science, history, etc.)

My mother enjoyed telling me of her childhood Christmases in Springville, Utah, when her family rode through the snow in a horse-drawn sleigh. She said she, her brothers, and her sisters each routinely received a single orange for Christmas—nothing more, or of course the threat of only a lump of coal if they were not "good children." Nevertheless, my mother spoke fondly of those bygone days. She also spoke of how amazed they all were each Christmas morning when a decorated tree magically appeared in their sitting room.

Culbertson Featurette

In the 1930s, after people did their household chores, we spent our evenings with conversation, singing, playing musical instruments, needlework, puzzles, reading books, listening to the phonograph, or listening to the radio—preferably on something other than one of those non-electric crystal radio sets. (Crystal radios consisted of a piece of crystal, a wire whose length determined the frequency picked up, and a pair of earphones, all of which left a lot to be desired.) I was a great fan of the *Orphan Annie* and *Dick Tracy* shows. I saved my Ovaltine labels and sent for my official Ovaltine Shaker and special badge with a built-in alphabet decoder. Exciting secret messages were broadcast over the radio, which I could translate with the help of my official decoder.

We also played games. For adults, the popular one of the time was Contract Bridge, with a gentleman named Ely Culbertson as its most famous proponent (the Charles Goren of his day). In 1933, I was hired to film a short subject with Mr. Culbertson. When I was introduced to him on the set, they seated me at a table that held a deck of cards. I asked Mr. Culbertson if he knew how to play "Steal the Pile."

He said, "No. Please teach me!"

So, to his great amusement, I'm sure, this six-and-a-half-year-old spent the next ten minutes teaching the great card expert how to play my own favorite card game.

I remember one earth-shaking event that happened in 1933. On March 10 at 6:54 p.m., a 6.4 earthquake

HOLLYWOOD HERALD

)W'VE YOU

SHOWING HIM HOW. Little Marilyn Knowlden, 6-year-old starlet, who appeared in "The onquerors" and "Call Her Savage," shows the famous Ely Culbertson a new wrinkle in cards. She is teaching him how to play the game of "Steal the Pile." She appears in the Radio Culbertson bridge shorts.

I was really teaching Ely Culbertson the game of "Steal the Pile."

hit Southern California! Centered in the Long Beach area, it was altogether too close to where we lived. At the time, I was suffering from the flu and was probably slightly delirious when the chandelier in our living room began swinging wildly. My father lifted me out of my Murphy bed and carried me outside, and I honestly believed that the world was coming to an end!

A few days later, we drove to Long Beach and saw whole sides of buildings torn away. Lots of area stores and schools had to be rebuilt. In fact, even today, Southern California is still rebuilding from that earthquake, but at least, the world hadn't actually come to an end.

Snickerty Nick and the Giant

In 1933, I went around singing "Who's Afraid of the Big Bad Wolf?" for Walt Disney had just produced the Technicolor short, *Three Little Pigs,* which used an innovative three-color process. Of course, that was the first time I had seen a color movie, for all films at that time were strictly black-and-white.

Later in the year, I met a most interesting, wealthy widow named Julia Ellsworth Ford. That lady, loaded with money from her late husband, decided to put her many dollars to a fun use. Her hobby was writing—particularly children's stories and plays. And so she spent quite a lot of money having those plays professionally produced and then later made into movies. I played the part of Spring, in both the play and the ensuing movie, *Snickerty Nick and the Giant.* The part of Snickerty-Nick was played by Angelo, the very small dwarf who sold newspapers in front of the Warner Bros Theatre.

Mrs. Ford also produced her version of *Goldilocks and the Three Bears,* and with a fancy blond wig, I played the part of Goldilocks. Amazingly for those early times, both films were shot in color, necessitating huge color cameras and expensive film. Because of the limited

Just me and the Three Bears, plus tiny Angelo, in the corner.

color technology of the time, that required special pancake makeup and blazing hot lighting. To this day, I feel sorry for the actors portraying those three bears, trapped in their heavy fur bear suits!

At that time, Hollywood was all abuzz talking about a new film Paramount was casting: *Alice in Wonderland*. Famous character actors such as Edna May Oliver and W. C. Fields were already selected, but the search for Alice continued, confined exclusively to adult actresses. In the August 4 edition of the *Los Angeles Evening Herald*, columnist Jimmy Star wrote: "While the search for Alice in Wonderland is going on, nobody seems to have remembered the tiny actress, Marilyn Knowlden, and there's an idea, a kiddie for the part."

Director Norman McLeod must have seen that column and

taken Jimmy Star's advice to heart, for I was contacted for a screen test. Everything was going famously, and Mr. McLeod had actually decided on using me, when the Art Director told him that he better check the sets. It seems they were constructed for someone sixty inches tall, while I only measured fifty-two inches. Since they wanted Alice to look like a child, not a midget, adult actress Charlotte Henry was cast in the part. My father was quoted in the newspaper: "She missed being Alice by eight inches!"

I was lucky because only a small part of my life was devoted to my Hollywood activities, and there was plenty of time available to me to play jacks and hopscotch with my little friends. For me, making a movie seemed like the most normal thing in the world. Nevertheless, although pushed at times into the recesses of my mind, being "in the movies" was an experience I would never forget.

8 Shirley Temple— I Knew Her When

In 1933, Warner Brothers filmed *As the Earth Turns* featuring a whole group of children. I was cast in the show, and when I showed up for wardrobe fittings, I had great fun throughout the day with one of the girls named Shirley, even though she was a couple of years younger than I was.

The first day of shooting was a snow scene. The prop man turned shaved ice into snow so we could throw snowballs, while a bunch of painted white cornflakes rained down on us. I looked around for my new friend, but she was nowhere to be seen. When I

Snow scene produced by the Prop Department.
(Photo courtesy of Warner Bros. Studios.)

asked the Assistant Director, "Where's Shirley Temple?" he told me that the other small studio to which she was under contract had insisted she return to work for them for a day or so. When I let out a disappointed sigh, "Oh!" the Assistant Director responded, "Don't worry about her, Marilyn! The woods are full of them like her!"

Shirley did shortly return to our set. It was obvious that she was never happier than when she was before the camera, and that Assistant Director certainly had to eat his words, for in a few months, Shirley made *Stand Up And Cheer, Little Miss Marker,* and *Baby, Take a Bow.* Those films started her on her illustrious career, and for many years, she was 20th Century Fox's top moneymaker.

A Peek into the Future

Toward the end of 1938, I made *Just Around the Corner* and had another chance to be in a motion picture with Shirley Temple, but oh, what a difference five years can make. By then, Shirley had become a famous child star, and her mother had successfully negotiated a contract giving Shirley's mother her own salary plus major control over her movies. Gone were my buddy and fellow-actor of *As the Earth Turns* days, where she had plenty of interaction with her fellow young performers, and by strict orders of her mother, Shirley was not allowed to even *talk* to other child actors—unless they were in a scene together—or the studio stagehands, except as necessary. Moreover, when she wasn't in a movie, she had a tutor who taught her all by herself in her little private bungalow.

Mrs. Temple probably wanted to avoid people fawning over superstar Shirley as much as possible, and so chose to insulate her daughter from children, other than the ones she had carefully chosen, such as Shirley's friends from the neighborhood and her stand-in, Mary Lou Isleib. (My parents had the same instinct when they drove to the rear of the Fox Oakland Theatre so I wouldn't see my name in lights, soft-pedaled any fan-mail I received, or when my father only discussed salary matters when I was out of the room.)

Every day, Mrs. Temple put exactly fifty-six pin-curls into her daughter's hair. As Shirley's contract guaranteed, Mrs. Temple was allowed to be there right next to the cameraman, encouraging Shirley before every scene to "sparkle!" In a position of power, Mrs. Temple saw to it that Shirley was not outshone by fellow child actors, either as to appearance or acting ability. No child was to be cuter or shorter than Shirley when she sang "On the Good Ship Lollypop."

Child actress Sybil Jason suffered from Mrs. Temple's interference, when the dramatic scene of Sybil's recovery of her ability to walk was cut from *Bluebird,* to the great detriment of the picture. I suspect that Mrs. Temple exerted power in my own case. In my part of "Gwendolyn," I had a few lines, and the script called for me to have a nice close-up as I said, "She has to cook, too!" As I said this line, I received no close-up—just a long-shot that only showed the back of my head! But my father, acting as my agent, got an A-plus on the billing he arranged for me on *As the Earth Turns.* In the screen credits, my name is listed five names *above* that of Shirley Temple!

> *Just a little girl in a grownup world,*
> *I'm always cheerful and willing;*
> *My life all costumes and hair being curled*
> *And people concerned about my billing.*

With a look even further into the future, I can report the very last time I saw Shirley. She was a young married lady known as Shirley Temple Black, and, of all things, was working behind the counter as a saleslady. No, she wasn't poverty-stricken. Instead, she was a volunteer worker in upscale Atherton's Assistance League Gift Shop.

Shirley no doubt loved the fact that her husband-to-be, Charles Black, was unfamiliar with her movie career. Her super-stardom did not keep her from having a real life outside of the Hollywood scene or of making a genuine contribution to the world. Looking at her entire life, including her years as the Ambassador to Ghana and Czechoslovakia and Representative to the United Nations, I think we have to congratulate Shirley and her parents. She turned out just fine.

9 Soft Soap and Music

The Great Depression was characterized by low wages, bread-lines, and extreme unemployment. During the dismal depths of that era, President Franklin Delano Roosevelt took office and promised a "New Deal." Sometime during that year, my parents took me downtown to join the crowds of people lining the streets. I saw the President and was convinced that he was waving to me, as he rode by in an open convertible, head tipped back and cigarette holder in his clenched teeth—a sight I have never forgotten.

Helping out and contributing more to our own finances, I began "selling soap." For several years, the White King Soap Company had been advertising their laundry soap through its trademark image. Appearing all over in magazines and on billboards was the painting of a young girl carrying a basket full of soap, her bloomers peeking out from beneath her dress, and a small terrier dog by her side. I was hired as the official "White King Girl" and filmed a short subject, with my basket in hand and a perky white fox terrier beside me. I made quite a few public appearances and posed for lots of photographs. When my mother began giving me suggestions on how to pose, my father announced, "Leave her alone. Let her be herself," and I was glad that he said that!

One nice dividend of my being the "White King Girl" was that for endless years to come, a full dozen bars of their other prod-

Posing as the "White King Girl" with a cute little fox terrier, both of us looking just like the White King Soap billboard.

uct, Lux Facial Soap, were delivered to our home each-and-every month. We used Lux Soap for everything—even laundry. Come to think of it, my mother was probably washing clothes the same way she had as a young girl—boiling them on the stove, scrubbing and rinsing them by hand, wringing out the water, hanging them up to dry on a clothesline, and then ironing them.

Later in 1933, we moved to a second-floor apartment on Vista Drive, and I began attending Hollywood's Gardner Street School, (where future alumnus Michael Jackson would one day donate an auditorium). One of my classmates was Jerry Paris, (Jerry on *The Dick Van Dyke Show*), who would someday receive two Emmys for his work as a director on *The Dick Van Dyke Show* and *Happy Days*. When I knew him, he was just tall, gawky, and a really nice boy.

Our new apartment gave me a bedroom of my own and backed up to Plummer Park. Plus, there were many open fields in which I could play baseball and kick-the-can. However, the most important thing about this new apartment was what came with it: the previous resident left behind for storage a lovely grand piano. My Daddy and I repeatedly pestered my mother to teach me to play that wonderful instrument, so she finally relented, bought me a John Thompson First Book, and began teaching me.

Since we didn't want to disturb the people who lived downstairs, my parents had a rule: "No practicing more than one hour a day!" I don't think my folks were deliberately practicing any kind of reverse psychology, but it certainly worked that way. After a few months, the owner of the piano took away his possession. However, my folks located upright pianos in a neighbor's basement—and later on another one in someone's garage—so I was able to continue my piano study in those locations, with my mother seated right behind me as my teacher and always-supportive audience.

There was a beehive on the side of Gardner Street School, up high on the top of the tall two-story building. Some of the bees would tumble down and be on their last legs, as it were. My girl-friend and I set up a Bee Hospital, rescuing the ailing bees and providing them with dandelion flowers, etc. Curiously, we let them crawl all over our hands, with no dire consequences.

One day, our school Principal visited us with a stern warning of the perils of bee-stings: "Don't come crying to me if you get stung!" I think our bees knew when they were among friends because, surprisingly, we never did get stung by any of those little bee-rescues, or their friends.

Another time, however, I did get in real trouble with the School Principal. There was a long, broad staircase leading up to the school entrance, and for safety's sake, there was a school rule that there should be no skipping up the steps. One day, I took two stairs at a time and ended up in the Principal's office. How times have changed, for she took a ruler and was about to whack me on the back of the hand, but she relented and just made me stay after school. I guess my preparation for composing future song lyrics began when I wrote a poem about the experience. The poem appeared in a 1933 edition of the school newspaper:

BEING REPORTED

Yesterday when I went to school,
I skipped up a stair and broke a rule.
A teacher saw me when
I skipped up that stair and then
She gave me such a dirty look
That in my shoes I trembled and shook.
I know what will happen to me today
And I pray
That I won't have to stay after school
Just because I broke that rule.

Music in the Air

In 1933, Jerome Kern, composer of such song classics as "All the Things You Are" and "Smoke Gets in Your Eyes," introduced his new musical, *Music in the Air,* and Edgar MacGregor was set to give it its first west coast production. Mr. MacGregor had seen me in the film, *The Mind Reader*, starring Warren William, and he sent a scout to get me for the part of Tina, a little girl in the Swiss Alps. Jerome Kern was there in person when I went to the Belasco Theatre in Los Angeles, but, of course, at my tender age, I didn't understand exactly whom I was meeting.

For motion picture auditions, if they really wanted to know how I'd do a particular scene, they'd give me a screen test, where I'd have a chance to learn my lines ahead of time. However, for that live theater production, things were different. Although I was only six-and-a-half, I was handed "sides," the abbreviated versions of scripts used by stage actors, and did a "cold reading." (Sides consist of a character's lines, plus the dialogue cues leading into them. A "cold reading" is one without time for preparation.) The audition must have gone okay, for I got the part.

Music in the Air, a cross between Wagnerian opera and a Broadway musical, does not refer to songs over the radio, but rather the singing of birds in the Bavarian Alps. In the musical, I played the student of Christian Rub. (He later was the voice of Gepetto in Disney's *Pinocchio*, and Gepetto's quaint physical appearance was modeled after him.) On stage, Christian Rub taught me dancing and yodeling. It was also fun singing "I've Told Every Little Star" and "There's a Hill Beyond a Hill" along with the rest of the cast.

Broadway stars such as Walter Woolf and Vivienne Segal were hired for the production, plus a fine twenty-piece orchestra and a hundred cast members that included some famous European opera stars. The scene in the Munich Zoological Gardens included live parrots, macaws, monkeys, goats, and a working merry-go-round. Of course, most of the performances were at night, and since a car ride did an excellent job of putting me to sleep, my parents would drive me around town in the afternoon for a nap. Since I was an only child, support such as that was feasible.

Music in the Air received critical acclaim, both for its singing and its acting. It was a beautiful show with fantastic music, but in that time when 25 percent of the population was unemployed, it was probably too expensive a production. After a couple of weeks, it closed, to everyone's dismay. I always think of that show and its sad cast members whenever I hear ". . . the closing when the customers won't come!" — lyrics from Irving Berlin's "There's No Business Like Show Business."

My singing, dancing, and yodeling teacher, Christian Rub.

10 Imitation of Life and Claudette Colbert

Filmed in 1933 by Universal Studios, *Imitation of Life*, written by Fannie Hurst, was way ahead of its time, for it was the first major motion picture to focus on problems experienced by a black woman in America. At that time, in some parts of the country there were separate drinking fountains, schools, and sections on the bus for "Blacks and Whites."

In Fannie Hurst's story, a very dark-skinned woman and her light-skinned baby come to live with a white woman and her child. Problems arise when eight-year-old Jessie (who was played by me) reveals to the other school children that light-skinned Peola is not the white child she pretends to be. Peola runs tearfully home to her mother, crying "She called me Black!" as if Jessie had insulted her! (This was long before the "Black is beautiful" slogan was heard throughout our land. The polite term of that time was "colored.") The rest of the story concerns grownup Peola's decision to live as a white woman and eventually disown her dark-skinned mother!

The script called for two mothers, one white, one Black, and two daughters, one white and one light-skinned Black. What's more, the daughters were to be shown first as toddlers, then as little girls, and still later as young women.

John Stahl first cast Claudette Colbert and Louise Beavers as the mothers. Claudette Colbert would soon win an Academy Award for Best Actress Award for her work opposite Clark Gable in *It Happened One Night,* which also won an Academy Award for Best Picture. Louise Beavers was a kind of perennial maid, taking that kind of role in some twenty films, but she often stated, "It's better to play a maid than to be a maid!"

Perfectionist director John Stahl was determined to get the best cast possible. To achieve this, he conducted 800 interviews and made seventy-five screen tests. In fact, more film was used during those screen tests than during the making of the actual movie. Universal advertised the movie as having the most carefully selected cast in screen history.

> *I'm waiting to be discovered. When will somebody see*
> *I'm just the one they're looking for? When will a big director notice me!*
> *I'm waiting to be discovered. I'll never understand*
> *When it takes experience to get a part, how do newcomers ever get a start!*
> *I'm waiting to be discovered, and when the day is through,*
> *I'm all too likely to hear the words,*
> *"Don't call us. We'll call you!"*

The children had to look like the same person at a different stage of life, and the white children all had to resemble Claudette Colbert. For the part of her eight-year-old daughter, Jessie, Director Stahl interviewed 164 children and made numerous screen tests before he finally selected seven-year-old me. "Baby Jane" Quigley was cast to play me as a baby. After numerous interviews, the two children scheduled to play Louise Beavers' daughter, Peola, were also chosen. Of course, for each child who was selected, there were dozens of others who were left disappointed, but that's Hollywood.

You wonder what's the matter when you're not the one who's chosen.
Your stomach feels all hollow, and your body feels all frozen!
You think you must lack talent, or perhaps your looks are lacking.
What made the proper people fail to offer you their backing?

Claudette Colbert proved to be a warm and delightful "mother." (I often felt a special bond with anyone who acted that role.) I did notice that she had one interesting personal preference: she

Having an important talk with my special new "mother," Claudette Colbert.
(Photo courtesy of Universal Studios.)

liked the camera to photograph her from the *left* side of her face. I remember what fun she had looking in the mirror at Rochelle Hudson, who played my character grownup, Juanita Quigley (the original "Baby Jane"), and myself, laughing as she compared her own nose and profile with that of the three of us. Her verdict: we were perfectly cast as her daughter, Jessie.

Have you ever wondered whatever happened to Baby Jane? (like the movie with that title). As for whatever happened to the real-life Baby Jane, early in filming, Universal decided they really had something with their tiny actress, so they put her under contract, featured her in their publicity, and listed her name—but not mine or any of the other children—in the opening credits of *Imita-*

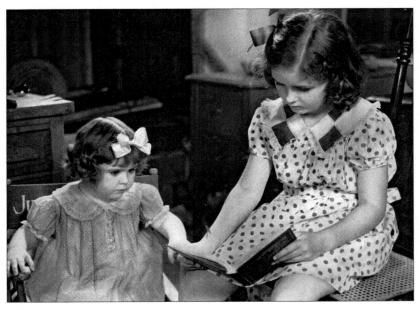

I'm shown reading to Baby Jane, who played me as a toddler in the movie. (Photo courtesy or Universal Studios.)

tion of Life. (The career of an actor can be affected by what "billing" he receives.)

The *Whatever Happened to Baby Jane?* screenplay by Lukas Heller was based on the novel of the same name by Henry Farrell, and the story sprang from the Quigley real-life family situation. Later on, like in the story, Juanita's career was overshadowed by that of her sister, Rita Quigley. However, unlike the book and film, Baby Jane in time became a nun, like a few other disenchanted actresses. However, eventually she left the religious order and married an ex-priest.

At the conclusion of *Imitation of Life*, a desperately remorseful Peola runs after her mother's hearse. A truly tragic tale, the film was widely dubbed a "five-handkerchief movie." John Stahl's perfectionism certainly showed itself in his directing style. He made a habit of shooting take after take, occasionally more than thirty. Of course, he ended up with a fine product, but those repeated takes were awfully hard on us actors and made it difficult for me to pretend everything was happening for the very first time.

In 1934, *Imitation of Life* was nominated for an Academy Award as Best Picture of the Year. Our motion picture no doubt benefited from the fact that by 1933, dialogue, music, and sound effects could be separately recorded, then through editing, combined on film. The Library of Congress has officially declared *Imitation of Life* ". . . of historical significance," and in 2007 *Time* named *Imitation of Life* one of "The 25 Most Important Films on Race."

Imitation of Life was remade in 1959, with Lana Turner in the leading role and Terry Burnham playing my part. Certainly, even twenty-five years later, the message of the film was appropriate, for there was still racial discrimination at the polls, on the buses, and in the schools, problems not at all addressed until the Voting Rights Act of 1954, the work of Martin Luther King, and the Civil Rights Act of 1968.

My favorite scene in our film is where stone-faced Ned Sparks offers to teach Claudette Colbert—in two words—how to make a million dollars. That, in exchange for a second order of pancakes in the little short-order place she is running. Sparks tells how the Coca-Cola fortune came to be when someone offered a $100,000 suggestion: "Bottle it!" His million-dollar idea was "Box it!" Miss Colbert's eyes widen, as she envisions something like Aunt Jemima Pancake Mix. Sparks responds, "Now, do I get those pancakes!" In the 1959 version, all of that is regrettably missing, including the pancake shop. No doubt that's because by then the studio wanted to be politically correct and avoid the "Aunt Jemima" mental image.

As a side note, if there is anything I hate, it's a missed opportunity. In September 2007, I was contacted by e-mail to film an on-screen interview for a documentary that would accompany Universal's 1934/1959 two-DVD special edition of *Imitation of Life*. However, I was concentrating on finishing this very book and did not keep up well enough with my e-mails, until it was too late. So, this eighty-one-year-old woman sadly missed out on that chance to reminisce on camera for Universal Studios. Oh, well . . . .

In the opening credits of the 1934 version, a certain "William Hurlbut" is listed as the screenwriter, whereas most of the actual screenwriting was apparently done by actor Preston Sturges. Despite the excellence of his screenplay, he no doubt chose to remain anonymous because of the controversial nature of the film's racial themes. Preston Sturges passed away in 1959, but 1934's *Imitation of Life* was included in a recent collection of Preston Sturges' films, so eventually the truth did come out.

In 1933, when we began filming, I noticed that each evening before we returned home, Louise Beavers gave Dorothy Black (her screen daughter, Peola) a nice hug and kiss on the cheek. I asked my mother why Miss Beavers never did the same for me. As I found out later, my mother passed on this bit of information to that fine black lady, who responded, "I didn't think you'd want me to kiss your daughter!" You can bet that from then on, each evening I also received a warm hug and kiss. I'm reminded of the lyrics to "You've Got to be Carefully Taught" from Rodgers & Hammerstein's *South Pacific*: " . . . and people whose skin is a different shade. To hate all the people your relatives hate, you have to be carefully taught!" Clearly racial prejudice was not something my parents taught me!

11 David Copperfield

Katherine Hepburn always maintained that her favorite director was George Cukor. In 1934, I went on an important interview at MGM, and once again—at his invitation—met that talented gentleman, who had been my director on *Little Women*. Cukor was considering me for the part of Agnes Wickfield in the film version of Charles Dickens' *David Copperfield*, starring young British import Freddie Bartholomew. It was an important role, for in the story, David eventually grows up and marries Agnes. Screen tests followed and more interviews.

Eventually, I was asked if I played the piano.

"Oh, no," answered my father."

"Oh, yes!" I replied, grateful for the year I'd spent with my John Thompson First Grade Book.

I was immediately referred to MGM's Music Department. They supplied me with a hand-written manuscript copy of "Beethoven's Minuet in G," asked me to study it over the weekend, and then return on Tuesday. Now as far as Beethoven compositions go, that piece is not a very difficult one, but with its tricky fingering, etc., it was certainly way, way beyond First Grade John Thompson and way beyond my seven-year-old piano expertise.

However when a studio asks us to jump, we ask, "How high?"

My mother spent all weekend teaching me that piece, mostly by having me imitate what she played. We worked and worked, and when Tuesday rolled around, I had it memorized, which I proudly announced to the Music Department.

They informed me that my character would first be seen playing the piano, with my father (Lewis Stone) and David nearby. A new problem appeared, for the studio had since decided that Agnes should be playing the theme song for the Wickfield scene. Instead of "Minuet in G," I was to play "Mendelssohn's Song Without Words." I timidly gazed at its many arpeggios, which are broken chords that need to be played rapidly hand over hand up the keyboard. Back to the neighbor's basement! Necessity being the mother of invention, I did learn the piece and played it in the movie. Of course, all of that made me leap way forward with my piano playing.

Now that I had the role, another challenge loomed. I had to play the part with an upper-class British accent. Someone could have taught me in a half-hour how to pronounce all the lines of my part, but this was to be an A#1 film, with no room for anything but the best. Consequently, Director Cukor assigned me to work with an English dialect coach. For six weeks, I worked with him and learned all the basics about speaking with a proper English accent. MGM, Producer David O. Selznick, and George Cukor all believed in grooming their actors for future performances and in doing things right.

Soon, they were filming me in various costumes. I even was photographed wearing the actual dress a little girl had worn back in the Nineteenth Century when she went to visit the President of the United States.

Lewis Stone plays my father in a scene where David Copperfield has joined the Wickfield household. (Photo courtesy of MGM Studios.)

Marilyn Knowlden Dolls

Because I was to play blond Madge Evans as a child, the powers-that-be decreed that I would once again need to have my hair bleached. They also developed a darling hairstyle for me—something like the future *Star War*'s Princess Leia—hair parted in the middle and braids twisted in buns over my ears. That same hairstyle could be found on Marilyn Knowlden Dolls that would soon be manufactured. For promotional purposes, MGM arranged with the Ideal Toy Company, manufacturer of Shirley Temple dolls, to produce a "Marilyn Knowlden as Agnes" Doll. No, there were no royalties involved, at least not for me. When I made a film, virtually all my rights were signed away—and that would include, of course, the future medium of television, years before anyone even dreamed of owning a television set.

I understand from my doll-collecting friends that my particular doll is today one of the rarest to be found. This I can believe, for even I didn't own one of the dolls. That is, I didn't own one until 2008, when I acquired my very first "Marilyn Knowlden as Agnes" doll through the magic of the Internet, which my daughter had located. A kind seller also mailed me a page from a catalog describing the "Marilyn Knowlden Doll." As I mentioned before, I didn't play with dolls much as a child, but had lots of fun with that latter-day doll. Moreover, as of 2010, I acquired a dozen dolls, all dressed by me in costumes from my favorite films—and my family continued to tease me about my "second childhood."

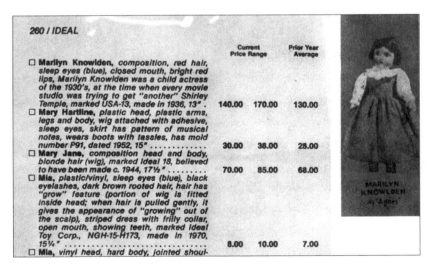

260 / IDEAL	Current Price Range		Prior Year Average
☐ **Marilyn Knowlden**, *composition, red hair, sleep eyes (blue), closed mouth, bright red lips, Marilyn Knowlden was a child actress of the 1930's, at the time when every movie studio was trying to get "another" Shirley Temple, marked USA-13, made in 1936, 13"* .	140.00	170.00	130.00
☐ **Mary Hartline**, *plastic head, plastic arms, legs and body, wig attached with adhesive, sleep eyes, skirt has pattern of musical notes, wears boots with tassles, has mold number P91, dated 1952, 15"*	30.00	38.00	28.00
☐ **Mary Jane**, *composition head and body, blonde hair (wig), marked Ideal 18, believed to have been made c. 1944, 17½"*	70.00	85.00	68.00
☐ **Mia**, *plastic/vinyl, sleep eyes (blue), black eyelashes, dark brown rooted hair, hair has "grow" feature (portion of wig is fitted inside head; when hair is pulled gently, it gives the appearance of "growing" out of the scalp), striped dress with frilly collar, open mouth, showing teeth, marked Ideal Toy Corp., NGH-15-H173, made in 1970, 15¼"*	8.00	10.00	7.00
☐ **Mia**, *vinyl head, hard body, jointed shoul-*			

Original ad for the "Marilyn Knowlden as Agnes" Doll, plus the page from a doll catalog.

**Enjoying my new kitten, while a studio photographer takes pictures.
(Photo courtesy of MGM Studios.)**

One day at MGM, a tiny kitten made my acquaintance. I just loved the little thing and, at day's end, uttered one of childhood's classic requests: "Please, CAN WE KEEP HIM?"

My mother explained to me that the kitten had to stay where he belonged—at the studio.

An assistant director quickly corrected her. "This studio is over-run with cats! We use them to keep down the rodent population. And sometimes we have to shoot them! If Marilyn wants that kitten, believe me, she can have him!"

And so, Patches-the-Cat became part of our household. When he grew up, he loved the large fields close to our apartment, but all we had to do was call "*Patches!*" from our upstairs back porch, and he'd come running!

Freddie Bartholomew, who played David Copperfield, was a really nice boy. Later on, I was invited to his birthday party, along with quite a few other child actors, such as Judy Garland, the Mauch twins, Spanky McFarland, Jackie Moran, Bonita Granville, June Lockhart, Dickie Moore, Jane Withers, Virginia Wiedler, Scotty Beckett and others.)

Eventually, I was introduced to most of the other members of the cast, such as W.C. Fields, Edna May Oliver, Maureen O'Sullivan, Roland Young, Arthur Treacher, Madge Evans, Hugh Walpole, Elsa Lancaster, Fay Chaldecott, Frank Lawton, Jessie Ralph, Basil Rathbone, and Lionel Barrymore. I remember so well the time we got together to autograph copies of the script. (In a 2003 auction on ebay, one of those autographed scripts sold for $12,000. Still later, it was auctioning for $35,000!)

David Copperfield represented what my father wanted for me: being part of something first class. There were times when—wisely or not—my Daddy turned down parts for me. He rejected a chance for me to appear in *Our Gang Comedies*. (Today, renamed *The Little Rascals,* and considered "classics," at the time they were B-rated low-budget shorts with largely improvised plots, filmed mostly

Freddy Bartholomew's birthday party. In back, Billy and Bobby Mauch are next to Judy Garland. Wally Albright is near Bonita Granville, Marilyn Knowlden (wearing a corsage), and Susannah Foster. At right, Ann Gillis and Fay Chaldecott are behind Dickie Moore. At far left, Jackie Moran and June Lockhart next to David Tillotson, while Virginia Wiedler, is next to David Holt and Billy Lee. In front are Baby LeRoy, Spanky McFarland, and Scotty Beckett. In the front row are Douglas Scott, Jane Withers, Tommy Kelly, Freddy Bartholomew, and Baby Jane Quigley.

with children straight off the street.) My father also chose not to have me under consideration for the "brat" role later spectacularly filled by Jane Withers in Shirley Temple's *Bright Eyes*. Sure enough, *David Copperfield* was nominated by the Academy of Motion Picture Arts and Sciences as Best Picture of the Year, and later the *New York Times* selected it as one of the "1000 greatest movies of all times!" The premiere of the movie was held at Grauman's Chinese

Theatre in Hollywood, which was another chance to watch the searchlights in the sky while I walked down the red carpet.

> *Everyone who's anyone is going to be there*
> *And arriving in a limousine!*
> *Later on we'll find them and those fancy clothes they wear*
> *Featured in some movie magazine!*
>
> *Join me at the Movies. They are having a big Premiere.*
> *Hollywood's most famous stars are going to be coming here.*
> *All of that elegance upon display. Join me at the Movies today!*

12 Music, Music, Music

Just before *David Copperfield* was released, Gardner Street School selected me to be their drum major in a school parade they were having. No, I would not be twirling a baton or attired like a cheerleader. With a tall plumed military hat a la *The Music Man*, I was dressed as the leader of the band, and my job was to smartly move my large baton up and down, and keep everyone marching and playing their instruments together in time to the music.

That was not my first experience as a "conductor." I can remember at my earlier Cheremoya School, at the age of five, standing on a box and leading the singing for an "Old California" festival they were having.

Perhaps I inherited my sense of rhythm from my ancestor, Gideon Wood, who was a drummer in a company of minutemen

I'm in the center of the group, after just having led the singing.

Little Girl Has Important Role

Marilynne Knowlden

Demonstrating that it does not take size and age to make a good drum major, diminutive Marilynne Knowlden, 7 years of age, has been selected to lead the band at the annual carnival to be held today at the Gardner School in Hollywood. Marilynne is no amateur at this sort of thing, having a record of twenty-three featured roles in motion pictures to her credit.

during the American Revolution. At any rate, having skipped first grade, I was now seven years old and in the third grade at my Los Angeles public school.

Helena Lewyn, a Hollywood piano teacher, was watching that parade, had read about it in the newspaper, and perhaps had read somewhere that I would be playing the piano in *David Copperfield*. She approached my parents, said she liked my sense of rhythm, and offered to be my piano instructor. She ended up giving me two lessons a week at her studio on Sunset Boulevard, in a place known as "Crossroads of the World." There was no charge for my lessons. She just wanted to use my name in her advertising and occasionally have me play somewhere. That was a good thing, for my parents could not have afforded her expensive lessons.

Several times I had the immense privilege of playing the piano together with fellow student Leonard Pennario, a young man so gifted that some believed he was the reincarnation of Mozart. He was able to

**Seventy-six trombones
did *not* lead our big parade!**

My "fellow student," twelve-year-old Leonard Pennario,
one day to be called "America's finest pianist."

sight-read difficult piano concertos. He ended up being a noted concert pianist, very much in demand on the concert stage throughout the world, and he has often been called "America's finest pianist." He benefited greatly from his training with Miss Lewyn, though eventually they came to a parting of the ways, when he was determined to play *Rhapsody in Blue* and other Gershwin material to which conservative Miss Lewyn objected—and which he later became famous for playing.

Miss Lewyn was a fine classical pianist, had studied in Europe with several marvelous classical musicians, and had performed as a soloist at the Hollywood Bowl. She gave several recitals a year at her studio in which I participated, playing strictly classical music—by memory. I also played duets with my girlfriend, Carlotta Laemmle, the niece of, Carl Laemmle, the founder of Universal Studios.

I was truly blessed to have a perfectionist such as Miss Lewyn as my piano teacher. Her system was to have me, as my very first task, completely memorize a piece; then the real work on it began. Miss Lewyn had several famous actresses as her students, but she told my mother that I had something she couldn't give me. Of course, that was my natural love and feeling for music. It has been such an important part of my life. Yet without Miss Lewyn, *David Copperfield*, and other Hollywood incentives, I might never have moved beyond my John Thompson Book One.

Performing a duet with Carlotta Laemmle.

Easy to Take

In 1934, Paramount was considering me for the part of a radio singer in *Easy to Take*, to star Marsha Hunt and Eugene Pallette.

"No," my father said, after Paramount executives asked if I could sing.

"Yes," I just as quickly answered.

"There seems to be a difference of opinion here," said the studio executive, followed by a visit to their music department. (The same thing happened at MGM for *David Copperfield,* when I was asked if I could play the piano.)

When they asked me to choose a song, I selected the kind of low-down "Let Yourself Go" from one of the currently popular Ginger Rogers and Fred Astaire movies. After I gave my all on that song, they responded, "Great! That's just what we wanted! And we'll try to get that song for you!"

They hired me for the movie, where I performed along with Carl "Alfalfa" Switzer (who sang off-key without knowing it in many of the *Our Gang/Little Rascals* films.) But when they tried to get authorization for me to sing "Let Yourself Go," they ran into quite a snag. You see, that was a song written by Irving Berlin, so there was no way they could get the rights to that song. They ended up obtaining the rights to "Crosspatch" for me. In an innovative technique for the time, they had me pre-record the song, and then lip-sync it while the camera filmed both long-shots and close-ups. Nowadays, on television, they would probably use multiple cameras, rather than lip-syncing, but this was 1934 and the movie business.

13 Movie Parents

I was very much a grown woman before it finally hit me that my father had given up *his* career as an attorney for *mine*—and there I was, just a child! Something powerful happened to my Daddy at all those times he took me on interviews: he fell in love with Hollywood! By the time 1934 rolled around, I had been in twenty films and had worked at Paramount Studios, RKO, MGM, Fox, Warner, and Universal, and my father had visited all those places, plus a few others. He was especially fascinated during my time at RKO, where he met stars like Cary Grant and Hopalong Cassidy's Bill Boyd. He also spent one memorable afternoon chatting with producer/aircraft builder Howard Hughes, at that time a producer at that studio.

My father was finding it increasingly difficult to maintain his Oakland law office, so he contemplated opening an office in Los Angeles. He ended up opening a Los Angeles office all right, but it wasn't a law office. His Hollywood time had given him an opportunity to employ his skills as a negotiator. So it was that in 1935, my father became a Hollywood agent. His new office was in the Equitable Building, at the Northeast corner of that famous intersection of Hollywood and Vine.

People like me, people like you,
Each with a dream that might come true,
Make up the heart and soul of Hollywood!

I must say, I was one of the very few movie youngsters whose father took them on interviews. Fathers in general were a rare commodity among child actors. Though he still loved accompanying me to the studios on interviews, now that he was a legitimate "artist's representative," my father decided it was rather unseemly for him to have me as a client, so I lost my Daddy as my agent, and a man named Al Kingston took over, followed later by Gus Demling.

As an agent, my father specialized in those non-star types who were found in most every film: cowboys, Indians, gangsters, and policemen—character actors who worked really often, though sometimes only in small parts. His most famous client was Bela Lugosi of legendary *Dracula* fame, as well as Susan Hayward and her sister before those ladies became real famous. I had no brothers or sisters, and,

Patches and I visit my Daddy's new office.

except when I was a small baby, I never had a baby-sitter. My Mother and Daddy and I were buddies who went everywhere together, including a lot of little theaters. There my father often acted as a talent scout, and all three of us enjoyed discussing the plays we'd just seen.

In those depression days, President Franklin D. Roosevelt established the Works Progress Administration, which provided "make-work" jobs for our citizens through the construction of roads, parks, bridges, theaters, etc. The WPA was also the employer of last resort for some lucky authors, actors, directors, etc., and we sometimes attended those WPA productions. Their pay wasn't very high, but people were just grateful to be working—especially in the type of business that they loved. I also had some interesting experiences meeting some of my father's clients, including time spent with a genuine Indian Chief, as well as an exotic dinner at the home of a Hindu family.

People sometimes ask me, "Was your Mom a 'Stage Mother?" If that means in the style of Mama Rose in *Gypsy*, or the mother of the little girl I replaced in *The Conquerors*, the answer is decidedly "No!" Fortunately, my gentle mother was no closet actress seeking to fulfill her fantasies through her child. It was only a kind of fluke that landed me in pictures, not some obsessive effort spreading over months and years. On the other hand, I can't forget my mother's diligence following our house-call doctor's advice, when an attack of laryngitis caused me to lose my voice. All through the night, she alternated hot and cold packs on my chest. The treatment worked, so I was able to be there on the set the next day. Yes, with her intense devotion to me, I'll have to admit that my "Mommy" did at least in *some* ways fill the bill as a Movie Mother.

Who gets them well quick when they're sick? The Mother, the Mother!
Bites her fingernails to the quick? The Mother, the Mother!
Shows them every camera trick? The Mother, the Mother!
Who in the world is anything like the Movie Mother?

Don't think that I am anybody's fool!
I teach my child what they don't teach in school!
I guide the hairbrush and the comb.
Remember there's no place like home.
And no one quite like me at all.
"If there's a part, be sure to call!"
No one quite like me, the Movie Mother!

All my life, I was only too aware that my happiness was my parents' happiness. How blessed I was to have a mother who liked to "spread a little sunshine" by stopping perfect strangers on the street to tell them she liked their hat or the tie they were wearing. And then, there was my father. He told the story of the man who wanted just two words on his tombstone: "He appreciated!"

One would think from their behavior that my parents had studied modern psychology books. I never was spanked—a scowl from them was punishment enough—but when I did something right, I knew I was appreciated. Mind you, I didn't get off too easy. My father insisted I read the newspaper every day. His attorney training also made him teach me to be very careful about any statements I made, as illustrated by his story of the man who commented on the white sheep on the hill, all facing into the wind. The lawyer's studied response was, "We only know for sure that all the sheep are white on their *left* sides!"

No complaints from me about *my* mother.

My mother always stressed the importance of honesty and encouraged me to tell her the truth, no matter what. She was also a stickler for proper grammar, didn't allow me to use phrases like "*Shut up!*" and insisted on proper etiquette—at both the table and otherwise—though not in a stilted manner.

Most of all, my parents taught me to be considerate of other people and to practice the Golden Rule, "Do unto others as you would have them do unto you!" But one of the main things my mother taught me was to look on the bright side of life. "Every cloud has a silver lining!" My father also stressed taking advantage of opportunities that came along. "When Opportunity knocks, answer the door!" He also taught me to strive for excellence, and to work and rework whatever I was doing. He learned this from his reporter friend, Bill Oliver, on an old unpaved Lincoln Highway during a long, early 1920s motor trip in a Packard sedan, a trip that Oliver would write up in a magazine.

I remember wondering how my parents would react when I brought home a C in penmanship. *Would they jump all over me?* Fortunately, they passed that test by encouraging me to take it all in stride. In other words, though they encouraged me to do my best, they were not unreasonable perfectionists.

A question I'm frequently asked is "Did your folks set your earnings aside for you in a trust account?" The simple answer is "No." I'm afraid that, in those depression years, my early Hollywood career was pretty much the Family Business, and none of us wanted to go hungry. My mother and I both tried to be as thrifty as possible. "Waste not, want not!" I never received a regular allowance, but rather asked for what I wanted—or, more accurately, what I needed.

As for pretty clothes and all that, I had more than I ever wanted. I often wished that my mother would spend more money on her own clothing, for when she shopped for clothes, they were almost always for me. I do remember my father's anger when my mother decided to supplement her broom and carpet-sweeper with an electric vacuum cleaner, which she purchased "on time" from Sears-Roebuck with monthly payments. From his unhappy response on that occasion, I can only conclude that our family was more "poor" than I realized at the time and, of course they never could afford to buy me my own piano.

When my father took me on interviews, he had a firm policy: he never discussed finances in my presence, I think probably for excellent reasons. I don't envy today's child actors who have so much money in their bank account that it must totally distort their view of things. I realize that there have been many instances where a child actor was taken advantage of by his family, Jackie Coogan being one notorious case. A famous child actor, Jackie discovered after his parents' death that they had squandered his sizable fortune, through gambling, etc. Because of his unfortunate situation, the Coogan Law was signed and implemented in 1939, setting aside 15% of a child actor's income. However the law only applied if the child were under contract—so that let me out. However, I have no complaints whatsoever about the way my folks treated me. Throughout my entire life, whenever I needed my family's support, financial or otherwise, it was there.

I'm proud to say that my father gave me the title for this book. In 1934, he placed an ad in a trade magazine that included my picture with the heading "The Little Girl in Big Pictures!" Even though she's been gone many years since I began this autobiography, if I have any collaborator on this book, it is my own dear mother!

Marilyn Knowlden as Little Cosette.
(Photo courtesy of Twentieth Century Fox.)

14 Les Misérables, Dancing with Charles Laughton

*E*ach time I see the Cosette logo for the musical, *Les Misérables*, my heart skips a beat, for I feel as if I'm looking at my own picture. You see, in 1934 I played eight-year-old Cosette in the 1935 United Artists/Twentieth Century Fox version of the famous Victor Hugo novel.

Both the logo for the much later *musical* version of *Les Misérables* and my costume as Cosette were taken from an Emile Bayard (1837-1891) lithograph illustrating Victor Hugo's 1862 novel. My own appearance, the headband that I wore, and my long, straggly dress and hair are all a dead ringer for the lithograph. On the other hand, the costume designers took my crisscross shawl and wooden shoes from a painting by Jean Geoffroy (1834-1924).

In the story, the little girl is rescued from a cruel innkeeper and his wife at the request of her mother, a dying employee of Jean Valjean. Played in the film by Fredric March, Valjean becomes the little waif's adopted father. A former galley slave who refuses to register with the police, his original crime was merely stealing a loaf of bread for his starving sister and her family. He ends up escaping with Cosette from the cruel law of the time, in the person of stern-faced Charles Laughton. His passion for justice, plus

**Emile Bayard lithograph that inspired
my appearance as Cosette.**

his love for Cosette, are the driving forces of his existence, and later on, he nearly loses his life trying to rescue grownup Cosette's sweetheart. In a very real sense, Cosette is Jean Valjean's "leading lady." So, the role of Little Cosette is clearly a child actress' dream-part.

What a treat I had waiting for me when I was introduced to Richard Boleslawski, hired by producer Darryl F. Zanuck to direct *Les Misérables*. Born in Russian-occupied Poland, Boleslawski was the product of the Russian School of Dramatic Arts and the most famous student of Konstantin Stanislavski (1863-1938), the Russian who originated what was later called the Method school of acting. As opposed to making faces and posing, the "Method" has each actor draw on his own emotional experiences as a way of understanding the inner life of the character he's portraying. Most of today's distinguished acting coaches rely at least partially on this technique. Both the Actor's Studio and the Strasburg School, for instance, are based on Method acting.

As the most famous student of Stanislavski, Richard Boleslawski was the author of the classic, *Acting: The First Six Lessons* (1933). The book is presented as a dialogue between a Teacher

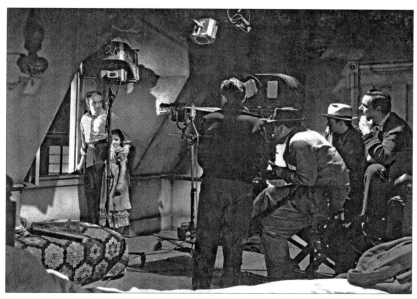

A behind-the-scenes look at 1934 movie-making. Director Boleslawski at right, and Prize-winning Cinematographer Gregg Toland behind the camera. (Photo courtesy of Twentieth Century Fox.)

and his Student. When the Student inquires how he can manage to evoke within himself the emotions of a murderer, since he has never felt like killing anyone, the Teacher's classic response is "Ah, but have you never killed a fly!" No one informed me of my director's background or the philosophy behind his directing style. A great bear of a man, he was certainly perfectly costumed in the role of the director, with his leather-front sweater, pipe, and ascot tie. I soon came to realize that he was someone who approached things differently—and wonderfully.

I did several screen tests and numerous costume and hairstyle photos before filming ever began. Although Hugo's *Les Misérables* mentioned an eight-year-old Cosette, W. P. Lipscomb's script called

Les Miserables **film crew, and Director Richard Boleslawski with
his traditional pipe, at center rear, next to Gregg Toland.
(Photo courtesy of Twentieth Century Fox.)**

for a thirteen-year-old in the part. Once I was chosen for the role,
however, he revised the script for an eight-year-old Cosette. I might
also add that it was a part considerably larger than in the musical
version of *Les Misérables*.

Each morning, the Hairdressing Department added a Vaseline-
like product called "bandaleen" to my hair to make it look dirty,
and they washed it out every evening. As usual, I still managed to
avoid makeup and the Makeup Department, except in the film's
early scenes, when a bit of Fuller's Earth was smeared on my face to
make it look dirty. It's hard to believe all the work, planning, and
research that goes into the sets, costumes, makeup, and hairstyles
for a top-level production such as those "big pictures" I was fortunate to be a part of!

I was delighted with my movie father, Jean Valjean, in the person of the handsome and kindly actor Fredric March. In 1932, he'd received the Best Actor "Oscar" for *Dr. Jekyll and Mr. Hyde* (and would later on receive a second Oscar for *The Best Years of our Lives*.) He told me he had a little daughter just my age, so that helped us both.

Most of my scenes were one-on-one with Mr. March, and I was soon calling him "Papa." We became fast friends and had great fun together around the set. I have an entry in my autograph book that reads: "To Marilynne (a coming star) – with much love from Jean Valjean (her Pop) Fredric March 2/23/35"

Big, Black Cigars – Part 1

Jumping into the middle of the story, the very first day of shooting involved a scene where Valjean, Mayor of the town, has for the first time taken Cosette to his lovely home. In preparation for dinner with her new father, the little waif has been cleaned and dressed up by the housekeeper, and during the dinner, Cosette is so overcome with emotion that she's moved to tears.

Director Boleslawski asked me, "Now, Marilyn, how are we going to get you to cry?"

I answered, "You don't have to do anything. I'll just cry."

Mr. Boleslawski really helped me by taking the time to explain to me the complex emotions that eight-year-old was feeling. During the scene, as I was sipping my bouillon soup, the tears came—to my director's delight.

He said, "Well, Marilyn, that deserves a Big, Black Cigar!"

I was thrilled!

Mr. Boleslawski apparently shared his pleasure with the front office, for a bunch of male visitors appeared at next day's shooting—("Suits" we call them today). Immediately, I had to plunge right in to the close-up of my crying scene, but then such is the lot of the movie actor!

> *It's true that acting I understand.*
> *It's just like dolls or playing house.*
> *But all that crying upon command,*
> *I'd like to leave to Minnie Mouse!*

To achieve spontaneity and genuine feeling from his actors, our director had a unique way of functioning. Once he had conferred with the crew, Mr. Boleslawski would often say softly, "Freddie and Marilyn, come on over here." He then would explain to us in low tones what the scene was all about, followed by our quietly rehearsing the lines while confusion was going on all around us. Finally, to everyone's surprise, he'd yell out "Okay, let's shoot it!" Later it was "Quiet on the set! Lights! Camera! Action!" Then, following the scene, "Cut!" and hopefully "Print it!" Sometimes, that first "take" was the one that ended up in the movie. All through the filming, whenever he was especially pleased with my performance, Mr. Boleslawski would say, to my great delight, "Well, Marilyn, that's another Big Black Cigar!"

Jean Valjean and Cosette, traveling on a fast-moving horse-drawn buckboard, appear in a wild chase scene fleeing from Javert (Charles Laughton) and the other mounted gendarmes. I'm sorry to report that two of the horses tripped during the filming of the chase, broke their legs, and had to be put to sleep.

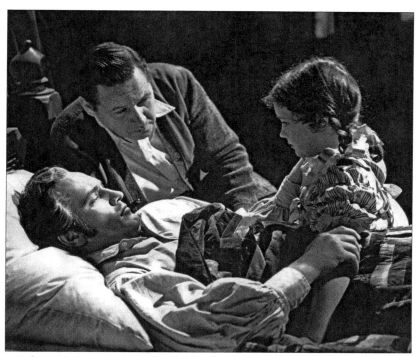

Soft words from our Director Richard Boleslawski—words that helped so much. (Photo courtesy of Twentieth Century Fox.)

Actually riding on that wagon, my screen "double" for that surprisingly dangerous scene was a small teenage boy. When shooting began, however, he turned white as a sheet and had to be replaced. His replacement stuntman turned out to be a former jockey in his sixties with a gnarled face, but wearing a silk dress, pantaloons, ballet slippers, cloak, braided wig, and poke-bonnet identical to mine. What fun I had saying to him, "Curtsy, Cosette!" The small, cooperative man would grab each side of his skirt, bend his knees, and do a dainty curtsy—for my benefit.

(I think I should explain here the difference between a double, a

The difficult chase scene, with Fredric March holding the reins and Marilyn Knowlden hanging on for dear life. (Photo courtesy of Twentieth Century Fox.)

stand-in, and an understudy: A "double" is someone who substitutes for an actor in the long-shots, either for convenience or to avoid danger to the primary actor. A "stand-in" is someone who substitutes for the actor, not on screen, but only when the lights and camera

Jean Valjean and Little Cosette hiding from Javert.
(Photo courtesy of Twentieth Century Fox.)

are being adjusted. Far more common on stage than in films, an "understudy" is someone who learns an actor's lines and is prepared to substitute for the actor in case he's sick or otherwise unavailable.)

In the long shots, the old man's face would not show, nor the face of the stuntman doubling for Fredric March, but the close-ups and medium shots needed to show both of us on the buckboard, standing, and hanging on to the back of the wagon's seat. We did a "process shot" where we were filmed in front of a large rear-projection screen that displayed passing forest scenery. The prop men placed long boards beneath the wagon and proceeded to yank them up and down, making our wagon bounce crazily. To add to the realism, a big wind machine blew in our faces as the cameras rolled. Believe me, I had to hang on tight to the back of that seat. Talk about your Disneyland rides. I was supposed to scream while all this was going on, and that just came naturally. That was surely one of those scenes where Mr. Boleslawski promised me another Big Black Cigar!

Dancing With Charles Laughton

I had the unique opportunity of visiting the soundstage where Jean Valjean carries a grownup Cosette's wounded fiancé through the sewers of Paris, pursued by the determined Javert. Imagine—the sewers of Paris on an indoor sound stage, where bits of wax floated in the water to make it look yucky! Apparently, Rochelle Hudson and I were look-alikes, for she played me grownup, as she had before in *Imitation of Life*. That gave me the chance to make friends with Charles Laughton, who played fearsome Javert, the villain of *Les Misérables*. (He had previously won the Academy Award for Best Actor for playing King Henry VIII and would soon earn one for *Mutiny on the Bounty*.)

In preparation for a particularly dramatic scene, Laughton would sometimes throw chairs around the set! His violent behavior scared me a bit, but they assured me that was his unique and effective way of getting in the mood. Although he was fearsome in his Javert scenes, Mr. Laughton and I struck up a friendship, and he promised that he'd pay *me* a visit. Later, when he visited *our* set location that was the exterior of the inn, my raggedy costume included a pair of wooden shoes—fortunately lined with felt—while Charles Laughton's costume included an awesome pair of hip-length boots. Would you believe, right there on the set, we worked out a spirited wooden shoe dance together? We did more than worked it out; we danced it! "Step, Kick, Hop. Step, Kick, Hop!"

The scene where Cosette first meets Jean Valjean takes place

Little Cosette meeting her new adopted father, Jean Valjean—Fredric March.
(Photo courtesy of Twentieth Century Fox.)

at night by the well, where Cosette is drawing water for Valjean's horse. In order to shoot that scene, Twentieth Century Studios had to get special permission from the Child Welfare Office for me to work at night. (Through financial dealings by Darryl F. Zanuck, the studio later became Twentieth Century Fox.) You needn't feel sorry for me having to carry such a heavy wooden bucket. It had a false bottom and only looked real heavy.

When I watch other versions of *Les Misérables,* I find myself waiting in vain for certain memorable lines. I discovered later that some of my favorites were written, not by Victor Hugo, but by the scriptwriter, W. P. Lipscomb. Two examples: when straggly-looking Jean Valjean asks the kindly bishop, who has allowed shunned ex-convict Jean Valjean to stay for the night, if he isn't afraid the parolee will murder him in his sleep, the gentle Bishop's reply is: "Well, how do you know I won't murder you?" In the scene where the Bishop not only allows him to keep the silver plates he's stolen, but in addition, gives him two silver candlesticks, the Bishop tells the awe-struck man, "Life is not to take, but to give!" On a personal level, throughout my life, that sentence has meant a great deal to me.

Richard Boleslawski had a birthday during the filming, and the crew gave him a party. Sadly, this was to be nearly the last birthday my Director was to experience, for he died suddenly at the age of forty-seven!

As you can see from the photograph of this event, I was one little eight-year-old girl in the midst of a sea of grown men. I must say that they were very protective of me, never using bad language or anything (although I'll admit it's possible that I just didn't understand the words they were using).

Cast and crew join forces to celebrate Richard Boleslawski's birthday.
(Photo courtesy of Twentieth Century Fox.)

This picture also illustrates the immense appeal that having a nice part in a movie can have for a child. As a featured player, I was treated with the respect due an actor of whatever age. The favorite theatrical quote, "There are no small parts, only small actors," reflects the simple truth that even an actor with the smallest part can have a huge impact on the overall success of a production.

Mr. Boleslawski gets my vote as my favorite director. He was always so kind to me. He was no mousy sort of gentleman, however. During the filming, he showed tremendous disgust and anger toward the actor playing the Innkeeper. I'm not sure of the reason, but I suspect it was because the man was over-acting, or "hamming it up," rather than showing the sincerity that our director so wanted. The end result was that Mr. Boleslawski cut several of the

Innkeeper's scenes, reducing his part to an absolute minimum. In his intense desire for realism, for the unbelievably miserable-looking galley slaves who were Jean Valjean's fellow inmates straining to pull their oars on the slave ship, our Director actually cast residents of Los Angeles' Midnight Mission! He also used those same hungry-looking men for the uprising sequences, altogether casting 200 of those unfortunates—truly "les miserables"—the wretched ones.

Big, Black Cigars – Part 2

Since I was always a freelance artist, rather than under contract to any one studio, the final day of shooting always meant a sad good-bye to my fellow actors. That last day, Mr. Boleslawski said he had a gift for me.

"Well, Marilyn, it's about time you received your 'Big Black Cigars!'"

Incredibly, resting in a long box usually reserved for long-stem roses, my accumulated Big Black Cigars turned out to be sixteen-inch hand-made chocolate ones, with wooden skewers for reinforcement and adorned with hand-painted cigar bands. I was so thrilled! But I wasn't thrilled by the picture coming to an end, and once I was out of sight of the studio, I sobbed uncontrollably.

"Marilyn, why are you crying?"

"Because I'm unhappy. I want to come some more!"

Les Miserables Postscript

Hollywood Cinema Fashions soon manufactured Marilyn Knowlden dresses, modeled after an outfit I'd worn in the film and sold at places like the Los Angeles and New York Saks stores.

My reward for performing to my Director's satisfaction—a box of Big,
Black Cigars! (Photo courtesy of Twentieth Century Fox.

Ad from a New York newspaper.

I learned of those dresses when my mother and I went shopping for a new dress for me at Bullock's Wilshire, and a saleslady said,

"Oh, we have the cutest dresses! They're Marilyn Knowlden Dresses."

"Well, here she is!" proudly announced my mother.

New York Gimbel's featured a Little Cosette headdress, and I appeared in person at the San Francisco Emporium, where they had a "Have your picture taken with Marilyn. Knowlden" contest.

The then-current *San Francisco News* mentioned ". . . an unnamed actor's standout performance as a half-witted convict" in the courtroom scene, where Champmathieu, a poor unfortunate mistakenly thought to be Jean Valjean, is brought to trial. Interestingly enough, that "unnamed actor" was none other than dual-role-playing Fredric March himself, his persona altered by a beard, long straggly hair, a squeaky voice, and one widened nostril, thanks to a tube in his nose! During that episode, I was able to visit the set and watch and listen to my "Pop" in action. Sometimes, Mr. March would tease me on our set by using that "other" voice.

During filming of *Les Misérables*, Fredric March presented me with something I would cherish forever: a darling marionette, "Clippo the Clown," who started me on a wonderful hobby. Once I outgrew "Touslehead," I pretty much lost interest in dolls. The only "dolly" that interested me was the small wagon with rubber wheels that moved the camera from place to place while a scene was in progress, but a marionette was something special. I made a puppet theater out of a wooden crate and a small velvet curtain, acquired other marionettes, and enjoyed putting on neighborhood puppet shows, including some for my friends' birthday parties.

In 1935, *Les Misérables* earned an Academy Award nomination as Best Picture of the Year, edged out only by *Mutiny on the Bounty* that also starred Charles Laughton. Much later on in 1999, the New York Times Company published *The New York Times Guide to the Best 1000 Movies Ever Made,* which named *Les Misérables* as one of those 1000 and included the 1935 newspaper review which had favorable things to say about me.

Sadly, Richard Boleslawski died suddenly in 1937 at the age of forty-seven. However, before he died, he cast me in his *Metropolitan* starring Lawrence Tibbett. It was the smallest of parts, but I was pleased that he had thought of me.

As if to confirm my feeling that the *Les Misérables* Cosette logo is really a picture of me, in 2008, a two-sided DVD edition of the 1935/1952 versions of *Les Misérables* was released, with the *only* photograph on the cover being a large headshot of me as an eight-year-old Cosette!

In the Cast of Characters for *Les Misérables,* my name is spelled "Marilynne," rather than "*Marilyn* Knowlden." There's a rather odd reason: my father, who was not normally superstitious, had a fascination with names and titles, but in 1934, some numerologist convinced him that things would work out much better for me if my name were spelled "Marilynne." My mother and I both thought that was silly. What's more, my mother had named me after that famous 1920s dancer, Marilyn Miller (who, in 1898 was named after her mother, Mary, and her father, Lynn). However, I'll have to admit that being in *Les Misérables* was one of the luckiest things that ever happened to me!

15 My "Mother" Katharine Hepburn

In 1935, I returned to RKO studios to film *A Woman Rebels* with Katharine Hepburn, with whom I'd previously worked in *Little Women* and *Morning Glory*. One benefit of my part in that movie was being assigned to Lucille Ball's dressing room-trailer, complete with a striking Art Deco style, smoky-blue mirrored radio. I fell in love with that very modern-looking radio, and later, for my birthday, my parents presented me with an identical one. Miss Hepburn and I became good friends, and we enjoyed chatting about the intricate details of the Eighteenth Century costumes we wore.

In that Victorian-era film, I'm pictured shooting a bow and arrow at an archery target! I didn't realize it at the time, but my nine-year-old character's use of a bow and arrow represented an early expression of "Woman's Lib," for in *A Woman Rebels,* the heroine expresses part of her rebellion by having her little girl engage in archery, a scandalously "athletic" activity in the Victorian era.

Miss Hepburn promised me a dollar if I could hit a bull's-eye during one of the "takes." As to the outcome of that challenge, I cherish an autograph that states: "To Marilyn — Hoping that her archery improves — Affectionately, Katharine Hepburn."

I didn't usually ask for autographs. Recently, I've learned a special

Archery—such a scandalous activity for a young lady— at least in the Victorian era. (Photo courtesy of RKO Studios.)

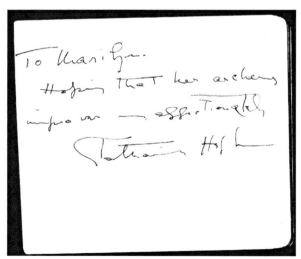

Page from my autograph book.

reason for treasuring that autograph: it seems Miss Hepburn did not usually permit them. I'm sure she realized how naive I was regarding her personal preferences because she gave me the autograph.

Skeletons Out of the Closet

While I was filming *A Woman Rebels,* I was under the impression that I was playing Katharine Hepburn's niece and assumed the newspaper clips that said I played her daughter were in error. After all, didn't the script call for me to refer to her as *"Auntie!"* Rather than the finished film, I think I only saw the "rushes" to the movie—raw footage printed up from the day before and shown in a private projection room. I was sixty years old when I mentioned to a friend something about playing Katharine Hepburn's niece in *A Woman Rebels.* My friend said, "Marilyn, you didn't play her niece! You were her illegitimate daughter!" And to think it took fifty-two years for that particular skeleton to come out of the closet.

When that extraordinary lady finally passed away in 2003, her actual niece, Katharine Houghton, was interviewed in *People* magazine, where she stated that she was the *only* one who had ever portrayed Katharine Hepburn's daughter (in the film *Guess Who's Coming to Dinner).* I knew that wasn't the case, so I wrote *People* magazine, and they kindly published my letter.

Her niece also appeared on Larry King's television show, where she declared that in Katherine's later years, she loved to watch her old movies and *A Woman Rebels* was her favorite. No doubt that was because she was certainly a bit of a rebel herself, or perhaps that fascinating lady, who never had any children of her own, liked picturing herself as a very independent-type mother.

16 Show Boat

1926, the same year I was born, marked the birth of *Show Boat*, first as an Edna Ferber novel, followed by the Ziegfield stage production with book and lyrics by Oscar Hammerstein and music by Jerome Kern. As I learned from Miles Kreuger's excellent comprehensive history of all the *Show Boat* versions, Carl Laemmle and Universal Pictures had purchased the screen rights in 1926, but didn't acquire the rights to the music until 1929, shortly after they'd already filmed a silent version of the story. In an attempt to salvage their *Show Boat*, they redid most of the scenes with sound and added in songs, producing a kind of patchwork version that Universal distributed in both sound-on-disk and sound-on-film versions.

Clearly, a remake was needed. It came into being in 1935, personally produced by Carl Laemmle, Jr. and with a screenplay by famed lyricist Oscar Hammerstein. It starred Irene Dunne and Alan Jones and featured heavyweights such as Helen Morgan, Charles Winniger, and Paul Robeson in the supporting cast. I became a part of that cast, playing daughter Kim (an acronym for Kentucky, Illinois and Missouri), probably because Jerome Kern recommended me, remembering me from his 1933 musical, *Music in the Air*, on Los Angeles' Belasco Theatre stage.

Although its historical significance was certainly lost on me at the time, once again I ended up in a motion picture that dealt with racial injustice—in this case, the prohibition against racial intermarriage. In the story, through a sharing of the blood of their hands, the lovers visually overcome the prohibition against miscegenation that was still on the law books in 1926.

The previous stage versions of *Show Boat* had gambler Ravenal singing the hit song "Make Believe" exclusively to leading lady Magnolia: "Only make believe I love you. Only make believe that you love me. Others find peace of mind in pretending. Couldn't you? Couldn't I? Couldn't we?"

I'm proud to report that before filming, Oscar Hammerstein wrote specially modified lyrics to "Make Believe" that would make the song appropriate for Alan Jones to sing to his young daughter. Hammerstein's specially modified lyrics were: "Only make believe I'm near you. Only make believe that you're near me. Girls and boys find it fun just pretending. Couldn't you. Couldn't I. Couldn't we?" And to whom was Ravenal singing? Why, I was that little girl, seated on the bench next to him, at the convent where he was visiting

That innovation of the father singing to his daughter has since been incorporated into recent stage versions of *Show Boat*. A few years ago, the American Film Institute's special on "Favorite Quotes" included one of my lines from that scene: "Don't you remember, Daddy. We could make believe!"

In 2006 the American Film Institute voted our version of *Show Boat* one of the Top 25 Greatest Film Musicals. It was certainly a thrill having Alan Jones sing to me, as well as being in a film with velvet-voiced Paul Robeson, whose rendition of "Old Man River" has probably never been equaled. Robeson passed away in 1976,

**Alan Jones is about to sing "Make Believe" to me.
(Photo courtesy of Universal Studios.)**

but in 2003, the US Postal Service issued a handsome stamp in his honor.

Alan Jones was feeling lucky that he'd been able to play Ravenal in *Show Boat*, instead of the part for which MGM wanted him, namely the singing lead opposite Jeanette MacDonald in the operetta *Naughty Marietta*. However, none other than Nelson Eddy was Jones' replacement at MGM, which meant that Alan Jones later lost out on all those marvelous roles opposite Miss MacDonald. Once again, we may not discover what is really "lucky" or "unlucky" until many years later!

17 Anthony Adverse

From 1929 to 1933, during the depths of the depression, a man named Hervey Allen was writing a novel. He finally produced the 1,200-page tome, *Anthony Adverse,* which told the life-story of an eighteenth century orphan raised in a convent. In 1936, Warner Bros. and Mervyn Leroy were busy doing a film version of that very-long book. The film was also a monumental effort, using 700,000 feet of film and featuring ninety-eight speaking parts. Warner Bros. built more than a hundred sets on their twenty-seven huge sound stages.

Fredric March was hired for the title role, Billy Mauch was chosen to play him as a boy, and I was hired to play Florence Udney, Anthony's convent-dwelling sweetheart, as a young girl. (Director Mervyn LeRoy had previously cast me in *The World Changes.)*

A bit of a conspiracy occurred during the production. You see, Billy Mauch had a twin brother, Bobby, who was hired to play his stand-in and was dressed in an identical costume. (Stand-ins relieve the main actors of having to stand there for the long periods when lights and props are being adjusted.) At times, much to their great amusement, the Mauch twins would trade places for a scene or so.

During the filming, I once again saw my dear friend, Fredric March, as well as the boy who would play his son, Scotty Beckett (the little boy with the heavy sweater over one shoulder in *The*

As Florence Udney, the little girl in the convent. Along with *Show Boat* and *Les Miserables* —the third time I'd been filmed in a convent! (Photo courtesy of Warner Bros Studios.)

My picture with *both* Mauch twins, taken for *I'll Tell the World*, a short we made for the 1939 World's Fair in New York.

Little Rascals), with whom I would later share many wonderful experiences.

Before shooting began for me, there was a big crisis. I lost two of my front baby teeth! A quick trip to Shirley Temple's own dentist solved the problem. Like some little old lady, I found myself wearing false teeth, all hooked to a plate that fit on the roof of my mouth. I presented other problems to the producers of *Anthony Adverse,* for I was scheduled to film *Show Boat,* and there were considerable scheduling difficulties.

Our famous director, Mervyn Leroy, was a polo player and big-time horse-racing fan. We all knew that he'd bet thousands of dollars on the oh-so-famous "Seabiscuit." That legendary horse was the favorite in an exciting, 1938 Santa Anita race that was about to take place. Our director's good friend, Bing Crosby, was rooting for a horse named Ligaroti. For fun, the cast and crew were running a pool on the big event.

My parents never went to the races. However, my mother had a warm feeling toward horses, since my grandfather, William Alma McKenzie, used to compete in races—even as an old man—driving one of those little trotter carts. Plus, her grandfather, George McKenzie, was one of the original stagecoach and Pony Express riders, delivering mail between Salt Lake City and California. For whatever reason, she gave me a dollar to be a part of the pool.

The pool was probably somewhat rigged, for I was handed the name "Stagehand" with opening odds of 150 to one, while Mr. Leroy was given the name of the favorite, "Seabiscuit." My mother explained to me that my horse had little chance of winning, but I listened excitedly to the radio broadcast anyway.

The race, with 70,000 in attendance, turned out to have a photo-finish ending. You should have seen the faces on the crew when we heard the results. My "Stagehand" had most unexpectedly defeated "Seabiscuit" and come in *first,* in a stunning upset that kept Mr. Leroy's choice from being the biggest money winner of that era! No, I didn't win $150.00, only the $14 or so collected in the pool, but the moral victory was terrific. We listened to the radio on a sound stage, so I thought the name "Stagehand" was entirely appropriate.

The premiere for the very long and expensive film was an extravagant affair at the Carthay Circle Theater in Westwood. Each person in attendance was given a copy of the *Anthony Adverse* book,

My mother and I walking down the red carpet at the *Anthony Adverse*
premiere. (Photo courtesy of Warner Bros. Studios.)

or so it appeared. What we were actually handed was a four-inch
thick covered box with the program pasted on top that was designed to look like the 1,200 page book. Though my mother wasn't
driving at the time of our 1931 auto accident, after that traumatic

event, she refused to get behind the wheel and left driving strictly to my father. While he parked our car, my mother and I walked down the red carpet, flashbulbs flashed, and enthusiastic fans asked for autographs!

> *May I have your autograph, dear celebrity?*
> *Please, may I have your autograph, something special for me!*
> *Such a very simple thing*
> *It should make you laugh:*
> *All the joy your words can bring.*
> *May I have your autograph!*

Long before the premiere took place, I was busy shooting *Show Boat* at Universal, the possible scheduling conflicts involved nearly costing me the part. *Anthony Adverse* won Academy Awards for Best Supporting Actress, Best Cinematography, Best Score, and Best Film Editing. One very nice postscript to *Anthony Adverse*: it was also nominated by the Academy of Motion Picture Arts and Sciences as Best Production of the Year!

> *Let's go to the movies; they are having a big premiere.*
> *Hollywood's most famous stars are going to be coming here.*
> *All of that elegance upon display:*
> *Let's go to the Movies today!*

18 Rainbow on the River

In 1935, when I was offered the chance to play the part of an all-time brat in *Rainbow on the River*, my father had a change of heart regarding not wanting me to portray little monsters, no doubt influenced by Jane Withers' success as a brat opposite Shirley Temple in *Bright Eyes*.

The film starred boy-soprano Bobby Breen and featured the all-Black Hall Johnson Choir. It also featured Louise Beavers, my special friend from *Imitation of Life* days, as the ex-slave Black woman who raises the little white orphan.

In the story, my father, played by Alan Mowbray, brings Bobby to the home of his grandmother, who at first doubts the youngster is really her grandson. I play the part of Bobby's spoiled cousin, who makes his life miserable and refuses to invite him to her birthday party. At this party, my character plays the piano for her many guests. Schumann's "Happy Farmer" was my piece, and my piano teacher, Miss Lewyn, was most upset that the script called for me to play it badly—even playing a wrong note or two on purpose!

Alan Mowbray was quite the comedian. We all wore elegant nineteenth century costumes, on which our oh-so-fussy costume designer Albert Diano was constantly checking. My on-screen father made the prissy costume designer's life miserable by repeatedly unbuttoning and buttoning his coat, with one-too-many buttons at the top and one-too-many buttonholes at the bottom. Yes, Mr. Diano really met his match in Alan Mowbray, and Bobby Breen and I couldn't help but be royally amused. Mind you, Bobby and I didn't dare do something like that ourselves.

Taking My Punches

In the *Rainbow on the River* plot, I supposedly get furious at Bobby when he starts singing from his room on the second floor, competing with my piano performance, right in the middle of my birthday party—to which I hadn't invited him. In an act of extreme cruelty, my character then has the butler drown Bobby's mice.

In the climax of the film, my mother, in a moment of supreme anger, slaps me on the face! Benita Hume played that part and had an unpleasant time with this bit of necessary business. There were plenty of hugs both before and after the shooting of that pivotal scene, but when I came down the staircase of the beautiful residence, Miss Hume gave me a resounding slap! "Mommy!" I wailed, as the cameras rolled.

Nowadays, the sound technicians would be able to skillfully dub in the very loud sound of a slap, timed to the mini-second, even with Miss Hume not laying a hand on me. However, for us no such sophisticated equipment was available, so the real thing was necessary, and I got slapped hard—once for the long-shot and once for the close-up!

Being a true "professional" by then, I had no hard feelings about that slap. Afterwards, my screen mother hugged me and, once again,

Group scene with Benita Hume, Charles Butterworth, and Bobby Breen, where I'm "offended" by Bobby's mice. (Photo courtesy of RKO Studios.)

apologized for her "dirty deed." Believe me, my character deserved it. Theater audiences clearly agreed. It was a strange feeling to be in a theater and hear the audience enthusiastically clapping when she gave me that wallop. I wasn't sure whether I should be proud, or a bit resentful. Of course, feeling proud won out.

Producer Sol Lesser was so pleased with the way that film turned out that he scheduled a well-received cast party at the conclusion of the picture. We all felt the exhilaration of a job well done, as our party spread over the entire sound stage.

Rainbow on the River contains some marvelous singing of Stephen Foster music by both Bobby Breen and the all-black "Hall

Johnson Choir." Like *Imitation of Life* and *Show Boat,* by showing a white boy successfully raised by a black woman, the movie was ahead of its time in the racial sphere.

Our motion picture received praise from the critics and success at the box office. However, perhaps because it was independently produced by Lesser, rather than one of the major studios, the film met with misfortune in later years. Perhaps the warehouse where the negative was stored burned down; perhaps it met the fate suf-

I was so mean. No wonder I deserved that slap
(Photo courtesy of RKO Studios.)

fered by so many other old films once they'd been distributed. Until the American Film Institute undertook the preservation of old films, they naturally crumbled with age. In other cases, the negatives were purposely destroyed for their silver content. Whatever its fate, it is clear that the negative for *Rainbow on the River* did not survive, and neither did even a decent print.

Apparently at some point, a very much-used print of the film was sold to some company that duplicated it as a VHS tape, which they distributed under the title *It Happened in New Orleans*. To add insult to injury, in the new opening credits, my name was misspelled as "Marilyn Knowlder." Fortunately, in recent years the film has been at least partially restored and issued as a DVD with its original title, *Rainbow on the River.*

A Small Confession

Even though he was several inches shorter than me, nine-year-old Bobby and I had a crush on each other. (David Durand had previously been my on-screen boyfriend in both 1933's *Best of Enemies* and *The World Changes*, but we were not at all interested in each other.) I'll never forget the day Bobby invited me into his dressing-room-trailer, complete with a star on the door. He then held my hand and sang me a beautiful love song in his extraordinary boy-soprano voice—followed by a kiss on the cheek. When he tried to kiss me on the lips, I think I automatically turned my head, as my parents had taught me to do. Before we knew it, the Assistant Director was going crazy and knocking loudly on the door, which I only then discovered to be locked. End of the incident.

Bobbie Breen and Marilyn Knowlden, next to their stand-ins, Jackie McGee and Gloria Thatcher, in-between scenes for *Rainbow on the River*

The Rest of the Story

Let me fast-forward a few years: Bobby Breen, my stand-in, Gloria, and I all ended up at the same Beverly Hills High School, yet Gloria was too embarrassed to reveal her *Rainbow on the River* connection to the two of us.

Let's fast-forward to the present day. Gloria(Thatcher) de Ment and I live fairly close to each other and give lectures on child actors of the 1930s in various public locations. Gloria recently succeeded in making telephone contact with Bobby, and I later spent an amazing few minutes on the phone with the former child star.

"Are you still as beautiful as ever?" Bobby Breen asked me—

one of those questions to which there is no satisfactory answer, but all these years later, which sure felt good!

We then recalled that afternoon when we'd given the Assistant Director fits when he was knocking on Bobby's locked dressing room door.

"You rejected me!" Bobby complained.

"No, I didn't," I truthfully responded.

When I reminded him that he'd held my hand and sung to me, he assured me that he didn't do *that* very often. There we were, two old people in our eighties, reminiscing about that incident in Bobby's trailer seventy-three years ago, when we were a couple of nine-year olds!

19 Mentors

I'm sure my life would have been less meaningful without the several mentors that came my way. The first one was Charlie Silber, our neighbor on Cheromoya Drive. He came to own the Hollywood Magic Shop on Hollywood Boulevard and gave me my first lessons in magic, a hobby I later pursued strenuously, reading all kinds of books on the subject and diligently practicing my sleight-of-hand, with both cards and coins. Then there were Lillian and Alfred Gay, she a fine operatic singer, he a violinist. They often picked me up and took me to their lovely home, where we enjoyed a three-way musicale, with me on the grand piano. And then, there was someone else . . . .

Through the Donut Hole

One day in 1935, I was lunching with my parents at a Hollywood Boulevard Coffee Shop, when my eye caught a white, very strange-looking backwards collar that was worn by a man in a black suit. When the man noticed my staring at him, he picked up the donut he was eating and gazed at me through its hole! Later he came over and introduced himself. He told us his name was "Father Smith" and that he was a retired Episcopal priest.

Strangely enough, we kept running in to him around town.

About the third time, my parents told him that in a couple of days I would be playing the piano on the radio on station KFWB. A radio commentator named Richard Blake Saunders was going to be doing a program on child prodigies like Mozart, and supposedly as an example of a modern day "prodigy," I was to perform Grieg's Papillon (which means "Butterfly" in French). Father Smith promised he'd be listening to my live radio performance.

The next week I received an illustrated fan letter from the "Butterfly" himself. I was sure it was my new friend who had written the letter. After that, Father Smith became a frequent visitor to our home and a frequent contributor to our mailbox. Many of his letters were illustrated with whimsical pictures of animals.

He was not a handsome man; he had a sizable hole at the back of his neck, where he'd been wounded in World War I, but Father Smith had enormous personal magnetism. Forty years older than I was, he also had had a coronary thrombosis and was retired from active work with the Episcopal Church. His enormous charisma really appealed to me, and in time, he became my best friend, taking me to such places as the Planetarium in Griffith Park, the Alligator Farm, Monkey Island, the Ostrich Farm, the Circus, Olvera Street, and the Huntington Library and Gallery. He taught me all kinds of things, from religion to theories of education. I knew all about checkers, but he taught me how to play chess, with all its fascinating strategies. He also encouraged me to write poetry and bought me my first rhyming dictionary. One summer, I spent nearly all my time writing poetry, and I spent hours during another summer studying the regular dictionary.

My father was not too enthusiastic about my friendship with

Saturday, March 14, 1936   Hollywood Citizen-News

Helena Lewyn's Pupil on Radio

MARILYN KNOWLDEN, juvenile actress and pianist, who will play on KFWB's program tomorrow at 9:30 a.m. with Richard Drake Saunders acting as commentator. Helena Lewyn, concert pianist, has been the young musician's only teacher. Marilyn will play Norma Shearer's daughter in the forthcoming "Marie Antoinette" at M-G-M studios.

A different experience for me, playing the piano on the radio!]

Father Smith, who was forty years older than I, but my mother found him to be a wonderful person and was delighted with the way our friendship was enriching my life. Of course, all this was years before today's scandals regarding men with backwards collars that spent "too much time" with youngsters.

My parents both attended Brigham Young Academy, a precursor to Brigham Young University. They were members of the Church of Jesus Christ of Latter-day Saints, but not really attuned to organized religion. As a child, I remember visiting a Mormon Church only once, when my mother's best friend, "Aunt" Cora Bird, was singing there. My only formal religious training occurred when I attended various churches and Sunday Schools at the invitation of several young boys my age. Bob took me with him to the Baptist Church; Mathew to the Catholic; and Carly talked me into regular attendance at the Episcopal Church, where the two of us each received a quarter for singing in the choir. I had plenty of girlfriends, but it was always the little boys who invited me to church with them. I also remember my parents once taking me to a tent where Aimee Semple McPherson was preaching, using a clothes line, complete with clothes pins, for taking up the collection! The not-so-subtle message was, "No small change, please!"

Father Smith had an idea for a worthwhile project. Since I was about to film Marie Antoinette, he asked me to be the hostess for a roller skating party with a Marie Antoinette theme. With Los Angeles' Bishop Stevens' blessing, it was to be for the benefit of the Neighborhood Settlement House, a charity of the Episcopal Church. With a loud organ playing in the background, the skating party went off as planned and raised quite a bit of money for the charity.

It All Started in a Barn

Before long, Father Smith got a good report from his doctor and decided that he could return to work as an Episcopal clergyman. He owned a small ranch in Sunland, but decided that Encino, in the San Fernando Valley, would be the ideal place for a new church. He heard that the actor Edward Everett Horton, who was perhaps best known in the movies for portraying a butler, had a converted barn that might be suitable for church meetings. After receiving permission from the Los Angeles Diocese of the Episcopal Church, he called on the actor and received permission to use his barn for church services.

I was very much involved in all of the above, along with preparation for the first services, which were attended by such people as the actor Andy Devine, Mrs. Spencer Tracy, and the man who played Lum in Lum and Abner. On the first Sunday, Bishop Stevens, head of the Los Angeles Diocese, attended and gave his blessings to the fledgling church. Barker Bros. Department Store loaned us an organ and, ignoring the foot pedals, I played it for the opening. I even helped Father Smith count the collection every Sunday.

I was eleven years old. Nevertheless, from then on I played the piano for the services, which became increasingly popular in the Encino community. I also taught Sunday school—to children my age or younger—which necessitated a lot of Bible studying. I remember when I asked the children about their fathers' occupations, one of them replied that his father "made worm holes," which was apparently his part of the antiquing process in furniture manufacturing. Father Smith continued to give me a ride each Sunday, and he rewarded me for my efforts by giving me a gold

Reverend Father Smith is pictured greeting congregation after opening of St. Nicholas Church on Encino estate of Actor Edward Everett Horton.

Clipping showing first service of St. Nicholas Church.]

cross inscribed "Coadjutor," which meant ecclesiastical or church assistant. My parents attended services a few times, but my father said it gave him a backache, and later events proved he wasn't kidding about that.

Before long, someone donated a full-size church-model electric organ to our Saint Nicholas Church—the "Children's Church," according to Father Smith. Six free lessons came with the organ, and I took advantage of two of those lessons. I also had a book that I studied, and I taught myself how to use the keyboard-type foot-pedals that are so important to that instrument. At first, Father Smith let me know in advance what hymns we'd be singing so I could practice ahead of time. Necessity being the mother of invention, I soon learned to sight-read the hymns by studying the shape of the intervals I would be playing. In time, that helped me to improve my sight-reading enough to be able to accompany soloists with no advance warning, a skill that would serve me well the rest of my life. People tell me that I'm lucky to be able to play the piano and the organ. Believe me, there's a lot more than luck involved; there's a lot of hard work!

Before we knew it, a very generous benefactor donated large acreage on Ventura Boulevard. A building fund campaign was begun, and soon a fine church building arose on that site. I loved the appearance of its altar that was styled like an ancient three-sided altar. Father Smith had a studio scene-painter decorate the ten-foot doors with paintings of Saint Nicholas and Mary-holding-the-Baby-Jesus, plus what appeared to be the sky behind the altar.

Father Smith lived on a five-acre Encino ranch, complete with a very lovely small chapel. To me, accustomed to a small apartment, those five acres seemed more like one hundred. Several times, I was able to have a birthday party at that ranch, inviting all my school chums. They were fascinated by the stone barbecue pit that Father Smith had built, burying a donut in its heart—in honor of the way we'd met. Before long, Father Smith was driving me and my girlfriend Mary Stewart to St. Nicholas Church every Sunday. One summer, Mary and I spent a few days at the ranch. While Father Smith and a housekeeper stayed in the main house, Mary and I slept in the tiny guest house and spent our days shoveling gravel, riding a donkey, or having fun with Father Smith's gorgeous talkative cockatoo and two Chow dogs.

Previously, Father Smith had presented me with my first dog, a darling Chow puppy I named Fu Lynn. He was a very intelligent dog that I was able to housebreak, plus teach him to sit, lie down, "speak," and shake hands. He did have one unfortunate habit though: he liked to run up one arm of our couch, across the back, then rapidly down the other arm. This habit did no harm, other than totally terrorizing any of our visitors!

I say "Thank You!" to my wonderful parents. But I also say "Thank You!" to all my mentors, including Miss Lewyn and Father Smith. I would be a different person without them.

20 Slave Ship, 1937, and Other Matters

1937 was a sluggish year for our pre-World War II economy and a lean year for my employment. That explains why, at ten years of age, I found myself looking very much out-of-place as I stood in the California State unemployment line along with various out-of-work adults, registering for my unemployment insurance. Wisely or not, my father had decided that, once he was an agent himself, he should refrain from having his daughter as a client. At any rate, 1937 was a slow year for my Hollywood career, but it was an exciting year for every child in America, for that was the year when Disney's first feature film, *Snow White and the Seven Dwarfs,* hit the silver screen. Soon, many of us could name every one of those Seven Dwarfs.

Slave Ship

The tradition of christening sailing ships goes back thousands of years. Until 1846, that honor was extended exclusively to males, but in 1846, a new tradition was established. A Mrs. Lavina Watson Fanning broke precedent when she sponsored a U. S. warship called *Germantown* in Philadelphia and christened the ship.

In 1937, I benefited from that tradition when Darryl F. Zanuck, producer of *Les Misérables,* cast me in *Slave Ship*. I was to portray the young girl who christens a nineteenth century ship that is destined to become a slave ship and carry young African men and women from that distant land to America. In the film, a portent of dark days to come occurs when, just after her christening, a worker is killed while caught under the ship during her launching. Fox Studios had built an expensive 180-foot replica of a nineteenth century schooner. My task was to christen the ship with a bottle of champagne hanging from a ribbon, and then scream hysterically when the terrible accident occurs.

The director called out, "Action!"

I gave a great heave-ho to the bottle—which continued to dangle intact from the ribbon. On the second attempt, there was still no breaking of the bottle. The Assistant Director told me he would demonstrate the correct way to fling the bottle.

"Action!"

The bottle flung in the right direction. Still no breakage of the bottle! It was only after the Prop Man drilled hole after hole in that bit of glass that I was able to get the stubborn thing to break. At least I was saved a bit of embarrassment when other people had similar trouble breaking that darn bottle!

The Birds and the Bees

About that time, I had a burning question in my mind: *Where do babies come from?* I confess that most three-year-olds of today, whether raised on a farm or in today's sophisticated television society, are probably better informed about the facts of life than I was at age eleven. The truth is, I was an "only child" and I was ignorant

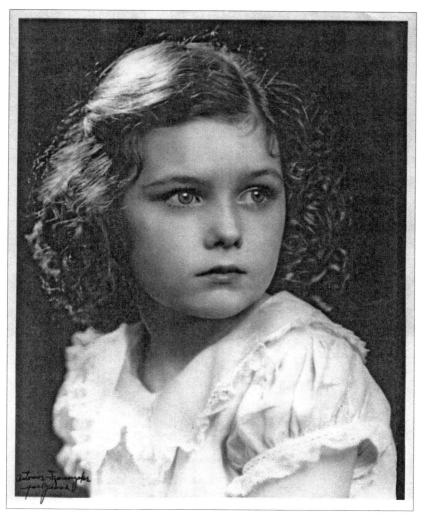

So much to wonder about.

about such matters, even though I lived in the heart of Hollywood. In our neighborhood, there were few pregnant ladies—or at least that I was aware of.

I had a hunch that it would embarrass my mother too much for me to ask. So the next time I visited the public library, I searched through the card catalog and selected a book I thought would be suitable. Since that book was in a special restricted area, I took courage in hand and requested *What Every Young Girl Should Know* from the librarian. My questions got answered.

A month or so later, my mother screwed up her courage and told me, "You know, Marilyn, when a girl gets to be about twelve years old . . . ."

"Never mind, Mother. I already know," I quickly interrupted. So that took care of that subject.

21 Marie Antoinette, Norma Shearer, and Tyrone Power

*Y*ou remember reading about Marie Antoinette. When the Eighteenth Century Queen of France was asked why the people were protesting, she was told, "Because they have no bread." She will always be remembered for her classic insensitive response, "Then let them eat cake!" Another way you may remember her: in 1792, thanks to the French Revolutionaries, she lost her head to the guillotine!

In 1938, MGM cast me as the daughter of Norma Shearer, who was playing the hapless queen. She had previously played Juliet in *Romeo and Juliet* and Elizabeth Barrett Browning in *The Barretts of Wimpole Street*. In portraying Princess Therese, I soon felt as if I was living through the French Revolution. The first filming for me occurred at night in a scene where Tyrone Power meets the carriage of the escaping royal family. Normally, the studio saves money by doing all the scenes for a certain location at the same time. In this case, they were forced to shoot all Tyrone Power's scenes at once, so he'd be free for another film. (Perhaps the most handsome actor of all time, he appeared in *The Mark of Zorro* and *Blood and Sand*.)

While shooting the scene with good-looking and very pleasant Tyrone Power, I met for the first time my new screen mother and father. I also renewed my friendship with Scotty Beckett, whom I'd met

The little Prince, Queen Marie Antionette, and Princess Therese—Scotty Beckett, Norma Shearer and Marilyn Knowlden. (Photo courtesy of MGM Studios.)

during *Anthony Adverse*, and who would be playing the little Prince. The two of us only had one scene with Mr. Power, but thanks to him, once filming had started for us, our employment had officially begun.

Nice Work If You Can Get It

For six weeks, other than when one of our scenes was scheduled, Scotty and I fulfilled our part of our contracts by attending school for three hours each day in MGM's famous "Little Red Schoolhouse," taught by a Mrs. McDonald. Our only other classmates were none other than Mickey Rooney and Judy Garland, the young lady who soon would be shooting *The Wizard of Oz*. (Occasionally, Susanna

Foster, who was filming *Phantom of the Opera,* also dropped in for a day or two. After school, Scotty and I, along with our mothers, would have a delicious lunch at the studio commissary, and then go home. For that, we were getting paid quite a bit of money.

Scotty and I were buddies, as were Mickey and Judy. Of course Scotty and I were children, while the others were teenagers. As such, they were hardly interested in us, and we were hardly interested in them. Judy had first received public acclaim in *Broadway Melody of 1938*, when she sang to Clark Gable's photograph. I met Gable again on the MGM lot, and this time received his autograph. Mickey and Judy had just finished *Love Finds Andy Hardy* and obviously enjoyed each other's company. I do remember thinking at the time that I preferred Judy's singing. Not so the studio. At that time, they were pushing Susanna, the star of *Phantom of the Opera*. Of course, the very next year, Judy starred in the unforgettable *The Wizard of Oz.*

Life in the Palace

Both in our schoolroom and on the set, Scotty and I, assisted by our tutor, studied the history of the French Revolution. Every day, there we were, in what surely seemed to be the real Palace of Versailles, with one magnificent room only leading to another. Most studio sets have no ceilings, but this one did, complete with many spectacular crystal chandeliers. The Art Director for the film had spent months touring Europe and buying up fabulous French antiques that now adorned our palace. While actual shooting was not taking place, many of the upholstered chairs were protected by a strategically placed cord, to prevent people like Scotty and me from sitting in them.

Costumes in Black and White

The legendary Adrian was our costume designer. He had a theory that we actors would perform much better if our costumes were authentic. So that's the way he had them made, right down to delicate, lace-trimmed bloomers and petticoats, things which no camera would ever photograph! Visiting the wardrobe department was an awesome experience. There were acres of brocades, embroideries, satin, ribbon, oversize gray wigs, and gigantic hats with feathers. There was a whole sea of talented seamstresses, on some days as many as 300! As the legendary queen, Norma Shearer had thirty-four costume changes and eighteen different wigs, not to mention the appropriate hats, shoes, gloves, trains, jewelry, and fans that would complete each outfit! On the set, the studio provided "leaning boards" for the supposed comfort of its female actors, since the skirts the women wore were so huge that sitting in a chair was impossible.

Just as huge as the wigs and skirts, there were ninety-eight massive sets, some shooting of the *actual* palace at Versailles, plus a cast of 5,500 extras. MGM surely made a mistake by not filming *Marie Antoinette* in color. When I now watch the film on my television screen, I am appalled at the missing mosaic of colors that I was so aware of! Perhaps the film was so over-budget that color was too expensive, or perhaps MGM thought that color would make the tragic story look too cheerful. I know there was a lot of opposition to Ted Turner's more recent colorizing of motion pictures, but *Marie Antoinette* is one film that surely would benefit from that process.

One of the gorgeous outfits designed for me by famous designer Adrian.
(Photo courtesy of MGM Studios.)

Our Movie Parents

Robert Morley played our father, King Louis XVI, complete with a padded stomach. Scotty loved playfully punching Morley in that heavily-padded tummy, and Robert Morley did his own bit of teasing when he would simply devastate fastidious Adrian by letting a bit of shirt-tail hang out. One memory I have is of Director Van Dyke's nodding to Miss Shearer and meaningfully pointing to his chest, when he thought her dress was slipping too low and revealing too much of her bosom. By today's standards, believe me, there was little that was shocking about her appearance.

Norma Shearer and Robert Morley were wonderful screen parents to us. When we returned to the set after lunch, Scotty and I headed to a delicate French porcelain box that was our "magic box" since, courtesy of our screen parents, there was often a little surprise inside for us, such as the little puppy-dog charm bracelet I still prize! But to this day, when I think of the French Revolution, I have a vision of an angry mob, upraised clubs in hand, storming the palace and coming after us.

Amazing Norma Shearer

Scotty and I were amazed by our "mother's" ability to produce tears on demand. If a crying scene for Norma Shearer was about to begin, she was able to chat pleasantly with us while tears began incongruously welling up in her eyes, in preparation for her next scene. I never could figure out how she was able to do that. Crying scenes are the bugaboo for almost all child actors, and many adults, as well, often necessitating the Makeup Man's blowing a glycerin inhaler in an actor's eyes.

It was only when I became an adult and read Norma Shearer's life history that I figured out her secret. To produce tears, we chil-

**An autographed photo from Norma Shearer, together with a
page from my autograph book, which continue to remind me
of our "good old days at Versailles!"**

dren perhaps thought about some pet we'd lost (in my case, a de-
ceased pet pink-eared rabbit). In Norma's case, I came to realize
that she was a grieving widow, no doubt recalling the recent loss of
her thirty-seven-year-old, frail producer-husband, Irving Thalberg,
who was indispensable to both her personal happiness and her career. For many years, her husband, father of her two children, had
been promising her the starring role in *Marie Antoinette*. At the
time of his death due to a congenital heart defect, the production
was well under way, and MGM had already spent a half million
dollars on the extravagant film. Sadly, her husband never got to see
the final product, so no wonder the tears came easily to her.

Like Bette Davis, Norma Shearer was more interested in doing
a fine job as an actress than in always looking picture perfect. As a
result, in her final scene, just before the queen goes to the guillotine,
she appears with her hair long and stringy and without makeup.

The premiere was held in Westwood's Carthay Circle Theater.

There was no limousine for my mother and me, but we did have our chauffeur, my faithful Daddy, driving our Chrysler sedan. Red carpet! Searchlights in the sky! Lots of fans asking for autographs!

> *It won't take a minute*
> *Of your precious time.*
> *Write a little something in it.*
> *It won't cost you a dime.*
> *It will mean so much to me.*
> *You don't know the half!*
> *I want the whole world to see*
> *That I have your autograph!*

While we were filming, Scotty and I questioned our tutor as to whatever had happened to the real-life Prince and Princess we were portraying. After all, the King and Queen had both lost their heads to the guillotine. From the movie script, we did know that the revolutionaries had dragged the little Prince away from his mother and sister. Our tutor explained that Princess Therese (my role) had indeed survived, although she never had any children, but that a mystery surrounded whatever had happened to the little Prince, popularly known as the "Dauphin," the designated future King of France.

The movie was behind me, but thoughts and memories of *Marie Antoinette* continued to haunt me, and I found myself composing my very first piece of music. At that stage of my life, I had almost no knowledge of harmony; I just kept poking piano keys until I found sounds that created the right tragic feel. Reaching way down inside, I managed to compose a short piano etude I called "Marie Antoinette." I treasure an entry in my autograph book that reads: "To Marilyn – To remind you of the good old days at Versailles – Norma Shearer."

22 Public and Private School Dilemmas

All during my time in the fifth grade, I kept worrying about going on to Junior High School, which in the Los Angeles public schools began with the sixth grade. My girlfriend, who was older than I, filled me with terrifying stories of the difficulties of Junior High School. I ended up in such a panic that my father said, "Don't worry, Marilyn. We'll think of something!" That something turned out to be my parents enrolling me in Miss Long's Professional School. Their "Alma Mater Song" *should* have been:

> *All hail our dear Professional School,*
> *Where we receive each useful tool*
> *We're going to need in our career,*
> *Though we just spend three hours here!*
> *Our afternoons we need to use*
> *For auditions, lessons, and interviews!*

> *To learn my lines, I'm going to need*
> *To learn the proper way to read.*
> *To answer my fan-mail each night,*
> *I'll need to learn the way to write.*
> *Arithmetic will seem sweet as honey*

When it's time to add up all my money!

Never before was I in such a place. The studio tutors had always worked out fine for me, but of all things, that school tested me and wanted to advance me two full years (and I was already ahead one year). The school was full of juvenile Hollywood extras and "wannabes," whose every moment was filled with talk of photographs, dance lessons, and studio interviews. (An "extra" is an actor without speaking lines.) I was not impressed, and I yearned for a school where I could really learn something. I confess, it was Miss Long's School I was satirizing in my 1993 I'm Gonna Get You in the Movies "Alma Mater Song" and the following duet:

Girl One: I am too younger than you. I am too younger than you.

Girl Two: Official records plainly do show that's really not true!

Girl One: Well, I am shorter than you. I'm way much shorter than you.

Girl Two: A minute ago I was on tiptoe. I'm way much shorter than you.

Girl One: I make more money than you. I've more screen credits than you.

Girl Two: My bulging scrapbook makes it clear I've had a glowing career.

Girl One: Well, I am blonder than you. Take a look at every root.

Girl Two: I'm way much blonder than you!

Girl One & Two: Well, who could be more cute!

My father thought over our situation and did a very smart thing: he moved us to a modest two-bedroom apartment in Beverly Hills. The entire town did not consist of mansions, but it did have a simply wonderful educational system. What's more, their elementary schools went through the eighth grade. I comfortably moved into Hawthorne School's Sixth Grade, and my school problems were solved.

Unfortunately no dogs were allowed in our new apartment, so Father Smith arranged for Fu Lynn to be retired to the country. Fortunately, Patches-the-Cat made the move just fine and ended up sleeping in my bed. Every morning I would be sneezing and coughing, while my father would say, "Now, Marilyn, that's just a bad habit you have!" At that time, the term "allergy" was unknown to us, and it would be many years before a doctor would determine that I had a severe allergy to cats!

My very first year at Hawthorne, I learned to play a newly-invented small flute-like object called a "Tonette." At the end of the year, the school performed The Prince Who Was a Piper, and I portrayed the Prince, adding authenticity to my part by playing "Kerry Dancers" on my Tonette. Sadly, we were unable to locate a garage or basement piano on which I could practice. Even though Miss Lewyn had plans for me to play my newly learned Mozart's "Piano Concerto in A Major" together with an actual orchestra, my piano lessons with Miss Lewyn came to an end!

Frankie Burke is about to shove my hat down my face.
He plays a young James Cagney. I play a young Ann Sheridan,
while William Tracy and Ann Howard watch.
(Courtesy of Warner Bros. Studios.)

23 James Cagney's Angels With Dirty Faces

While I was still eleven, the famous director, Michael Curtiz, cast me to play glamorous Ann Sheridan as a child in the James Cagney/Pat O'Brien/Humphrey Bogart film, *Angels With Dirty Faces*. (In 1943, Mr. Curtiz would receive the Academy of Motion Picture Arts and Science's Best Director Award for the nation's all-time favorite, *Casablanca*.) No doubt our film benefited from his typical careful attention to the smallest point. He certainly demonstrated that with me, paying attention to every detail, including exactly how I was to be dressed. The 1938 film received three Academy Award nominations for Best Director, Best Actor (Cagney), and Best Original Story.

Near the beginning of the film, Frankie Burke, playing James Cagney as a teenager, playfully pulls my hat down over my face. (Later in the movie, as a grownup Ann Sheridan, my character does the same thing to James Cagney!) Our scene was shot on the Warner Bros. "New York City Street." The setting was all too familiar to me, since I'd previously filmed four other movies at that studio.

In 2007, I received an e-mail from Frankie Burke's granddaughter pleading with me to tell her about the grandfather she'd never met. I did send her a photograph of her grandfather that was taken from our scene together in the film, but I'm sorry to say, I couldn't tell her very much about him. Frankie was a teenager with no interest in a girl my age, and I certainly had little interest in him. I'll have to admit, though, when James Cagney visited our set, I noticed that he did look a lot like Frankie Burke.

All his life, Frankie looked forward to an opportunity to take advantage of that uncanny resemblance. When the eighteen-year-old read that Angels With Dirty Faces was to be filmed and that Warner Bros. was looking for someone to portray James Cagney as a youngster, Frankie lost no time in journeying to Hollywood. Before he even had time to request an interview, a Warner Bros. talent scout, Solly Belno, spotted him at a traffic signal and arranged for him to screen-test—which, of course, led to Frankie's playing Cagney as a youngster.

A Movie's Life Expectancy

What happened to all my motion pictures after they'd been shown in movie theaters around the country and overseas was that they often disappeared into vaults somewhere. I could never see them again, except in the unlikely event that they were reissued to theaters or released on 16mm film. Even if you could get your hands on a film, only the very wealthy could afford to buy a 35mm print or a projector with which to display it. With time, many early movies crumbled into dust, or were destroyed for their silver content.

All that changed with the advent of popular television and the later invention of the home video recorder/player. Suddenly, I could see many of my films on my private television screen, or perhaps on cable television on Turner Classic Movies. Before I knew it, there were copies available on VHS tapes that I could actually own.

Little did I dream that *Angels With Dirty Faces* would become a classic, not only popular as a VHS tape, but also when it was issued as a DVD! I may not have had a giant part, but it feels wonderful to have appeared in a movie with such longevity. After all these years, being a small frog in a big puddle suits me just fine!

Another postscript to all this: in 2008, the Breygent Company asked me to be part of an *Angels With Dirty Faces* autograph trading card featuring the film poster and my current photo, bio, and signature. As I signed those 300 cards with my eighty-one-year-old hands, I couldn't believe that I was actually capitalizing on my work as an eleven-year-old.

24 Director and Producer Power

Woody Allen has a saying: "Half of life is just showing up!" I agree. Perhaps much of whatever success I experienced in Hollywood can be explained by the fact that *they knew they could count on me!* Throughout my more than fifty films, (thanks to cooperation from my parents), I never missed a day, never was late, never failed to have learned my lines, never complained about my costumes, never failed to have my hair right, and never lost a crucial item. That may explain why, as I look over a list of the films I've been in, I notice some of the same names reappearing—directors such as William Wellman, Mervyn LeRoy, Richard Boleslawski, Irving Cummings, and George Cukor. I am also amazed by how often the same producer names show up—such as Darryl F. Zanuck, Jack Warner, and David O. Selznick. Hollywood actors are conscious of the immense power of the Director. Behind the scenes, however, their professional fate is often determined by that ghostlike creature, the Producer. Some claim that in Hollywood, it's "who you know." I would submit that even more important is probably "who knows you!" Of course, all that may make you wonder:

> *When it takes experience to get a part,*
> *How do newcomers ever get a start?*

In 1938, David O. Selznick, who had been my Producer on both *The Conquerors* and *David Copperfield,* was casting *The Adventures of Tom Sawyer,* which was to be filmed in color. Selznick was considering me for the part of Tom Sawyer's girlfriend, Becky Thatcher. For most of the year, I'm afraid I violated my family's policy of "No great expectations," for I really coveted that part.

Two young boys were being considered for the part of Tom: Jackie Moran and Tommy Kelly. It was rather clear that I was way too tall for Tommy, (despite my agent pointing out the reality that little girls were often taller than boys of the same age) but Jackie was just the right height for me. There were lots of interviews involved. Then, screen tests were made of me paired with Jackie, while Tommy was filmed together with ideally short Ann Gillis.

There was lots of excitement in my family when I signed a seven-year contract for the film. It consisted of an as-yet-unsigned-by-Selznick one-year contract, followed by six yearly options, with the salary increasing each year up to great heights, or so it seemed to me. After considerable debate, Selznick and the powers-that-be made a big decision—or should I say a "little" one—they chose the smaller pair of youngsters!

At the time, I was really pained by that loss, but the passage of time cast quite a different light on the wisdom of a child signing a seven-year contract. Actors like Judy Garland and Mickey Rooney ended up bemoaning the loss of their childhood, thanks to such contracts, which decreed that children will attend school at the studio. The in-studio tutors are competent, all right, but they can provide none of the social benefits of school attendance. For me, that was one of those times when—over the long run—so called bad news indeed turned out to have a silver lining.

Strictly Gone With The Wind

A year later, Selznick was considering me for the part of Carreen O'Hara, youngest sister of Scarlett, in that blockbuster of all times, *Gone With the Wind*. Once again, I suffered great disappointment when Ann Rutherford was given the part. Once again, my high hopes were "gone with the wind!"

> *It's tough to get a part,*
> *But it is tougher still to lose one.*
> *Don't let them break your heart*
> *When out of many they must choose one.*
> *If you are in this business, you just better get used to it,*
> *For if your life is show-biz, you are certain to go through it!*
> *You better learn to be a little philosophical*
> *In case you don't receive that one important call!*
> *It's tough to get a part,*
> *But it is tougher still to lose one.*
> *Don't let them break your heart*
> *When it turns out that you lose one,*
> *For it's not you they choose*
> *When they choose one!*

A little postscript to all this: in 2010, I had occasion to be introduced to eighty-nine-year-old Ann Rutherford. I jokingly complained to her that she had gotten the part for which David O. Selznick was considering me. She told me of all the unbelievable dividends she'd received from playing the part of Scarlet's sister in *Gone With the* Wind. (I can just imagine!) When I asked her for her autograph, here is what that gracious lady wrote: "To Marilyn. I didn't mean to be Carreen! You would have been perfect!"

25 Act in a Movie and See the World

All my childhood was spent in California, except for one trip to Springville, Utah, where I met lots of relatives and became a country girl for a day, sliding down a haystack, milking a cow, and almost everything. Then in 1939, I was cast in Jam Handy's short subject, *An Evening With Edgar Guest*. Edgar Guest (1881-1959) was a grass roots poet, who produced an endless stream of home-spun poems. His most famous poem, "Home," goes:

"It takes a heap o' livin' in a house t' make it home,
A heap o' sun an' shadder, an' ye sometimes have t' roam
Afore ye really 'preciate the things ye lef' behind,
An' hunger fer 'em somehow, with 'em allus on yer mind.
It don't make no differunce how rich ye get t' be,
How much yer chairs an' tables cost, how great yer luxury;
It ain't home t' ye, though it be the palace of a king,
Until somehow yer soul is sort o' wrapped round everything."

Because Edgar Guest had a weekly radio program in Detroit, Michigan, that film had to be shot in that location. A fellow child actor, a twelve-year-old like me named Mickey Rentschler, was also cast in the show. Mickey and his mother, my mother and I, and

Publicity still with child actor Mickey Rentschler, Poet/Broadcaster Edgar Guest, and Marilyn Knowlden having a cracker barrel chat.

our tutor spent three days journeying to Detroit by train. Each day, our teacher, who was paid by the studio, gave us three hours of instruction—a most delightful sort of school. Often glancing out the window of the train, we mostly studied the various states we were passing through. Mickey and I really enjoyed ourselves. At night, our upper berths were opposite each other, so what fun we had fun chatting about the events of the day.

We were scheduled to be there for just a few days. However, the producers hadn't counted on Edgar Guest's priorities. His daughter was about to be married, and he couldn't have been more excited. After a short time shooting, he would often cry out, "I can't stand it. I'm missing so much at home. Let's call it a day. I'll see you all tomorrow!" As it turned out, we spent a total of three weeks in Detroit, so we were able to visit Canada, as well as the Ford factory in Dearborn,

We also saw that town's reconstruction of the Menlo Park, New Jersey laboratories of Thomas Edison. Yes, that same Thomas Edison, who in 1877, invented one of the very first phonographs and was one of the main developers of the motion picture! Most evenings, for the only time in my life, I partook of frog's legs in our hotel's luxurious dining room. Yes, they did taste like chicken. They really did!

At the conclusion of the picture, Edgar Guest presented me with a beautiful leather-bound collected edition of his poems. It was inscribed with a lovely message, and I promised I would treasure the volume forever. However, at some point in my childhood, I loaned the book to a girlfriend. So, to my sorrow, I have it no more.

Carmen of the Golden Coast

The same fate befell my autographed copy of *Carmen of the Golden Coast,* presented to me by popular children's author Madeline Brandeis. The book tells the story of both old and modern California. I was the model for that book's "Carmen," and we filmed quite a few of the shots at the Hollywood Bowl. I attended several autograph-signing sessions with the author, a wonderful lady who certainly knew how to get along with children. My personally inscribed copy of *Carmen of the Golden Coast* with a lovely statement from Miss Brandeis, would have been a wonderful keepsake for me. However, as before, I loaned it to a girlfriend—and I never saw it again either!

Autographing copies of *Carmen of the Golden Coast,* **Madeline Brandeis,**
author, and Marilyn Knowlden, model.

Barefoot Boy

With the exception of Columbia and Monogram, I had now
worked for every major studio in Hollywood. As if part of an overall plan, in 1938 I made *Barefoot Boy* for Monogram and in 1939,
Hidden Power for Columbia.

Barefoot Boy brought me once more in contact with teenage
Marsha Mae Jones, as well as the actor who would play my boyfriend, Jackie Moran, my friend from *Tom Sawyer* screen tests. Part
of that film was shot at Lancaster Lake, which was well-stocked
with catfish. That was my first fishing experience—a challenge I
enjoyed—but who wants to eat food so indelicately acquired. I
threw every fish back into the water!

Ice cream parlor scene. Bradley Metcalfe is chatting with me while Ralph Morgan watches. Seated at table: Jackie Moran, Marcia Mae Jones, and Johnnie Morris. (Photo courtesy of Monogram Studios.)

The Hidden Power

In 1939, Columbia filmed *The Hidden Power*, starring Jack Holt. Some eight years after Dickie Moore and I played brother and sister in *Husband's Holiday*, he was also now a teenager and in the movie. The main thing I remember about that particular low-budget picture is that when someone tripped on the rug, the director merely stopped the camera at that point, then resumed filming—without taking the scene from the beginning! Director Frank Capra, with his *Mr. Deeds Goes to Town* and *Lost Horizon* had done wonderful things for Columbia's position in the industry, but it still could not begin to match the lavish spending of MGM, Paramount, Universal, Fox, RKO, and Warner Bros. The super-thrifty production techniques employed in that movie really amazed and offended me. (Does the term "B-Movie" come to mind?)

Condemned to Live

My father would be so amazed to learn that this less than spectacular movie ultimately became important. Featuring Ralph Morgan as a midnight predator, the film has today become a popular cult horror movie! Fortunately, my own scenes did not involve my being attacked by predator Ralph Morgan!

26   Beverly Hills 90210?

There we were, living in what would one day receive the zip code 90210, except that zip codes were not put into use until 1963. One of my memories from my Hawthorne School days has to do with the Cotillion my friends and I attended with the blessing of the school. There, attired in their Sunday best and sporting white gloves, young boys and girls learned both dance steps and dance floor etiquette. The boys even learned how to carry cups of punch to the girls.

In the eighth grade, my best friend, Janet Bone, let me know about a little conspiracy in which she was engaged. Aware that our classmate, Peter Frank, had a crush on me, she told Peter she knew a sure way to win my heart: he should *serenade* me! No, he didn't grab a guitar or ukulele and position himself beneath my window, but he did ask me to dance, and I was close to cracking up when he began singing "Rosalie" in my ear: "Marilyn, my darling, Marilyn my sweet. Since one night when stars danced above, I'm oh, oh, so much in love!" Oh my! Later on, did that ever give me and my girlfriends lots to talk and giggle about! But Peter was a sweet boy (and later a successful attorney!)

Beverly Hills High School

The latter part of 1939, (with no trauma this time) I entered Beverly Hills High School. Our high school had a wonderful policy: if you did real well in English your freshman year, you could choose English electives during your next three years. That's how I managed to squeeze three years of my Radio Speech classes into my years at Beverly Hills High School. How exciting an experience it was, for each week our class produced a live fifteen-minute drama or comedy on radio station KMPC.

Each semester, we were required to write two fifteen-minute radio scripts, either comedies or dramas. That meant that in my days at Beverly Hills High School—including Summer School—I wrote a total of fourteen scripts. Our teacher, Harriet Louise Touton, selected a Producer, who selected a Director, who in turn cast the show and appointed the music and sound effects technicians. The music consisted of recorded phonograph selections. The sound effects included such items as coconut-shell horses' hoofs, a thunder-simulating sheet of metal, bells of all kinds, plus a miniature door that opened and closed. Since the show was broadcast live, everything had to be timed down to the second.

Incubator for the Famous

That program, *The Norman Parade,* gave me lots of experience as an actor, director, scriptwriter, producer, music director, and sound technician. Our classroom was probably the only one in America that contained a "sound mirror," an early form of wire recorder, which we used to record, listen to, and work on our speaking voices, with many repetitions of "How now, brown cow." No squeaky voices or glottal shocks were allowed, nor Midwestern twangs such as "inny" instead of "any." Beverly Hills High School certainly spawned a whole bunch of famous people, for we had lots of talent among our students.

There was Joy Paige, who was later featured in such films as *Casablanca.* There was Bob (Robert D.) Wood, who eventually became president of CBS. (He was the man who eventually fired the Smothers Brothers for ridiculing a Catholic priest.) Then there was Bobby Breen, that former boy soprano movie star with whom I worked in *Rainbow on the River.*

Not to be forgotten was darling Jerry Paris, my former third grade classmate from Gardner Street School, who went on to win Emmys for directing *The Dick Van Dyke Show* and *Happy Days,* as well as playing Jerry Helper on that, directing some episodes of *The Mary Tyler Moore Show*, directing *Police Academy II and III*, and most episodes of *The Odd Couple,* for which he received another Emmy. Also in our class was Frank Mankiewicz, who was later the campaign chairman for Robert Kennedy and the one who announced his death on television. A year behind me was musician/composer Andre Previn.

We also mustn't forget Bob Sherman, best known for writing the script and lyrics for the motion picture *Mary Poppins.* You remember "Supercalifragilisticexpialidocious!" You also may remember "It's a Small World," as well as many other Disney songs for which he was the lyricist. His younger brother, Richard, wrote all the music, and the Sherman Brothers won an Oscar for composing "Chim-Chim-Cher-ee!" More recently, of course, they've been involved in the hit Broadway musical version of *Mary Poppins,* plus a stage version of *Chitty-Chitty-Bang-Bang.*

I really enjoyed playing opposite Jerry Paris in a script I'd written, but my favorite part was playing the title role in Bob Sherman's *Naiveté,* whose script dealt with European refugees. When I listen to the recording of that show, I am amazed at its quality, and all done by high-schoolers! Bob used to tell us, "My name is Robert Barton Sherman, and I'm going to be a writer!" Most weeks of the year, I could be found after school rehearsing for the Saturday morning broadcast.

At the end of the year, we held an "Academy Award" dinner at Trader Vic's Restaurant, where cardboard Oscars with a small wooden base were handed out. (The "Emmy" had not yet been invented.) I still have the "Best Actress" Oscar I received at one of those dinners, and I bet that Jerry Paris was nearly as thrilled by the Oscars he received on those occasions, as he was by later winning two genuine Emmys!

Family Business

My father's agency business moved to Sunset Boulevard and did fine as long as the rule remained in place that an actor could not leave his "artist's representative" as long as he got him at least one part every six months. Once that rule was abandoned—probably because it represented a kind of captivity for the actors and violated their civil rights—it became very hard for small agents like my father to survive. After all, the minute an actor became successful, he'd switch to the William Morris Agency or MCA.

To help out our family finances, halfway through my sophomore year, my family moved back to Hollywood so my mother could manage the Formosa Apartments. Consisting of 200 formerly high-end apartments favored by silent screen actors, the rather somber-looking place was located right on Hollywood Boulevard, just a couple of blocks from Grauman's Chinese Theatre, as well as Brown's famous Hot Fudge Sundae Shop. (Their scrumptious sundaes came complete with a small pitcher of hot fudge sauce.) My father did his part by finally giving up his agency business and going to work as an attorney for the Lands Division of the Federal Works Agency.

Of course, moving to Hollywood placed me out of the Beverly Hills High School boundaries. However, since I had good grades, I received special permission to continue to attend the school, with transportation assistance from bus service and Hollywood's famous Red Cars—electric street cars that ran on tracks, powered by an overhead electric cable. Beverly Hills High School was indeed an outstanding school with college-caliber instructors. My fabulous English teacher, Wendell Black, eventually became president of Harbor College.

In 1940, I was cast in the school play, *All About Eve*. Also in the cast were my soon-to-be boyfriend, Ray Page, plus a pretty young girl with whom I shared a desk in A Cappella Choir, June Haver. Tiny as a sparrow, she would bring a huge sack full of her lunch and devour it all on the spot! An actual talent scout from Fox Studios was in our audience, and he arranged for both June and me to film screen tests. However, it was June who received the studio contract and went on to movie fame, starring in such films as *The Dolly Sisters* with Betty Grable.

Entertainment at our High School was enhanced by free costumes from the Western Costume Company, owned by a relative of one of our classmates. The Shakespeare Festival was always well attended. My sophomore year, I played Ophelia to my boyfriend's

Ray Page's Hamlet. A year later, I played the role of Lady Macbeth opposite Jerry Paris' Lord Macbeth!

I'll never forget our school's Talent Show. I performed a magic act, my tricks including the production of a fish-bowl full of live fish; making a pitcher of milk disappear; the amazing linking rings, and producing both billiard balls and coins, one by one, from the air. On the same program was an excellent ballet duet, performed by two sisters dancing to the music of Ravel's *Pavanne.* You may wonder why I remember their music, even after all these seventy years. Well, the two young ladies who gave such a memorable performance were Maria and Marjorie Tallchief, who were later on individual Honorees at *Kennedy Center Presents.* Maria became the Prima Ballerina of the *Ballet Russe* and married the choreographer Ballanchine. I now shake my head over the huge line my friend Bill Stroud dared give me: he told me his favorite dance partners were me and Marge Tallchief!

27 Bette Davis and Other Teachers

Before I finished High School, my father decided maybe it was time for some acting lessons. After making a few inquiries, he settled on a lady named Josephine Dillon. She had gained fame as the acting teacher—and first wife—of legendary actor Clark Gable. She sounded impressive enough, but oh, what an acting teacher she was! There I was, accustomed to the very finest directors in the business, such as George Cukor, Mervyn LeRoy, John Stahl, and Richard Boleslawski. Yet the style of acting she was trying to teach me was that favored in the movies' silent era. In other words, she tried to teach me the facial expressions connected with each and every mood (surprise, anger, fear, etc.) After a couple of lessons, I pleaded with my father, "Please, Daddy! No more lessons with Miss Dillon! No more!" Showing respect for my opinions, my father gave in to my request.

During summers, Warner Bros. ran a kind of tuition-free drama camp right there on the studio lot, which was considerably more to my liking. A lady named Sophie Rosenstein conducted acting workshops for a few young actors, including myself and Alexis Smith. Then after a few weeks, not worrying about the expenses involved, they filmed some of our scenes using 35mm film. For me, nothing much came of that, but Alexis Smith went on to Hollywood stardom.

Now that I was older, one time they did want me for a part where I'd appear topless. My parents always taught me to hold my standards high, so you can imagine how quickly that idea was vetoed. My father did discuss the so-called "casting couch" road to fame with me. He told me that, in his experience, the good directors would in the long run choose those actresses who'd had a good night's sleep the night before!

All This and Heaven Too

In 1940, I acquired another legendary star as my tutor, none other than Bette Davis! An Academy Award-winning Best Actress for *Dangerous* and *Jezebel*, plus star of *All About Eve* and *Whatever Happened to Baby Jane,* she played my teacher in *All This and Heaven Too.* Most actresses did everything they could to look beautiful on screen. Not so Bette Davis, an actress who favored realism over cinematic beauty. Anything that would improve the picture, she was ready for.

The plot for this film revolves around a girls' school, whose students spread stories about their instructor's having an affair with a gentleman played by Charles Boyer. It was truly "old home week" for all us girls, and I was able to renew my acquaintance with Cora Sue Collins, Ann Gillis, June Lockhart, Ann Howard, Peggy Stewart, and Virginia Weidler.

The thing that really impressed me about Bette Davis in addition to her acting ability was her fantastically small waistline. The other notable item was, of course, her incredible addiction to cigarettes.

I did not get real close to Miss Davis the way I did to most other actresses. After all, I was just one of her many "students," and there wasn't that special relationship I felt when an actress played my mother. However, without me even requesting it, she did present me with an autographed photograph of herself. Of course, for me the thing of eventual significance about *All This and Heaven Too* is that it now joined *Little Women, Imitation of Life, David Copperfield, Les Misérables,* and *Anthony Adverse* as one of the six films in which I appeared that were nominated by the Academy of Motion Picture Arts and Sciences as Best Production of the Year.

The Way of All Flesh

Later in 1940, Paramount was looking for someone to play Akim Tamiroff and Gladys George's nineteen-year-old daughter in *The Way of All Flesh*. For some unfathomable reason, they hired me, though I was only barely fourteen years old. Certainly, the normal practice of the studios was to hire someone of *nineteen* to play a *fourteen*-year-old, not the reverse!

As a child actor, I was not used to makeup, but the studio bestowed on me all the resources of the makeup, hairdresser, and wardrobe departments. False eyelashes, a sophisticated hairstyle, and "falsies" did a fair job of turning me into a nineteen-year-old!

I'll never forget one interesting result of that subterfuge. One day, Gladys George, my new "mother," told the group a joke that I can only assume was an X-rated story. I looked at her blankly, at which point she looked pointedly at me and asked, "How old are you?"

"*Fourteen*," I answered.

Scene from *The Way of All Flesh*. (**Courtesy of Paramount Pictures.**)

She was really embarrassed and apologized profusely. As I write this, I can't help but be sad that times have changed so drastically.

Why are the standards of decency so different today? Well, in 1934, the Legion of Decency pressured the film industry into enforcing their 1930 Production Code, with its accompanying Seal of Approval. No profanity or suggestive scenes were allowed, and all criminal activity had to be suitably punished in order for a film to receive their Seal. Even married folks had to sleep in separate beds. Suffering from an over-abundance of censorship, in 1968 the industry abandoned the Production Code.

28 Current Events and College

On December 7, 1941, I was at church, when a car's radio brought us the news that the United States' own Pearl Harbor had been bombed! "Where's that?" was our initial reaction. We finally figured out that Pearl Harbor was a port in Hawaii, but little did we realize that the attack would mean the beginning of the United State's entry into World War II, nor did we dream of the impact that bombing would have on our future lives.

Little did we appreciate the immensity of the assault on our country, for the Pearl Harbor bombing left over 2,000 dead, 110 were wounded, eighteen warships were sunk, and 188 planes were destroyed. Of course, in 1941, those facts were carefully concealed from us so as not to provide valuable information to our enemies.

My Hollywood career was winding down, but being a member of Beverly Hills High School Latin Club, Tri-Y, the Alpha Girls, and president of the History Club, I was too absorbed with my high school studies, clubs, plays, and Radio Speech classes to pay much attention. Most of my afternoons were spent at school, followed by a trip home by bus and trolley. There was our ice cream parlor and Simon's carhop drive-in, and at noon, we often had a "sock hop," where we danced in our stocking feet to phonograph records featuring the current Hit Parade favorites.

We also often had dances where the girls would wear formals. Oh, the excitement when our date would arrive proudly bearing an orchid and perhaps even a white one. Although they served liquor at Hollywood's Palladium night club starting in 1940, we high-schoolers were permitted to enjoy dancing there to the music of the latest Big Bands, including Woody Herman, Glen Miller, and Tommy Dorsey featuring new songsters like Frank Sinatra. In other words, my high school years were a very happy time.

I always enjoyed school, as well as discussing and debating the events of the day with my father, who always encouraged me to read the daily newspaper. Early in my high school days, I began dreaming about going on to college, and I pestered my Daddy about which one I could attend. One time he told me, "I've often thought that, for a girl, instead of college, travel might be a wonderful idea," but I didn't really buy that particular plan.

In 1943, fate intervened on my behalf in the form of a letter from Mills College, Oakland's exclusive woman's place of higher learning. They wrote to Beverly Hills High School and asked them to choose an outstanding girl from their most outstanding department. "English" was the department selected, and I was the lucky girl who was awarded a full scholarship!

Not so lucky were some of my fellow child actors. The little girl I replaced in *The Conquerors* went on to become a queen of the burlesque, a crude and vulgar form of vaudeville. June Haver, my a cappella choir seatmate, had a fine Hollywood career. However, having sung with Ted Fiorito's band while still a child, she apparently suffered from her early entrance into the entertainment business, for after who-knows-what trauma, she became a nun. Happily, she later in life married movie star Fred MacMurray. In 2007, Michael Jackson sang "Have you seen my childhood . . . I've never known?" And we're all aware that Judy Garland, who complained that she'd never had any childhood, died at an early age of a drug overdose.

> *For a little girl in a grownup world,*
> *Where is there time to be free?*
> *For a little girl in a grownup world, tell me,*
> *Where is there room for just me?*

Although there are people like Ron Howard, Jackie Cooper, Jody Foster, and Gene Reynolds, who followed juvenile careers by becoming successful directors, there are others like Scotty Beckett, my buddy and "brother" from *Marie Antoinette* days. Like the unfortunate little Prince that he portrayed, Scotty's life was doomed at an early age.

The mystery regarding the real little Prince was solved in 2001, when DNA tests proved that the tiny child's heart claimed to be that of the little Prince was indeed really his, after the child had been murdered. Not any happier was Scotty's life. He played Al Jolson as a boy in *The Jolson Story*, but he never went on to college, never prepared himself for anything other than a Hollywood career. He was talented, but as an adult, his baby-face appearance was against him, for he was not suitable for either a leading-man or a character part. (Male child actors are often chosen because they're short and/or have cherubic features, neither of which leads to success as adults). For a while, he tried selling automobiles, but it is said that at the age of thirty-eight, following a beating, he succeeded in committing suicide.

Fame while still only a child is hardly the norm, and the probable outcome of loss of popularity can be devastating. Of course, even adults, whether in or out of the entertainment industry, have trouble with sudden fame and a sudden fall from grace. Some lottery winners have trouble with their sudden notoriety and their sudden loss of it. However, there is nothing quite like the pampering that a Hollywood career can generate—even for those who are not big stars!

Being in this business can be rough;
You've got to be tough.
All those interviews and being inspected.
And sooner or later you're going to be rejected!

It's hard to be a "has-been;"
The future looks mighty cold.
It's awful to be a has-been
When you're just fifteen years old!

29 Farewell to Hollywood

$\mathcal{S}$urprisingly, it was probably lucky for me that I didn't become so famous that I had no childhood. Only in hindsight did I realize how fortunate I was in managing to weave my way through the minefield that was Hollywood with barely a scratch. (In writing this autobiography, I have that wonderful perspective supplied by the passage of time.)

Perhaps it was because of my early Hollywood career that for so much of my life I've felt like I have to have some "project" going, whether writing, directing, playing the piano, composing music, stamp-collecting, magic, or studying the dictionary. I do think it was good (like Freddy Bartholomew, who became a successful advertising executive) that I worked hard in school, went on to college, and did not limit myself to the field of acting. Unquestionably, the main reason for my fine experience in that unusual place called Hollywood was my good fortune in having the parents I had. They were supportive, but not pushy.

> *When I need someone to care for me,*
> *I always know my Family is there for me.*
> *No matter where you're born or neighborhood you're in,*
> *Your family is where they always take you in!*

Families can be large – or very small.
The Family of Man is largest of them all.
No matter what happens, it's easy to see,
I want them there for me, my family.
I need them there for me, my family!

Shortly before I left home for college, my grandfather, William McKenzie, passed away and left my mother some money with which she purchased a spinet piano. We were sorry to hear of his passing, but at last—my own piano to practice on, instead of the high school auditorium's grand piano I'd been using for practice. However, that piano would not be mine to play on for very long, for I would soon be traveling to my new school.

As I was about to leave home, once again my mother's good friend, Cora Bird, who had driven me to my very first workday in Hollywood, stepped into my life. She called and wondered if she could introduce me to her eighteen-year-old nephew, who was then at nearby Camp Roberts, and who would shortly be going overseas, since World War II was just heating up.

Father Smith was there when I met Cora's nephew, Dick Goates, and played *Warsaw Concerto* for him on our new piano. I'd learned the piece without Miss Lewyn's help, practicing occasionally on our high school piano. Dick was a tall, thin teenager, who had enlisted in the Army as a seventeen-year-old Private, but I certainly wished him well, as off he went to fight for our country.

I think that moment pretty much represents the end of the First Act of my life. I was about to leave for Mills College, 400 miles to the north. I dearly loved my parents, but was really look-ing forward to the college experience. I was planning on being a drama major, with the thought of perhaps eventually becoming an attorney like my father, but I knew that, whatever I decided upon, my family would be squarely behind me.

Be yourself. Just be whatever you want to be.
Be yourself. Don't try to live your life for me.
Parents, of course, are good at making plans,
But your life is yours. Your future lies right here within your hands.

In my eyes, you're always going to be a star.
Doesn't matter what you do or where you are.
In the star's dressing room, or in our living room,
You will always be my Star.
You're always going to be my Star!

Part Two

Me as a seventeen-year-old Beverly Hills High School graduate.

30 College Ho!

The year was 1943, and I was leaving my parents, my friends and Hollywood, but looking forward to whatever experiences awaited me at my new college in Oakland, California. Quite coincidentally, Oakland represented a return to my roots; the town where I was born and where, as a tiny girl in 1931, I'd made an on-stage appearance at the Fox Oakland Theatre. No, I didn't suffer homesickness, despite the fact that this was my first time away from home. Although I'm sure that she missed me terribly, my mother really seemed to thrive now that I was away at school and, for a change, actually began buying clothes for *herself*.

Mills College had all the traditions and ambience of an Ivy League college. A total of 300 students walked handily from class to class, many of which contained as few as eight students. Built in the 1800s exclusively for women, Mills prided itself on its religiously-followed honor code. Its motto was: "Remember who you are and what you represent!" Respecting that tradition, when we took the train into San Francisco on weekends, we always wore a very proper hat and gloves, plus high heels and long silk stockings that were held up by a miserable girdle or garter belt. Also as part of that honor code, we were allowed to take makeup tests, sitting all by ourselves in a room containing books with all the answers inside, and no, we didn't peek.

Mills College did not allow sororities. I was slated to live up the hill in Ethel Moore Residence Hall with my assigned room-mate, who was also a drama major. We ate breakfast in turn-of-the-century Mills Hall and our lunch and dinner in our Ethel Moore dining room, where we sang our special college songs with an enthusiasm reserved for college students. No, there weren't any men on campus, but this was during wartime, anyway, so all of the institutions were pretty much women-only, except for military cadets and those who had failed physical exams. Mills College did hold dances and often arranged to bring in enlisted men, cadets, or officers from neighboring institutions, so we didn't feel deprived.

To assist in the war effort, we rolled bandages. This consisted of folding gauze in a strange way to create surgical sponges that would later be sterilized. Sugar, gasoline, meat, butter, and silk stockings were rationed through a coupon system, and heavy blackout drapes covered our windows at night to thwart possible enemy aircraft. Who knew that World War II would result in the deaths of nearly 406,000 American military? I was blissfully ignorant of the fact that the majority of the boys I'd dated in high school were destined to be killed, either in the air, at sea, or on the battlefield.

The classes I signed up for included Beginning Harmony, plus Intermediate Drama. I figured that, with my acting experience in Hollywood, I wouldn't need the Beginning Drama class. I couldn't have been more wrong. After all, I'd never had the type of acting instruction where one tries to portray an alligator or a tree in a windstorm. My guidance counselor was head of the drama depart-ment, so I don't think she took too kindly to my wanting to skip the beginning class. I was soon to realize, she was a "stage" devotee who took a dim view of "the movies." At any rate, the Beginning Drama class is where I ended up.

I received quite a surprise a few months after my arrival. Our room was at ground level, with windows that opened out by first sliding up a screen. The school was abuzz that week with news of a prowler on campus. I was lying in bed thinking about that when I heard an unwelcome sound. I let out a small shriek as I plainly heard the sound of a screen slowly being slid open! A loud scream from the room next door corroborated my worst fears, and I ran down the hall, screaming: "There's a man in my room!"

Of course, the campus police were summoned, and the Head Resident called all concerned parties to a meeting in her room. My next-door neighbor recounted how she had gone to open her window. She had slid open her screen when she heard my shriek from next door, which caused her to scream. It was terribly embarrassing, but I had to confess on the spot what I came to realize was behind that midnight caper: I had heard my *neighbor's* sliding screen, followed later by her scream, and she had heard my shriek, followed later by my widespread announcement! In other words, we were (especially me) two delusional females! My confession was supremely embarrassing, but I knew I'd eventually get over it.

In my freshman year, I did receive a couple of interesting visitors. From Camp Roberts arrived Private Dick Goates, Aunt Cora's nephew, whom I'd met shortly before coming to Mills. Dick took me out to breakfast, and it was nice seeing him again. I knew he was about to be sent overseas, so that was worrisome, to say the least.

Later when I received a letter from him, I noticed from the envelope that he'd been promoted to Private First Class. When I wrote him back, congratulating him on the promotion, he wrote me back, "Thanks for the congratulations. Just think, at this rate I'll be a general by the year 2010!" I was sincere with my congratulations, not realizing that Dick had planned on a military career and been given a commission to West Point but had been turned that down because of his eyesight and so had enlisted as a Private, earning $50 a month, $2 less than his Private First Class salary.

Of course, the irony of his situation was that he would soon spend his military service as a Forward Observer with a Field Artillery unit, a position that demanded good eyesight! We corresponded some during the war, though it was difficult for him to be much of a pen-pal when he was mostly unable to send mail *to* anyone, including his mother.

Later, Ray, my high-school boyfriend, paid me a visit and wanted to get very serious about our relationship. At the age of seventeen, I was hardly ready for any such thing, plus Ray struck me as a little too much of a "wild card." He was a struggling actor, smoked cigarettes, and, in general, kind of scared me.

Giant Surprise

Near the end of my Freshman year, I received the biggest surprise of all: news of the marriage of my eighteen-year-old girlfriend, Mary, to my childhood mentor, fifty-eight-year-old Father Smith. I was simply devastated! I felt as if I had been stalked myself! My father said he never had much liked the idea of my spending so much time with Father Smith, and my girlfriend Janet's father remarked, "There, but for the grace of God, goes Marilyn!"

One of the main things I've learned from writing this auto-biography is how the passage of time can change one's perspective. Let's fast-forward around forty-nine years from the previous paragraph's story to our fiftieth Beverly Hills High School reunion. There, Mary Stewart Smith took me aside.

"You know, Marilyn, *I* was the one pursuing *him!*" she confided. "He resisted for a long time. Then, I guess he finally thought, 'Well, why not!'"

Mary had lost her own father when she was just a little girl, so I'm sure that was part of the appeal of an older man. Believe it or not, before his death at age ninety-eight, Mary and Father Smith were married for *forty* years and had three beautiful children, all of whom graduated from college, and he maintained his mental faculties to the end. Even today, Mary is so smitten with love-of-her-life Father Smith that she refrains from dating. Like I said, the passage of time can certainly change our perspective.

Another Minister

I had mentioned to my Harmony instructor that I had been an organist at St. Nicholas Church. When the minister of All-Saints Episcopal Church in San Leandro phoned her for a referral to a potential organist, she gave him my name and number. The only telephone in Ethel Moore Hall was the one in the office. Who-ever answered the phone that day was intrigued by the masculine voice at the other end of the phone and began drumming up an interesting scenario that was somewhat reminiscent of Janet Bone's behind-the-scenes work with my friend Peter.

The afternoon that the Reverend came to drive me to his church for an audition on the organ, all my friends were abuzz with excitement, even though at that point, no one had seen the man. *Would this gentleman turn out to be old, fat, and married?* Funny thing was that he turned out to be none of those things.

Before long, I became the official organist for All Saints Church, which was small, all redwood, with an authentic pipe organ. Amazingly, my girlfriend's scenario came to pass. Although ten years older than I, the Reverend later invited me out to dinner, which began an interesting relationship. He took me to concerts, the ballet, gave me fine books as gifts, and, in general, pursued me. What a shock, my girlfriends' wildest dreams had come true.

I'll never forget the day he invited me to a church picnic. The congregation was really excited when we showed up together, and that felt so funny. Eventually, he proposed marriage, which gave me all kinds of problems for I didn't want to hurt his feelings. I cared for him, but I was not in love with him. Plus, I couldn't really see myself as a minister's wife. After all, I was only eighteen years old. I'm sorry to say that this story ended when he asked to be transferred out of our parish.

31 Music vs. Drama

Although I was a drama major, I got my best grades in music and was always grouped with the music majors in classes like Music Appreciation. There were small music practice rooms where I could maintain my piano skills. I never bought any sheet music; I just took copies from the college library and memorized them, including "Grieg's Piano Concerto." Miss Lewyn had always taught me to work on the hard parts first, and I continued that policy on my own.

Malcolm Gladwell claims that "Talent is the desire to practice," and I think he has something there. I might as well mention here my secret for avoiding nervousness when playing the piano. I abandon any search for absolute perfection and tell myself that my audience would benefit more from my performing than from their listening to nothing but silence; more importantly, they aren't truly listening to *me,* but rather to the *composer* whose music I'm playing. The same kind of self-talk helped me to stay grounded when acting on the stage.

I also participated in college plays. Since there were no men on campus, girls had to play the male roles. I ended up playing the part of Paris in *Romeo and Juliet,* where I had to learn how to fence. My instructor was no less than Helene Mayer, the 1937 Olympics Foil World Champion and considered one of the greatest female fencers in history.

In the audience were my parents. Whether he had requested it or not, I still don't know, but the Federal Works Agency had transferred my father to Northern California, and my parents had rented an apartment in Berkeley. My mother called it "The Tree-tops," since it was on the third floor and looked out on the tops of beautiful jacaranda trees, with their intriguing purple blossoms. Some people might have described those living quarters as being miserably located on the third floor of an apartment house and hated climbing the steps to the third floor, but my mother always made the best of any situation, so there she was, happy to be living "in the Treetops."

Darius Milhaud

I wrote movie reviews and other articles for the college newspaper, and one of my assignments was doing an article on Darius Milhaud. He was the most famous professor at Mills College and composer of fifteen operas, thirteen ballets, twelve symphonies, six piano concertos, eighteen string quartets, plus the scores for several motion pictures. He was part of a group of outstanding French composers called "Les Six," his close associates being Igor Stravinsky, Satie, and Poulenc, and he was then teaching jazz innovator Dave Brubeck as a graduate student. He was certainly a fascinating man to interview.

I learned from his wife, Madame Milhaud, that he was absolutely compulsive about his music, composing something each and every day of his life. I loved his music, often featured in our Mills College concert hall. Both melodic and full of fascinating rhythms, his music inspired me with a unique goal: some day I would study composition with the master himself! That meant that I would most definitely need the three prerequisites of Beginning and Advanced Harmony, followed by Counterpoint.

In my Sophomore year, I signed up for French Conversation with Madeleine Milhaud, Monsieur Milhaud's wife. She had been a famous actress in France, and their home had been filled with the renowned artists, actors, and musicians of France. I had studied French for only one year, instead of the two I was supposed to have studied. However, the conversation we heard in her class was so utterly engrossing that I hung onto her every word, struggling to understand what she was saying with all my might, and did all right in the class.

I had become increasingly drawn to music and especially composing. In planning my junior year, I told my advisor I would like a double major in Drama and Music, even though a double major was not mentioned in the college catalog. My advisor, the head of the Drama Department, went into orbit! Did I or did I not want to be a drama major? She said I had to choose, and if I wanted to be a drama major, she wanted me to take a class in Esthetics (the philosophy of beauty and art), offered at the exact *same hour* as the Counterpoint class I'd requested, Counterpoint being a prerequisite for the Composition classes with Darius Milhaud that I wished to take in my Senior year.

I think at that point I sorely needed a course in Assertion Training. I had appeared in plays my advisor had directed, so perhaps I was too conditioned to doing whatever my "Director" told me to do—and I didn't want to be disloyal to my precious Drama. So, with an ache in the pit of my stomach, I chickened out and did what my advisor told me to do—signed up for the Esthetics class, for which, unlike the Counterpoint class, I would have no practical use.

In my junior year, I did have the title role in *Iphigenia in Tauris* at Oakland's impressive Greek Theatre. I also took private lessons in voice and appeared in a concert of classical music in our extraordinarily beautiful concert hall. I managed to get an A in my Esthetics class, all the while mourning the fact that, without Counterpoint, I would *never* be able to have private composition classes with the Master. I may seem to be wasting my time talking about my choice of college classes, but as it turned out, those choices would have a major impact on the direction my life would take just a few years later. Life is like that—small choices with major implications.

32 Merrill's Marauders and Other Visitors

Richard Bird Goates was the young man with the funny animal name about whom Aunt Cora Bird had told me all my life. Apparently, he knew all about me, for as a boy, he used to invite his little friends to go with him to see my movies. We were both only children, he being just a year older than I, and our mothers were old friends. More than that, my great-grandparents, the George McKenzies, had lived in Springville *right next door* to his grandparents, the Birds, who lived at 58 West Second North. Of course, Cora was my mother's lifelong best friend and the one who had escorted me to my very first day on a Hollywood set, way back in 1931. While Aunt Cora was only my pretend "Aunt," she was the real thing for Dick, as she was married to Dick's mother's brother.

Dick couldn't tell me about it at the time, but he spent World War II in a mule pack outfit with the dangerous volunteer group, Merrill's Marauders (about whom a movie was later made). Their goal was to prepare the way for a pipeline to be built from India to Burma. No, they didn't ride the mules; the animals carried their supplies while they fought beside the Chinese against the Japanese, operating behind enemy lines with an eight-to-one ratio at times favoring the Japanese. With a Burmese tribe of Kachins as their guides, they hiked over the Himalaya Mountains, cleared their way through the jungles with machetes, and traveled *on foot* from India to Burma through an area for which there were no maps! One time, a soldier began singing "On the Road to Mandalay," when the other battle-worn men quickly pounced on him with a loud "No!"

Their supplies, including food and letters, were airlifted to them, but they frequently went to the wrong outfit, or else were intercepted by the Japanese. When food was scarce, Dick and his fellow Chinese and American soldiers frequently ate what their guides taught them to eat—roots and grasses, mixed with *beetles* for protein. After his superior officers were killed off, Dick received a Bronze Star for bravery and a field promotion to Second Lieutenant—which is not the easiest way to become an officer.

I wrote Dick from time to time, but he was usually unable to get letters *to* anyone, including even his mother. The only news she received about him was an occasional V-Mail from the government informing her merely that her son was still alive. With equally poor communication, Dick's father was a Colonel in the Army, fighting in the Solomon Islands, plus the fierce battles of the Philippines. With the dropping of the atomic bomb on Hiroshima on August 6, 1945, World War II began coming to an end, and Dick did manage to send me a cute Signal Corps photograph of him beside a Howitzer cannon. After the peace treaty with Japan was signed on September 2, 1945, he was stationed in Shanghai, so we were able to exchange letters once he was in that Chinese city.

Not too long after the end of the war, I received a visit from Colonel Goates, Aunt Cora's brother-in-law, who was Dick's father. General Douglas MacArthur had just appointed him the new head of Information and Education for the Army of Occupation in postwar Japan. That entailed the huge job of his starting high schools throughout that country, plus heading up all its colleges, newspapers, and radio stations. He was in the United States to recruit talent, and knowing of my background and the training I was receiving at Mills College, he spoke of wanting me to be the civilian Program Director for Radio Tokyo once I'd graduated, a position that certainly sounded intriguing to me.

Colonel Goates invited me to go with him to a showing of *Oklahoma*. I'd seen several Rudolf Friml operettas, such as *The Vagabond King*, but that was to be the first modern musical I'd seen. Right then and there, I decided that the most wonderful thing I could imagine would be writing one of those musicals, the kind where the songs are very much a part of the story line.

After interviews throughout the country with various prospective reporters, teachers, and broadcasting talent, Colonel Goates took a military flight for Japan, where Dick's mother had just arrived on a military transport ship. Unexpectedly, his plane developed engine trouble and was forced to return to Travis, Fairfield's military airport. In the Post Exchange, the Colonel noticed a tall, slender soldier buying military ribbons and said, "Pardon me, Lieutenant, but aren't you my son?"

"*Dad!*" was Dick's reply.

For the past three years, Dick had been serving in China, India, and Burma, while the Colonel was in the Far East. Incredibly, both of them *accidentally* ran in to each other in Fairfield, California—truly the *very* long arm of coincidence!

Father and son, Colonel and Lieutenant Goates, *accidentally* meet, after a
World War II-caused, three-year separation.

33 Lightning Strikes!

Before long, twenty-one-year-old Lieutenant Richard Goates, traveling from Shanghai to the United States on six weeks temporary duty, paid a visit to our Berkeley apartment, bringing me a coolie outfit—a little silk pajama set. My mother fixed her famous short ribs for all of us, and I played my "Grieg's Piano Concerto." Dick was a trumpet player himself, so he appreciated music.

Dick left town for a few weeks, then phoned, inviting me to go to dinner- dancing at Berkeley's Claremont Hotel. After hitchhiking and arriving by bus, we walked to the hotel, where Dick bought me a camellia corsage and arranged to have our picture taken together. I only had eyes for him, as we had a lovely dinner, and then danced to Jack Fina and his band.

From Irving Berlin's brand-new musical, Annie, Get Your Gun, they played "The Girl That I Marry" and "They Say That Falling in Love is Wonderful." Wonder of wonders, as we danced, that's what happened to us—we fell in love! Yes, we really did. Talk about a romantic moment! Then, as the band played "Full Moon and Empty Arms," with music from "Rachmaninoff's Second Piano Concerto," we both kept thinking about Dick's return to China in just three short weeks.

It's a little hard for me to explain what happened next. Perhaps it all goes back to the fact that our mothers were girlhood friends in Springville, Utah, which was where Dick's aunt had introduced us; that his father had recently paid me a visit; and that his grandparents and my great-grandparents had been next-door neighbors and close friends. Moreover, Dick's mother and my mother and father all had ancestors who probably knew each other in Kirtland, Ohio, and Nauvoo, Illinois, in the early 1800s, where they were some of the earliest members of the Mormon Church. Also, they probably knew each other when they prepared to hike across the wilderness, pushing their handcarts to Utah, some ending up in those ill-fated companies.

On the long walk home, Dick kissed me (our first kiss). He talked about burnt toast and other domestic matters and then proposed—even offering to get down on his knees to me! It must have been a good kiss, for as another wonder of wonders, my reply was that I'd try to be a good wife to him.

One kiss and we were engaged! Like my start in motion pictures, that scenario would not pass the plausibility test as a movie plot, but that was the way it happened. Let's face it: he was about to return to Shanghai and I might never see him again. There he was, tall, nice looking, very intelligent, considerate, wonderful sense of humor, and we both had a nearly identical cultural background. What's more, he combined a strong masculinity with tremendous sensitivity, including a love for ballet and music. I just didn't want him to get away, and I guess he felt the same way about me.

I told Dick that he'd have to talk to my parents. After all, I wanted their approval to be engaged during my senior year in college. As a kind of courtesy, we made a date with them. However, when Dick asked for their blessing on our engagement, my father surprised us by saying "No!" He plainly did not want me to be out of circulation my last year in college!

Well, "love laughs at locksmiths," as the old saying goes, and we had no intention of letting his objections stand in our way. Later I tipped off my mother (who just loved Dick) that he was about to buy me an engagement ring, hoping she could soften up my father a bit. With time in short supply, we set a time for buying the ring and planned to have another important conference with my parents.

I confess, we were a couple of giddy people, buoyed up by very new, very intense emotions as we took the train to an exclusive jewelry store in San Francisco. On the way there, Dick had a brainstorm. Reminding me of the "full moon and empty arms" we would soon be experiencing, he came up with a remarkable solution: instead of buying just one ring for me, why not buy two? That way, we could get married immediately, have a short honeymoon, and then in a few months, I could join him in China and share that part of his life with him.

So, there it was—the choice between my senior year in college and travel to the Orient to be with the man of my dreams. I'm normally a very careful person. Speaking from a purely rational standpoint, (and who am I kidding?), I'd already finished my classes in Stagecraft and Directing. Because of the limitations imposed by my college advisor, I couldn't even look forward to composition lessons with Darius Milhaud. I'm afraid the scales weighed heavily against Mills College in favor of Dick's rather wild idea. Even more to the point, I was really in love!

We visited the fancy jewelry store and bought a set of diamond rings for me and a gold one for Dick, and Dick signed an install-ment contract to pay for them. The diamond in my engagement ring weighed 0.25 carets, but it seemed like the Hope Diamond to me! While in San Francisco, another "long arm of coincidence" reached out to us: Dick ran into Pres Albertson, an old fraternity brother from his two years at the University of Utah. Dick delight-edly asked him to be his Best Man at our upcoming wedding, and he accepted. Yes, things were really rolling along!

"A wedding in a week?" Of course, that evening, my father was completely nonplussed by that bombshell! Never before had there been even a hint of me not completing college. I had been nominated to Phi Beta Kappa while still a junior, and my daddy was looking forward to my receiving that honor in my Senior year!

"What are you thinking?!" he demanded to know.

Then, I struck the coup de grace. I reminded my father of long ago, when he told me, "You know for a girl, I've often thought that travel would be just as valuable as college." Not only would I be traveling to the Orient, which was most rare in that era, but I would even have the chance to actually live there. What could the poor man say? His own words had defeated his best arguments!

The Rest of the Story

I was oblivious of a few facts in those happenings. I was unaware of the conversation that Dick and his father had had at their surprise meeting at the Fairfield PX. The Colonel had told his son, "I just returned from meeting with Marilyn Knowlden. If you're smart, you'll plant a big Hong Kong diamond on her finger. But go slow, son. Take your time!"

After we became engaged, three weeks after his arrival back in the United States, Dick sent a telegram to Yokohama, Japan: "DEAR DAD: ARRIVED THURSDAY MORNING. ENGAGED THURSDAY NIGHT. TOOK IT SLOW LIKE YOU SAID. LOVE, DICK."

I also didn't know that he'd later sent this telegram to his parents: "HAVE RECRUITED ANOTHER MRS GOATES. WILL REQUIRE A FEW SHECKELS TO COVER INCIDENTALS. URGENT PLEASE. DICK."

The next few days were as fast-paced as television's Ambush Makeover. Dick and I had dinner with my chosen bridesmaids from Mills College, who delegated assignments among themselves for selection of matching bridesmaid dresses, flowers, and a photographer. Meanwhile I contacted the minister of the little Episcopal Church where I'd been playing the organ and arranged for my minister, the church, an organist, and a soloist. We got blood tests and a marriage license, and I bought my wedding gown at Nancy's Dress Store on Hollywood Boulevard, a beautiful dress for which I paid the princely sum of $35.00. Dick and I met with Reverend Praed, and he presented us with the Marriage and Sexual Harmony book by a certain Dr. Butterfield. A main point of the book was, "A good bed does not squeak!"

Aunt Cora was the one who had introduced us, and Dick and I felt that we simply had to have her at our upcoming wedding. In order to make sure of that—although time was at a premium—we grabbed our book and took an overnight trip on the Owl, the #40 sit-up-all-night train to Los Angeles, and to Aunt Cora. Her husband was Dick's mother's brother, Uncle Vern, so we also wanted his blessing on our very sudden nuptials.

I'm sure that Uncle Vern must have been mightily amused to see us, two virgins sitting side-by-side on the couch and reading together Dr. Butterfield's Marriage and Sexual Harmony. As for Aunt Cora, she worried about our getting increasingly cozy together on that couch and warned us, "Hey, you two, you're going to be married soon enough!" Anyway, our trip's mission was successful, for a day after we arrived back in Oakland, so did Aunt Cora!

34 Wedding Bells

July 30, 1946, dawned bright and beautiful as a perfect day for a wedding. I was not nervous in the slightest. I was twenty years old and just knew I was doing the right thing, and I was *so* in love! The seed-pearl-encrusted headpiece with new attached veil that Aunt Cora brought me was my "something old;" my dress was my "something new;" my mother's handkerchief was my "something borrowed;" and my little flowered garter was my "something blue."

A relaxed bride.

Daddy marched me down the aisle, and Reverend Praed conducted the ceremony. My mother loved every minute of it. Besides Aunt Cora, even Dick's Aunt Louise and Uncle Joe were there, as were about half of my church's regular congregation, along with many of my friends from Mills College.

Dick looked so handsome in his uniform with beige trousers and long olive-green jacket, his chest ablaze with colorful ribbons representing all the medals he'd won, including the Bronze Star, for bravery! The little all-redwood church looked so mellow, lined on both side-walls with *lighted* candles. The bridesmaids looked wonderful in their matching pastel gowns, and the flowers were simple but perfect. A soloist sang "Oh, Perfect Love," and it all created a

My parents look on as our wedding takes place.

Two happy people—Marilyn & Dick Goates.

perfect day! At the end of the ceremony, Dick turned to Aunt Cora and told her, "Watch our smoke!"

I think it's safe to say that I was really in love. No lyrics from *I'm Gonna Get You in the Movies* fit here, but this is the sonnet I wrote for Dick in 1946:

I do not marvel at each breath I spend,
Nor at the stretching distance of the stars,
Nor strain to understand how He who jars them
From the heavens has no birth nor end.
I wonder not that night must follow day,
Nor at light's speed, nor at a leaping fire.
I marvel not that from two lovers' desire
A child may grow to live and love like they.

To comprehend one thing I have to strain,
That I may feel this deep a love for you,
And past my grasp, beyond my finite brain,
Beyond all wonders here or in the blue,
The marvel of the universe is plain —
That I may love and find you love me too!

Dick had rented a Plymouth coupe, which our friends had adorned with tin cans and a "Just Married" sign. With only a week left of Dick's temporary duty in the U.S., time was of the essence. We skipped having a wedding reception so we could get on our way to our planned destination—Lake Tahoe. When we stopped for dinner at a restaurant in Sacramento, a gentleman gave a close look at my left hand and the look on our faces and said, "That's an awfully shiny set of rings!" We couldn't get away with anything!

A tiny very rustic cabin at Duff and Jean Dean's Lakeside Cabins became our "honeymoon hotel." If we didn't sleep on a non-squeaky "Dr. Butterfield bed," we didn't notice. The next morning at breakfast, Dick ordered an omelet made with a full dozen eggs! Later, we went swimming in the ice-cold water of Lake Tahoe and hiked around our scenic surroundings. The knowledge that being together would soon come to a grinding halt made our time together all the more precious.

After a few days at Lake Tahoe, we rented a motel room near Oakland's waterfront, which turned out to be right next to the railroad tracks. In the middle of the night, the roar of a train woke me just soon enough so that I could grab Dick, shake him, and scream, "It's coming through! It's coming through!" He could have asked for an annulment right then and there, but he didn't.

Dick must have used his best powers of persuasion on the military, for they extended his leave for one week, but before we knew it, that week was also nearly over. My parents drove the two of us to the Fairfield Airport, where I said a difficult goodbye to Dick. I kissed my new husband goodbye. He got on the plane, and I watched it take off, keeping my eyes on the plane even after it had disappeared into nothingness.

35 The Lonely Months

North Wind, South Wind, gently you are blowing,
Whispering tales of cities far away.
Oh, how I wish I could be
Some of the places you're going to see.

North Wind, South Wind, find for me the answer:
Will I too be traveling soon your way?
Hurry off and bring back the news, North Wind, South Wind,
For here I must stay!

At first, Mother and I kept busy sending out wedding announcements, for there certainly had been no time to send out invitations. Dick and I had promised each other daily letters, and we kept that promise, although mail service by steamship was our only form of communication. There were no telephone calls and no airmail, (and instant messages and e-mails were years ahead in the future). Because of the slow mail service—truly "snail mail'—it took over four weeks before I received Dick's first letter, but when it did arrive, it was a beautiful love letter.

Since I knew I would not be starting the fall semester at Mills College, I found work in the Music Department of Breuner's

Department Store, which was my very first ordinary type of job. There, we sold 78 rpm phonograph records of both popular and classical music. My Mills College music training actually did help. In a few weeks, they wanted to make me an Assistant Buyer, but I had to decline their offer. I had other plans.

Since I would soon be traveling to a part of the world filled with horrendous diseases, the Army sent me notification of all the vaccinations I would need. For over a month, I traveled to the Presidio in San Francisco for weekly shots against tetanus, typhoid fever, encephalitis, small pox, diphtheria, whooping cough, Yellow Fever, and on and on. During my first vaccination, I actually fainted dead away, but they revived me, and I soon got very used to that weekly invasion of my body.

When it was time for my smallpox vaccination, I kept thinking of the ugly scar my mother had on her upper arm. I therefore asked the doctor to use a spot just above where my hip meets my leg. The doctor did as I requested, reminding me that when one day he spotted such a smallpox scar on a burlesque dancer, he'd know it was me! When my leg later swelled up like a balloon, I came to realize why the upper arm was the usual chosen site.

My new home would soon be the Republic of China, with Chiang Kai-shek in power, at a time *before* the takeover by the Communists. There would be no American-type stores or cafes; nothing like that, and I wouldn't just be there for a short trip; I would be living there.

My mother and I had great fun searching the antique stores for just the right Christmas gift for my new husband. We finally settled on a unique antique alarm clock, whose alarm was a real music box. Packing was a big project. I filled a tall old-fashioned steamer trunk—complete with drawers—with all sorts of things I feared I would be unable to buy in the Orient. We had received lots of congratulatory letters, and my parents had helped out our financial situation by paying off Dick's installment contract with the jewelry store. We might not be rich, but at least we were starting out free of debt.

Dick and I made up for our brief courtship by writing each other daily letters. Eventually, I received a prized letter from the War Department, setting a November 1946, date for my embarkation from San Francisco. Was I excited! I really felt sad for my parents when the day came for them to say goodbye to their one-and-only child. There I was, a bride of four months, setting off for a journey that would prevent any visits or phone calls for at least a year. As I looked down at them from the deck of the *Admiral Benson*, they waved me a fond goodbye. I felt so sorry for them, but that feeling was balanced by the thought that I would soon be seeing my almost-brand-new husband!

My slow boat to China, the troop transport ship, Admiral Benson.

36 Slow Boat to China

The *Admiral Benson* was a troop transport ship with none of the luxuries of a cruise ship, and there were few other military dependents like myself on board. I shared a room containing two bunk beds with three female civilian employees traveling to the Orient. In addition to military personnel The *Admiral Benson*, unlike today's vessels, did not have modern equipment in its heart to keep the ship from rolling. I did pretty well in the seasickness department. My secret was to position myself so the ship was like my rocking chair. Some of my shipmates were not so lucky.

During the twenty days we were on the high seas, we experienced one horrible storm that was so severe that it was impossible to keep our meals from sliding off the table! To solve the problem, the crew turned our chairs upside down, lashed them to the table, and then placed our meals in the center of the little box so created. We ate standing up—and hanging on—grateful for the crew's ingenuity. Yet every time the ship lurched, we would hear the loud crashing of china, sounding as if every dish on board was breaking.

The Army Chaplain on board recruited me to play hymns for non-denominational services held outside on the deck for three hours each day. My instrument was an Army field pump organ, a tiny instrument powered by pumping pedals with my feet. That

My instructors in Chinese—these Chinese Air Force officers.

was no problem for me as long as the sea was fairly calm, but when it wasn't, I had to spread my knees to prevent that organ from sliding clear across the deck of the ship!

Also on board our ship were 390 Chinese Air Force officers, who had been training in the U. S. They set up Chinese language classes for anyone interested, and that definitely included me. In addition to the "classroom instruction," I spent many hours with those gentlemen as they patiently taught me a bunch of Chinese words, phrases, and even a song. Chinese is a language that's very difficult to learn, since a great part of the meaning is conveyed by voice inflection. I could hardly wait to try it all out in my new home.

After nineteen long days, we made our first stop in Yokohama, Japan, where my new mother and father-in-law were clever enough to meet our ship. They took me to lunch at the Fujiya Hotel. That was the first time I'd ever met my new strong and very intelligent mother-in-law, although, of course, Colonel Goates and I were old friends. It was only when Dick's plane had landed in Japan for a brief stop that his parents had learned for sure that we were actually married. Then for me, it was back on board, for the final leg of my journey to the port of Shanghai, China.

37 Shanghai'd

After a four-month separation from my new husband, I was more than ready for a reunion. As we pulled close to Shanghai, a harbor craft sailed out to meet us. In the morning sun, who should be standing at the bow of that boat but my very own Lieutenant Goates, looking to me as impressive as Leonardo de Caprio at the bow of the *Titanic*!

Soon, he boarded our ship, and it was so wonderful to be with him again. Then, he gave me the unwelcome news that, as Troop Movement Officer, he'd be the last one off ship and that he'd be tied up that afternoon playing football. He introduced me to a Major Troyiano, who would be escorting me to the Army-Air Force football game, taking place at Britain's old Shanghai Race Track.

I knew little about football, so all I did was watch Number 24, hoping he would not get hurt. I'm sad to say that during the game, a player with the Air Force team from Okinawa, a professional ball player named Tommy Thompson, broke his wrist when he was tackled by a player who accidentally stepped on his wrist. The announcer delivered the news, plus letting everyone know that the man who had tackled him was Number 24, Lieutenant Goates!

Immediately, a chant erupted from the stands: "GET GOATES! GET GOATES!"

I couldn't sit still for that, so I stood up, shook my fist at the crowd, and yelled out, "No! That's my husband!"

Dick had written me that we would be living in Broadway Mansions. *Ha!* I said to myself. *Mansions? I don't think so!* But Broadway Mansions turned out to live up to its name, being a fine hotel that the Chinese government had turned over to the American military. We would be lodged on the eleventh floor in #1111, a room that boasted the very best view of Shanghai, one which even to this day is the favorite of photographers. (Considered the symbol of Shanghai, today the Broadway is a four-star hotel renamed the Shanghai Hotel.)

Unless we had other plans, we would be eating all our meals in the elegant hotel dining room, whose kitchen was staffed by gourmet chefs. At times, they prepared really exotic food, such as venison or pheasant under glass, and they occasionally made ice sculptures for us. We were each charged a mere 25¢ for all our meals. The price was the policy of the military, and the food was mostly courtesy of Madame Chiang Kai-Shek's Officers' Moral Endeavor Association (OMEA). The Generalissimo's wife, she was a favorite of America, having been educated in the United States. OMEA meant "Morale" but said "Moral." Dick and I continued to get along famously, and he announced to his friends, "We should have been married off as kids!"

Shanghai was a city of tremendous contrasts. From our eleventh floor room toward the left, we looked out at the intersection of the Huangpu River and Garden Bridge Park, American gunboats rather threateningly on display in the middle of the river. Our view toward the right was of the Bund, Shanghai's financial district, with tall

Broadway Mansions, our surprisingly nice hotel
in Shanghai, as seen from Garden Bridge.

View from our hotel room, small sampan boats in the foreground, Chinese soldiers marching in the park in the middle section, and American gunboats on display in the distance.

skyscrapers that had been built in 1921. Immediately across from Broadway Mansions was Soochow Creek, whose small bridge led to an area that would later erupt in tremendous labor unrest. Soochow Creek was jammed full of sampans—very small boats upon which people lived with their families—sleeping, cooking, eating, washing clothes, and from which they were not allowed to go ashore. The sound of hawkers was deafening, and the outdoor smell was an overpowering combination of mold, ammonia, unfamiliar foods, various unmentionables, and the Huang Pu River.

There was a lot of political agitation in Shanghai because the Communists were on the move in a big way. I was advised that the

Shave and a haircut and washing—right on a Shanghai street.

prudent thing to do was to limit my excursions to a stroll to the Army Post Exchange a few blocks away. The city was a veritable anthill teeming with people, and walking was extraordinarily difficult. Much activity took place right on the street, such as haircuts, shaves, the washing of clothes, cooking, and of course, hawking of wares and strange-looking food. "I think I'll pass on the eel, snake and dog!"

Some of the men wore western clothing, but most of the people wore traditional coolie-jackets and pants or Chinese-style robes that were padded for the winter season. Rickshaws and Pedi-cabs were everywhere, and drivers sometimes pulled their two-wheeled vehicles along *barefoot,* even in harsh winter weather. Yet, by contrast, when we attended a party at the French Club, I learned that

Shanghai beggar woman.

its dance floor was on springs, a luxury that seemed incongruous in the face of so much poverty.

Beggars filled the sidewalks, a woman occasionally even having cut off a baby's arm or leg to make her appeal for donations more effective! If someone had the misfortune to pass away on the sidewalk, that's where they just might be left. Folks might chuckle as they passed them by and were glad that they had been spared that fate themselves. They were also grateful that they would not be hauled away by the "dead truck," its driver kicking each body to be sure the corpse was not still alive!

I now realized that I had been living in something of a "bubble." For the first time in my life, I was confronting abject poverty, and I experienced something of a cultural shock. How could I be so privileged while surrounded with so much misery? Away from Hollywood, away from Mills College, away even from the United States, and away from North America, I could indeed confirm in writing to my father that living there was an education in itself.

I had so looked forward to using the elementary Chinese I'd learned aboard ship, but when I tried speaking Mandarin to our waiters, the "boys" who made our bed, or various shopkeepers, I only met with frustration. It wasn't just my lack of expertise. I discovered that everyone to whom I'd tried speaking spoke the *Shanghai dialect,* almost as distinct from Mandarin as a completely foreign language.

Before traveling to China, I was curious about the local women I'd find. I seriously doubted that any of the local Shanghai girls could have provided me with much competition in the dating department. Then I met Dick's secretary, a stunning Russian blond, plus a former girlfriend, a handsome Russian ballet dancer. I was shocked, but I felt both relieved and proud after surveying the competition.

Merry Christmas

I was lucky enough to arrive in Shanghai in time for Christmas, and we received a pair of Chinese porcelain bowls and spoons from the then-current ruler of China, Generalissimo Chiang Kai-shek. Following Japan's 1937 attack, he had united the Nationalists and the Communists under him and led the country to a 1945 victory. Dick gave me a beautiful cultured pearl necklace, and I gave him that musical alarm clock Mother and I had purchased. The only Christmas tree we managed to find was a very small potted Juniper plant. We decorated it as best we could, but then discovered that the tree contained its own "decorations" in the form of a colony of stinkbugs!

When Dick first drove me to our new hotel in his Army jeep, he had remembered something he'd tossed in the back—a present for us that his good friend, Mischa Kluge, had handed him that morning. That wedding gift, resting in a fitted case, turned out to be a beautiful six-piece engraved solid silver tea-service that included a large silver tray inscribed with our names. I couldn't wait to meet my new friends, the Kluges!

Mischa & Galia Kluge.

On January 6, we were invited to Mischa and Galia Kluge's home for an elaborate tea celebrating Russian Christmas, its timing based on the old Julian calendar, not our current Gregorian calendar. Mischa was a civilian who worked for my husband as a dispatcher in his Motor Pool. Inflation was so horrendous that employees had to be paid with a whole wheelbarrow full of Chinese currency!

I was thrilled to meet those brilliant "White Russians," who had fled from Russia's Communist Revolution. In old Russia, Mischa had been a professor of history and mathematics, while his wife was a chemist who ran a soap factory. Galia was currently a much sought-out dress designer, and their two little daughters were equally intelligent, the older girl later receiving her PhD from Columbia University at the age of twenty-one.

Dick and I were amazed by their Christmas tree that they'd decorated with *lighted* candles. We entertained them with a duet of "Skaters' Waltz" on the two Tonettes I'd carted overseas. Then, I played Beethoven's *Moonlight Sonata* and *Appassionata Third Movement* for them on the piano, plus my own composition, a setting of the Eighth Psalm:

> *When I consider Thy Heavens,*
> *The moon and the stars which thou ordained,*
> *What is Man that Thou art mindful of him?*

As Troop Movement Officer in Shanghai, one of Dick's more interesting assignments was the result of the War Powers Act authorizing war brides to be returned to the United States, courtesy of Uncle Sam. Dick was called in to General Lucas' office to help decide whether that act, no doubt designed to help British and

Australian women, would also apply to some 400 or so Chinese war brides scattered throughout China. The act did seem to apply, so Dick's next job was to arrange for their transport. Not surprisingly, the descriptions he had of those brides were all remarkably similar: "Short, with black hair and olive eyes."

Dick arranged to mount posters on the sides of junks sailing up the river. Remarkably, 330 of those women were rounded up and set to sail to America on an Army transport ship. They arrived with an interesting assortment of baggage that included caged chickens or other fowl, as well as bedsprings, that were highly prized in rural China. After being advised that they were sailing to "the land of bedsprings," they finally reduced the amount of baggage they were taking on board. Dick found out later that their ship had run out of rice two days at sea, that most of the passengers refused Western food, and that they were seasick to boot. Apparently their voyage turned out to be the true voyage from hell.

During the day, I could only get Chinese music on our little radio, and since I was mostly confined to the hotel and had no access to a piano, I was really missing music. Acting on a whim, while Dick was away at work, I purchased a crude two-string snakeskin-covered bamboo violin from a street peddler. That was the first time I'd ever touched any kind of violin, so when Dick came home and heard the other-worldly screeching my violin was emitting—sort of Chinese sounding, I guess—he decided I'd gone bananas!

38 Nanking

About that time, we received "horrible" news: Dick was being transferred to Nanking. Nothing wrong with the transfer except for one thing: there were no quarters for dependents in Nanking! Even the General's wife had to stay by herself in Shanghai, about 400 miles away. Another separation seemed ahead for us!

Dick refused to take this forced separation lying down and claimed he'd think of something—and he did! He did some investigating and learned that there was an opening for a "Radio Engineer," a kind of disc jockey/talk show host job at XMAG, the Armed Forces Radio Station in Nanking. As a civilian employee, I would be authorized living quarters of my own, which Dick could then share with me. What was required was for me to audition for the job.

Getting to that audition was no simple matter. I had to board a military aircraft, an unheated, unpressurized, bucket-seat type of plane used to transfer paratroopers as they sat along the sides of the aircraft. I was suitably dressed for the occasion, wearing long-johns, wool slacks, fur-lined boots, a fur-lined hooded parka, and a parachute! My "bucket-seat," unlike those in today's automobiles, had no padding in it at all, just a scooped out place in the metal bench that would fit the parachute I was wearing and sitting on.

I was met at the Nanking airport by Sergeant Laisure, who

drove me to the Radio Station in his jeep. At an intersection on the way to the station, we ran into a Communist uprising! That was February 1947, about a year-and-a-half before the Communist takeover, when Chiang Kai-shek and his group would end up fleeing to Taiwan. A rioter lunged at my arm and tried to grab me out of the jeep, but I yelled at Sergeant Laisure, "Drive on!" Fortunately for us both, he did! It was only later, as I recalled that incident that I began to grasp the actual danger I was probably in. No, I didn't report the incident to my parents. I figured they had enough to worry about with their daughter so far away.

I passed the audition okay, so I would soon be working for XMAG, Nanking. The "MAG" stood for "Military Advisory Group." My employment meant that I would be granted living quarters of my own, so Dick and I could be together in Nanking after all. Our problem was solved!

On my return flight to Shanghai, much to my great distress, our pilot, Captain Petch, proceeded to fill the aircraft with the smoke from his big, black, smelly cigar, Unfortunately, he also chose to use the occasion to practice his instrument flying. He covered the windshield of our plane with black paper, and then proceeded to circle and drop, and circle and drop, which was somehow involved in his navigation of our plane. The black paper was still covering up the windshield when we landed, and was I ever grateful to be back on the ground!

My new job began on the same date as Dick's, so we were able to journey to Nanking together, our transfer involving an overnight trip on a Chinese railroad. On the train, as throughout China, they served hot tea, which you could let cool down if you liked, but that was one way of assuring that the water had indeed been boiled. We didn't choose to use the upper berth in our tiny compartment, and the dimensions of the lower berth were not at all suitable for Dick's six-foot three-inch size, but we managed.

Dick was able to share my commodious quarters in the compound reserved for civilian employees. I'm kidding, for we lived in a modest little one-room cabin, probably made of mud, straw, and judging by the smell, either animal glue or cow dung. We did, however, have a very sturdy concrete bathroom that we dubbed "Siberia!" It was constructed of ice-cold concrete, which caused water to drip down the walls and turn into mold. We had no electricity during the first two weeks. We had no water on the first evening, and from then on, we never knew when or if hot or cold water would be flowing from our faucets. Oh well, we couldn't drink unpurified, non-boiled water anyway.

The first night, I made quite a discovery. "Chintz sheets!" I exclaimed to Dick. They weren't really chintz; they were just thin cotton sheets with a lot of starch or sizing in them. Later, I announced another discovery: "No mattress!" We had been supplied with two single beds that contained box springs only. The next day, Dick, ever resourceful, managed to locate two mattresses that we stretched crosswise after pushing the two beds together, forming a rather peculiar—but acceptable—queen-size bed.

Every morning about 3:30 a.m., one Chinese "boy" would light a fire in the small potbelly coal stove that was our heater. An hour later, another boy would enter, add more powdered coal, and extinguish the fire! We never did manage to communicate our wishes in this matter, so we always awoke to a cold room! The "boys" were very good about knocking before entering, but no matter what our reply, they always entered anyway.

In Shanghai, I had felt rather foolish surveying all the personal supplies I'd carted overseas. After all, our nearby Post Exchange carried plenty of makeup and items of feminine hygiene. However, in Nanking, I was grateful for my well-stocked cupboard once I learned how poorly supplied our local PX was. Since I was the only military wife in town, not surprisingly, the Nanking PX carried absolutely *no* supplies for women, not even so much as lipstick.

The first woman disk jockey was "Tokyo Rose," who during World War II, broadcast American songs and seductive Japanese propaganda to American troops. The Armed Forces Radio Service was established to counter her unfortunate influence, and in the first part of 1947, fortunately with World War II over, there I was in Nanking being part of the service that was usually staffed by men. As part of the AFRS, XMAG was the largest American station in China, covering in the evenings the Shanghai, Peiping, and Nanking areas. Patriotic American companies provided large sixteen-inch wide recording transcriptions to the Armed Forces Radio Service. Those contained programs such as *The Jack Benny Hour, Lux Radio Theatre,* the *Bob Hope Show,* and musical programs with stars like Dinah Shore, Kate Smith, and Frances Langford.

On XMAG, I played recordings each evening, with suitable announcements between. It was necessary to hold the disk in place with my left thumb, start the motor, and then release the recording in such a way as to prevent a "wow" sort of sound that is much like the kind today's rap musicians purposely make when they use a turntable as an extremely crude form of "musical instrument." In the standard announcement I was instructed to make, I always impressively stated that I was "broadcasting from XMAG, Nanking, high atop the XMAG Building." How Dick and I used to chuckle over that announcement, since said building was only two stories high!

I soon became Assistant Program Director and was given my own program where, with comments each evening, I played records "from Gounod to Gershwin, from Corelli to Carmichael." A little later, I added a weekly show called "Nocturne," where I played strictly classical music, with suitable "talk show" comments in-between numbers, and Dick apparently loved gathering his friends around him and listening to my programs. I was usually all alone in the XMAG building, with the exception of Chiang, the radio engineer who kept us on the air. While the recordings played, I often chatted with Chiang. Happily, in addition to English, he also spoke Mandarin Chinese, as almost a second language, so I finally was able to try my wings at that incredibly difficult language.

Nanking local man-power.

I did receive some fan letters, including a nice one from a woman working in the State Department, who claimed she thought my programs were superior to the regular recordings we played. When our Program Director was away on a trip, I acted as Chief Program Director. Later on, I was offered the opportunity to replace him in that position when he was scheduled to be transferred in a few months.

Shanghai had been a cosmopolitan place in which to live. Nanking had previously been the capital of China, but when compared to Shanghai, Nanking was just a country town full of farmers tilling their rice paddies, often with the help of a water buffalo. I failed to see any reminder of its being the locale for "The Rape of Nanking," the 1937 incident where Japan committed atrocities against Chinese civilians. It was a place where it was finally safe for Dick to give me some driving lessons in our trusty jeep. The transmission for an Army jeep was much more complicated than that of an ordinary automobile, and of course, it was a manual one. Happily, gasoline still cost us a measly 5¢ a gallon.

I was thirsty for milk, but since we received a stern warning never to drink any possibly tubercular milk produced in China, I used to gaze longingly at the cow painted on the wall of our local dairy. We continued to eat all our meals in the Army mess hall at 25¢ per meal. Those particular Chinese cooks were anything but skilled at American-type cooking. More often than not, we would return our food to the kitchen with a request for toast and peanut butter!

My musical skills were once again called upon when I ended up as the organist for interdenominational church services on Sunday. This time, I had a nice Hammond organ on which to play, and I put to use some of my organ books that my mother mailed me.

Dick and I did what today are the usual tourist things, visiting a place featuring large statues of animals, as well as another with huge stone statues of emperors.

We also visited the elaborate setting for the tomb of Sun Yat-sen, who had become president of the Chinese republic in 1911, when the Manchu Dynasty was overthrown. The weather was cold and there was some snow on the ground, so we usually wore fur-

That's me, just another stone emperor!

lined parkas with nice fuzzy padded hoods. That funny white stuff was a real novelty for this California girl. I managed to scrape together enough snow to throw a few snowballs, something I hadn't done since some prop man produced snow for us in 1933 while I was filming *As the Earth Turns* with Shirley Temple!

Dick was an "Army Brat," whose father had served in the Army's Cavalry. Since horses were readily available to them, Dick and his father were both expert horsemen—even polo players. Dick had an Army friend in Nanking who was also quite a horseman, so Dick and Harry Roussom went riding one day, inviting me to be a kind of observer on horseback. Instructing me to stay put, the two men went charging down the field. Suddenly, my horse decided to catch up with them! With me hanging on for dear life, he bolted ahead until the two of us came to a fence. My horse skidded to a stop, and then lowered his head, allowing me to do a slow-motion somersault to the other side of the fence! Fortunately, only my ego was injured, but that horse was considerably more to handle than the beast I was used to, Father Smith's donkey Susan Jane.

When Nature Calls

Since I was the only military wife in our Army compound, one perennial problem I seemed to face was trying to locate a ladies' restroom. I pretty much had to settle for Dick—or some other cooperative soul—to first case the men's latrine, and then stand guard while I used the facilities, where fifty or so porcelain urinals would be standing at attention, like so many straight-backed soldiers. I'll never forget the time when Dick cased the men's room, then stood guard while I entered one of those forbidding places. Amazingly, just a few moments after I walked out of the room, out behind me marched a soldier, just as calm as can be—an embarrassing moment!

Another time, when we were visiting the central compound, I spotted a Russian woman—a female librarian—and excitedly ran up to her, inquiring, "Oh, please, can you tell me *where* is the ladies restroom?"

In a calm, satisfied voice, she replied, "They're building it now!"

I was so pleased when I was offered the chance to become Program Director of XMAG, but other plans were in the works, since Dick received orders for a transfer to Yokohama, Japan. However, that so-called bad news seemed to have a very real silver lining. Dick's parents were living in that city, and Dick's father, Colonel Goates, was head of Information and Education in Japan. That meant he was in charge of Radio Tokyo, former the home of Tokyo Rose, so I hoped that I could take up the Colonel on his previous offer of a Program Director job at Radio Tokyo.

I experienced another trip on the Chinese railroad, when I waited in a room at Broadway Mansions while Dick made a required flight to complete some military business in Hong Kong. During the time I was waiting for him, my shopping genes were activated by the knowledge that we would soon be leaving China. For reasons of personal safety, I had been advised to confine my excursions to within a couple of blocks of Broadway Mansions, but, throwing caution to the winds, I set out to brave the frenzied crowds of Shanghai! Lured by the carrot of Chinese art objects, I soon learned the secret of maneuvering my way: I scooted along the sidewalk in the same jerky manner as the Chinese.

When I think of today's shopping situation in the U. S. where so much of everything you pick up was made in China, it amazes me how limited was the selection of Chinese manufactured goods in 1947. There was an abundance of art objects to be bargained for, however, and that happened to be was what I was interested in.

Having become accustomed to the fact that one should *never* pay the asking price, in one shop I successfully negotiated the purchase of a large beautifully decorated serving platter. Then, I noticed in the distance what appeared to be a department store. I was correct in my assumption. However, I failed to notice on which side of the four-sided building I was entering. When I left the place, I unfortunately chose the wrong door. After some time walking, I came to the horrible realization that I was lost. Lost in Shanghai. Oh, my!

After several false starts, I decided I needed to follow my mother's excellent advice: "If you're ever lost, just ask a policeman for help!" I followed that advice, but sadly, my policeman spoke only the dialect used by Shanghai residents. I finally gave up my attempt to communicate with him or translate "Broadway Mansions" into Chinese. Instead, I decided to try my luck with the local version of a taxicab.

Approaching a Pedi-cab driver, who drove a combined version of a bicycle and a rickshaw that I'd never seen in the U.S., my negotiations were not any more successful. Worse still, within a few moments, a frighteningly large crowd completely surrounded us and began pressing closer. Just when despair was about to overtake me, I heard a most welcome sound—proper English coming from the lips of a European gentleman who had decided to rescue this damsel-in-distress. Not only did he tell my driver *where* to take me; he also completed the very necessary *financial* negotiations. Telling me exactly how much to pay my driver upon arrival, he saw me safely aboard my Pedi-cab and waved me goodbye, to the sound of my profuse thank-you..

I experienced an exciting ride through the streets of Shanghai and had decided that the worst was over when we finally reached Garden Bridge. Just as my driver began pulling my vehicle up the slope of the bridge crossing Soochow Creek, a burly Chinese fellow grabbed the side of my Pedi cab, and I thought it was all over! I don't think my driver noticed my trembling, but fortunately, I misinterpreted what was actually happening. On the way across the bridge, my driver had handed a few coins to the fearsome looking Chinese coolie. It seems his job was to use his abundant muscle power to _assist my driver in hauling the Pedi cab across the bridge. His tip is known as "kumshaw," and I really hadn't been in any danger, after all.

Our friends, the Phillips, accompanied me to the airport, where I then eagerly awaited Dick's return flight from Hong Kong. We waited and waited hour after hour. Sadly, Dick's plane never arrived, nor were there any messages advising us what had happened. There we were with our mouths hanging open!

Later, I learned that Dick's flight home had been delayed by a classic demonstration of RHIP (Rank Has Its Privileges). A certain Admiral Charles Cook absolutely *insisted* that Dick's pilot return the plane to Hong Kong to pick up the Admiral. Even though the pilot told him there was probably not enough fuel on board for such an endeavor, the naval officer was adamant.

Sure enough, there were serious headwinds, and at the pilot's request, Dick found himself scanning maps for an alternative landing site. Years before, the Flying Tigers, a volunteer group that opposed the Japanese before an official war was ever declared, had established some airports in a place called Swatow, and that was the location selected for their forced landing. Yes, they managed a successful landing, although it was some time before I heard that bit of good news, for their radio had conked out and no communication was possible. The only good news I heard on the radio was that Dick had made the All-China football team. (He later received the Chinese Grand Star of Honor, announced in a scroll signed by Chiang Kai-shek.)

Landing the plane was one thing, but refueling was quite another matter! It took days of searching the Flying Tiger's abandoned airports scattered throughout the area before the military men on board scrounged enough airplane fuel in five-gallon containers for the flight to Hong Kong.

When they finally landed there, Admiral Cook said to Dick, "So, Lieutenant, how did you like Swatow?"

"Oh, very well, sir!" was my good soldier's reply!

One bright spot was that Dick had been able to tell his fellow passengers that they had landed in the heart of the lace-making industry of China, so that had set off a shopping frenzy. Of course, Dick had to bring home a large all-lace ecru tablecloth, complete with twelve matching napkins. What a wonderful reunion we had when it was all over!

We were about to leave China, hopeful that I could take up my new father-in-law's offer to be Program Director for Radio Tokyo. The year was 1947, and we didn't realize how soon the Communists would be wresting Mainland China away from Chiang Kai-shek. He and his people would end up fleeing to Taiwan, and by 1950, China would be a Communist nation.

I certainly had mixed feelings when later I read in *Time* magazine how our military had destroyed all of XMAG's recordings and equipment before they abandoned our American radio station. I would miss chatting with my radio engineer friend, Chiang, and I couldn't help but wonder what had happened to him.

Though the most affluent among them were safely residing in their walled residences, I could only feel sorry for most of the Chinese I'd met. It had surely been interesting living in a place as different as Nanking and in a job as different as the one I had. Thank goodness I received frequent letters from my mother, for I had no family nearby and almost no female companionship. But I did have my best friend—my husband, and my time in China was something I would never forget!

Chinese amused by funny American lady in rickshaw.

39 On to Japan

$\mathcal{D}$ick and I boarded a military flight for Japan (no parachute this time). During the flight, Dick shared some of his wartime experiences with me. He skipped the gory battle details, but found plenty to talk about, as illustrated by the following:

When they left India, Dick's Merrill's Marauders compatriots were loaded down with military paraphernalia. As the grueling hike across the Himalayas wore on, they coped with tigers, elephants, malaria, and the Japanese, who often stole the food that was dropped to them by parachute, including gifts for Christmas and one greatly mourned, complete Thanksgiving dinner!

To lighten their load, the men began ruthlessly discarding various items. That is, all of them except a certain Private Peter Schmoller, whose pack, if anything, seemed to grow larger each day. Finally, a bamboo pole was procured, the heavy backpack suspended from it, and the men then managed to share his burden. Why was his pack so heavy? The close-mouthed soldier kept that secret to himself until a certain day months later.

When the battle-worn group had arrived next to the banks of the Schweli River, the outfit was plagued with scrub typhus, and the order went out for the men to eliminate *all* body hair. The only cutting tools they had were trench knives or twenty-four-inch machetes, so that's what the troops were using.

Suddenly, an unexpected sound pierced the jungle. A shrill, hawkish voice called out, "Razor blades! American beer! Cigars! Cigarettes! I will sell them to you for just what they cost me!"

It was none other than Private Schmoller himself, a born capitalist, putting the laws of supply and demand to powerful use. At other times, that enterprising gentleman collected all the leftover silk parachutes used in dropping supplies to the troops. Disappearing in remote regions of Burma to the famed Boudoin Jade Mines for hours at a time, he proceeded to trade those parachutes for the prized jade for which the country was famous. A jeweler by trade, he later opened up a successful business in New York City. It seems that some people are able to make the best of any situation!

During our flight, Dick became strangely quiet. Later on, I figured out what was eating him. He was questioning how he was going to function in the land of his previous enemy. At Tokyo's airport, Dick's father and mother were waiting for us, and we dined at the Fujiya Hotel, where the giant goldfish known as Koi actually ate bread out of our hands. Of course we ate with chopsticks, for by then we were both quite proficient with those implements. Dick eyed our Japanese waiters with some suspicion, but soon began making the adjustment to our new homeland.

Explaining that there was currently no housing for dependents in Yokohama, Colonel and Mrs. Goates invited us to share their comfortable quarters at Yokohama's Helm House. We were relegated to a sleeping porch on the second floor, but that was all right with us.

That first morning, the Colonel emerged from his bedroom all

Cherry Blossom time with my husband and in-laws.

white-faced. It seemed that during the night our quaint little music-box alarm clock—my Christmas gift to Dick—had gone off in the middle of the night. The otherworldly sounds it made led our host to believe that he was hearing heavenly music! In other words, at some point during the night, my father-in-law was convinced that he had died and gone to heaven!

The Japanese have a delightful custom of *formally* addressing everyone and everything. Thus their famous Mount Fuji is called "Fuji-san," meaning literally "Mr. Fuji" or "Honorable Fuji." We quickly began addressing Dick's parents as "Papasan" and "Mamasan," terms that were both convenient and affectionate, as well as solving the age-old problem of how to address one's in-laws. As an Army officer, Papasan was entitled to six servants, courtesy of the government of Occupied Japan. He settled for just one, a charming young Japanese girl named "Toshiko," or "Toshiko-san" as we would soon be calling her.

As in my early Hollywood days, I found myself in a strange Wonderland! We arrived in Japan just as Cherry Blossom time began, and the Japanese would spend a whole day hiking across town in order to view those trees. Of course, they had to walk, for in the Japan of 1947, as a result of the sacrifices required of them during World War II, none of them owned cars or even bicycles, all having been melted down for their war effort! The only truck you were likely to see was an odd three-wheeled vehicle with a kind of garbage can on top that burned charcoal for fuel. However, we sometimes saw a crude wagon loaded with wooden "honey buckets" that was pulled by some beast of burden. Imagine: I had found a China short of manufactured goods and a Japan without automobiles!

My father-in-law was head of Information and Education in Occupied Japan, which meant he was in charge of all the colleges, universities, high schools, newspapers, and radio stations in the country. Family and friend connections can be a wonderful thing, but they can also backfire. When Papasan tried to give me a Program Director job at Radio Tokyo such as he'd offered me in 1946 and similar to the one I had in Nanking, a woman at the station complained to the Adjutant General about favoritism. It was made clear to Colonel Goates that I was not to have *any* position at all at Radio Tokyo. So much for the flip side of nepotism!

Sleeping Giants

Dick's job was that of Barge Control and Petroleum Products Supply Officer for Yokohama Harbor. He ran a fleet of 300 barges delivering materials to the Eighth Army and to rebuild Japan, plus a fleet of seven-yard tankers that delivered oil to the economy of Japan and Korea. Working for him was a group of former Japanese naval forces who wore their old military uniforms—without insignia. Commanding Dick's fleet was English-speaking and USA-educated Mr. Saito, who came into Dick's office each day for dispatches, bowed, clicked his heels, and placed a single flower in a Coke bottle.

One day, Mr. Saito opened his navigation drawer, and Dick spotted the shoulder boards of an Admiral. Yes, Mr. Saito had been Vice Admiral Saito on the staff of Fleet Commander-in-Chief Admiral Yamamoto and actually present at the meeting where the decision was made to bomb Pearl Harbor! Saito claimed to have been there in person when Admiral Yamamoto, educated in the USA, made the accurate prediction, "I fear we will awaken a sleeping giant and fill him with a terrible resolve!" Mr. Saito's version differs from the *Tora! Tora! Tora!* movie with a similar quote, "I fear all we have done is to awaken a sleeping giant and fill him with a terrible resolve." According to Mr. Saito, the "sleeping giant" reference was uttered shortly *before* the attack on Pearl Harbor, at the time of intense debate among the Japanese high command.

Evidence of our victory over the Japanese in World War II was hard to miss. The area between Yokohama and Tokyo, which is similar to the distance between Oakland and San Francisco, had once been filled with buildings, but was then reduced to rubble by American bombs. It was largely a vast expanse of nothingness, with the exception of twisted steel, smoke stacks, and kitchen sinks!

Clear 1947 evidence of World War II damage—
the highway between Yokohama and Tokyo.

Japanese ways and customs seemed even stranger than those we found in China. Their constant bowing up and down as a greeting, as a farewell salute, as a gesture of apology, or for seeking permission; the removing of shoes before entering your house; all were so different from what we were used to!

The countryside managed to look surprisingly like Japanese paintings. What picturesque sights we witnessed, as the local farmers, wearing mushroom-shaped hats, waded through the water to grow and harvest their rice. Land was so scarce that not one square inch was wasted, even though that meant farming on the side of a mountain. I decided that the Japanese invasion of America was probably motivated by that land shortage.

One remarkable trait of the Japanese was the average person's appreciation of beauty. Even the most humble hut or corrugated tin shack was likely to boast a lovely flower arrangement, perhaps constructed only of weeds or branches. The arrangement might well be situated in a special alcove called a *tokomma*, perhaps with a painting or Japanese writing on a scroll placed above it. When a plumber came to call, he was likely to carry his tools in an artistic flowered scarf called a *feroshki*. I soon learned that you had to be careful what you admired in someone's home. They were all too likely to present the item as a gift!

Fortunately, Dick's parents were very much plugged-in to Japanese life, so many unusual opportunities were presented to me to learn of local culture and customs. These included visits and overnight stays at homes where we were provided with slippers—and sometimes kimonos—as we entered and removed our shoes.

The older homes had ancient sod roofs and large Japanese-style soaking bathtubs where you wash and rinse yourself outside the

In kimonos lent to us, Dick and I admire the Japanese garden.

tub, then soak in the hot water. In earlier times, those tubs were heated by charcoal, but more recently, they just threw an electrode in the water and threw the switch, warning, "Don't forget to turn off the current before entering!" For our overnight stays, there were no beds. Instead, the Japanese slid aside the panels in Tansu chests and produced padded quilts called futons, probably made from old kimonos. Tansu chests were surprisingly modern-looking modular wood chests with large round black locks. Since the floors on which our futons rested consisted of straw woven into thick *tatami* mats, the sleeping arrangements were not all that uncomfortable.

Instead of lording it over the Japanese, my father-in-law chose to build on the good parts of their culture. Searching the country for the best talent, he had the US Army sponsor concerts and plays, the first such presentations in all of Japan in many years. The talented performers sang, played their violin, piano, or xylophone

As part of Nikko festival, Shinto priests and children in fancy costumes.

in concerts, and they usually only owned the clothes they wore on their backs, but, to their great delight, Papasan obtained tuxedos for the men to wear for their concert appearances. The magnanimous attitude of people like Colonel Goates no doubt helped bolster the surprising respect which the Japanese of postwar Japan afforded America, democracy, and all things American.

Traveling together, Mamasan and I witnessed the Portable Shrine celebration in Nikko, then opened for the very first time since World War II. We were enchanted by the colorful costumes and enthusiasm of the celebrants, both the impressively costumed priests and the darling kimono-clad children.

The four of us were also among the fortunate few who were invited to attend both a Noh Drama and a Kabuki play, and to visit backstage with the actors. As with all classic Japanese theatre, there were no actresses, so all female roles were being played by men. I had studied about such theatre in my years at Mills College, but seeing it in person was something else.

I took a brief class in flower arranging and learned of other Japanese arts such as Bankei, consisting of "landscaping" on an extremely miniature scale, namely with clay in a plate full of sand. Then there was Bonzai, which is the art of growing miniature trees in a small pot. I quickly became quite intrigued with things Japanese, as well as the intricacies of the Tea Ceremony. The latter was mainly an exercise in discipline, to show how well one could conform to the very strict rules of the tea ceremony. After all the energy expended, I had fully expected the final product to be infinitely delicious, but it was not; it was just dull green, powdery, and somewhat bitter to taste, a supreme disappointment.

Mamasan was determined to pay a visit to a geisha house, which was off-limits to all military personnel, and she talked her friend, Mr. Mochizuki, who was the Mayor of Yokohama and head of the Yokohama Chamber of Commerce, into arranging such a visit for the four of us. Papasan's chauffeur drove us way out in the country, where the most delightful old Japanese home was located, complete with sod roof, sliding shoji screens, tatami mats, and charming gardens decorated with stone lanterns. (Shoji screens are rice paper panels supported by interlocking pieces of wood; tatami consists of three-inch thick finely woven rice straw mats, so delicate that walking on them in shoes would ruin them. Our "stone lanterns" in the United States may look similar, but they are made of poured concrete, not carved out of granite like these Japanese ones.)

Most important of all, of course, were the geisha who lived at that place. The girls wore tall Japanese-style black wigs and the most gorgeous kimonos I would ever see. Around their waists they wore an *obi*, an individually loomed or embroidered long silk sash, wound over and over and folded at the back to form a small pillow. Leaving their *getas* outside, the girls shuffled about in their cotton *tabis*, the Japanese version of socks, which had a separate compartment for the big toe. Only worn outside and removed at the entrance to a home, *getas* were the original model for our now ubiquitous flip-flops. In rainy weather special *getas* on short wooden stilts were worn.

Mr. Mochizuki explained to us that the geisha were quite at a loss as to how to treat Mamasan and me, the only non-geisha women to ever enter the place. They finally decided that their best course was to treat us the same way that they treated the men, which meant that they extended every courtesy to us. Of course, we ate with chopsticks and, sitting on the floor, we were served saki—which we didn't drink—in a tiny vase the size of a bud vase. Fortunately for Dick's six-foot, three-inch frame, rather than kneeling, he was able to dangle his long legs in the hole in the floor under our table, since there was no fire in the small charcoal burner resting beneath it.

Following the meal, the exquisitely dressed geisha entertained us with their music, played on a shamisen, a drum and a koto. The shamisen was a sort of Japanese guitar or banjo, and the koto was a kind of horizontal harp. The music had a certain hypnotic quality, even though it was not too likely to appeal to Western ears.

The Japanese men who were frequenting the place that afternoon had lots of fun imitating the girls' dancing, similar to the horsing-around that might take place at one of our girl-oriented American restaurants. The geisha were highly trained singers, dancers, and musicians, not prostitutes, as some might suppose. The latter all-too-common misconception explains why servicemen were supposed to stay away from such places.

40 General MacArthur and Sea Serpents

For centuries, the Japanese had been living under an emperor whom they believed to be of divine origin. Following Japan's surrender in 1945, their Emperor Hirohito fully expected to be tried for war crimes. Instead, in exchange for his cooperation with the United States and especially General MacArthur, the Emperor was permitted to remain in his moat-encircled palace. General MacArthur, the Supreme Commander of the Far East, was of course the general famous for returning to the Philippines in triumph after vowing "I shall return!" when our Army was forced from that country.

Promptly at noon, General MacArthur would arrive every day at Tokyo's Dai-Ichi building (the government headquarters) in his formidable, curtained limousine, while Americans like me and crowds of awestruck Japanese lined up to greet him, a dashing officer in purple tie, chest full of ribbons, and cap filled with "scrambled eggs" insignia. This impressive ceremony served both the needs of the Japanese and our own purposes, as occupiers of Japan, for General MacArthur gave them a new leader to honor and even worship. This may partially explain the respectful attitude of the Japanese toward the United States and Americans, an attitude that really amazed me as, of course, it did my husband.

Before long, it was time for my father-in-law, Colonel Goates, and his wife to return to the United States. For nearly two weeks, the colonel had been relieved of duty as head of Information and Education for Occupied Japan, when the four of us decided on a peaceful farewell vacation together at the Fuji-View Hotel, located on Lake Kawaguchi, at the base of Mount Fuji.

My husband and I rented a sailboat and sailed to a small island in the middle of the lake, where the only thing we discovered was a small Buddhist shrine, the inside of which was inexplicably covered with hairpins. Little did we realize what events were transpiring while we were so enjoying ourselves. An ambitious woman at Radio Tokyo, the same woman who had complained to the Adjutant General about my proposed employment at Tokyo Rose's former station, had been agitating, without success, to have her *own* script produced. It was similar to Orson Welles' October 1938, *War of the Worlds* radio drama—the one that sounded exactly like an actual news broadcast covering an invasion of creatures from Mars. That broadcast had resulted in mass panic, since not everyone heard the explanation that it was all just a radio drama. For security reasons, my father-in-law had previously nixed the airing of such a realistic broadcast, but with Colonel Goates safely out of town, the woman went ahead and produced the program.

One evening in June 1947, with radio music playing softly in the background, General MacArthur and his wife were visiting their son, Arthur, who was recovering from a broken arm at Tokyo General Hospital. Suddenly, an announcer interrupted the music with what seemed to be an authentic, urgent announcement reporting the presence of a "giant sea serpent in Tokyo Bay!" The broadcast was then supposedly switched by remote to the Kawasaki shore, where it was augmented by the voices of panicked crowds. General MacArthur, upon hearing the broadcast—complete with the moans and groans of the great sea monster—of all things, called out the fleet!

Soon, Naval cutters from nearby Yokosuka Naval Base were frantically searching the waters of Tokyo Bay for *sea serpents*, orders of General MacArthur. Since my husband was scheduled to be Officer of the Day in the Harbormaster's office, if he hadn't traded duty with a certain Captain Boyle, Dick himself would have been a part of that remarkable search party. Mounted with fifty caliber machine guns, all available crash boats were searching the harbor looking for a sea serpent, as ordered by General MacArthur!

General MacArthur hurried back to his office in Tokyo. You can imagine his reaction when he learned he had been duped, that the broadcast was a hoax, a total fake!

"Who is in charge of Radio Tokyo?" the humiliated 5-Star General demanded to know.

"Why, Colonel Goates, but he's already been relieved of duty."

"GET GOATES!" General MacArthur ordered.

So, General Willoughby, a two-star General, was the Army messenger sent on the two-hour trip to our Fuji-View Hotel, and he forced my father-in-law to cut short his vacation. My husband and I watched in amazement as the staff car with driver sped off, hurrying the Colonel and Willoughby back to Tokyo. There, a *personal reprimand* from General MacArthur was put in my father-in-law's personnel file—the kiss of death for an Army career officer! (Although eventually, General Robert Eichelberger, commanding the US Eighth Army, was able to remove that reprimand from his file.)

General MacArthur had by then assumed God-like proportions in Japan, with both the Japanese and many of the Americans. President Truman later had to deal with General MacArthur's seeming omnipotence in the Korean War, when General MacArthur disobeyed Truman's orders not to go beyond the Yellow River and was summarily relieved of duty. About General MacArthur, President Truman stated in one of his letters, "He's worse than the Cabots and the Lodges. They at least talked with one another before they told God what to do."

Captain Boyle never forgave my husband for that wild night he spent as Officer of the Day, searching the dark waters of Tokyo Bay for sea monsters, with deck-mounted 50-caliber machine guns at the ready, I have never read a biography of General MacArthur that mentions this Sea Serpent incident. One can only wonder why. Yet perhaps that incident met the same fate as General MacArthur himself, who was correct in his prediction that "Old soldiers never die; they just fade away!"

41 Settling On To Japan

I could scarcely have imagined teaching English to a bunch of Japanese, but my mother-in-law *had been* teaching an advanced English class to a group of Japanese students. Since she was leaving, I volunteered to take over her responsibilities. The class was held in a room of a building that had been bombed during the war. Every time I walked into the room, the students showed their respect by standing up and bowing. Those students claimed that they disliked the Japanese warlords nearly as much as we, but were obedient to their superiors.

It was exciting to see the enthusiasm with which those people, both young and old, approached the learning of a vastly different foreign language. As students they were unbelievably eager and a true delight for any teacher. Of course, it wasn't just the English language they were enthusiastic about. They were just as anxious to learn about the *country* that had so successfully defeated them.

We finally acquired our own residence, a converted barracks with a formidable pole right in the middle of the living room. An enterprising soldier who was one of our neighbors chose to cut down his pole—with quite disastrous results! We chose to place the hand-carved wooden chest we'd bought in Shanghai right next to that pole, as if some interior designer had planned the post there on purpose.

One day, I mentioned to my little maid not to hang up my

wool suit since I was going to have it cleaned. When the girl heard the word "cleaned," she took immediate action and *washed* the suit—undoubtedly in nice hot water! Of course, my beautiful red wool suit was shrunk to a size that made it impossible to wear!

Our army-issue home looked exactly like the ones next to it, with predictable results. One evening when Dick arrived home and bounded up the stairs, he felt that something looked a little different. Sure enough, he was all the way upstairs before he realized that he was in the wrong house!

After a whole year as "Mrs. Marilyn Goates," I had yet to cook a single meal. I then took courage in hand and opened a can of spaghetti! Dick was so impressed by my ability to prepare a meal that the very next day, of all things, he invited a whole group of his Army friends to dinner! Somehow I survived the challenge. I also wrote my mother, sending an urgent request for my *Joy of Cooking* cookbook. Instead, unfortunately, she sent me *It's Fun to Cook*, a children's novel with recipes interspersed.

I have mentioned the wooden "honey buckets" carried on local wagons. Those substitutes for modern plumbing were often placed strategically beneath a hole in the "bathroom" floor of Japanese homes since there were no outhouses. Their plumbing solution accounted for our being unable to eat locally-grown vegetables, since the soil was contaminated by their use of such easily-obtained fertilizer. The military occupation had an answer for that situation: they operated local hydroponic farms, where vegetables to be sold at the PX were grown in water.

Before long, many of the Japanese customs that had seemed so foreign to me now seemed quite wonderful. What kind of barbarians were we to walk into our homes wearing the footwear sullied by the dirt and mess from the streets; taking off one's shoes really made a lot of sense. I found myself using bowing as a form of greeting, apology, thank you, or farewell. And the custom of hot moist washcloths distributed before a meal seemed most appealing.

With Papasan and Mamasan returning to the United States, we acquired Toshiko as our maid. Like Papasan, we could have had up to six servants, courtesy of the Japanese government. I decided that was the moment of truth and I should gird up my loins and learn to cook! My mother later apologized to me for ill-preparing me to be a housewife. "But, Marilyn, you were always just so busy!" With Toshiko's assistance, I tackled the basics of cooking.

Although Toshikosan was actually a year or so older than Dick, she more or less became our "daughter" with her own bedroom. Whenever she went out with a date, Dick really quizzed the fellow. Incidentally, a few years later, she married an American Warrant Officer and moved to the United States.

I had lived in a China with few manufactured goods available, and I was soon living in a Japan almost completely devoid of automobiles! It's hard to imagine, but in the Japan of 1947, there were almost no cars on the road, other than some American Army vehicles and a few strange, three-wheeled, charcoal-burning trucks. I was anxious to continue the driving lessons I'd begun in Nanking, but I was sadly out of luck, for as in Shanghai, there were thousands of naive pedestrians to contend with. I couldn't forget the accident we'd had when Papasan's chauffeur hit a pedestrian; so, my driving lessons were put on hold

I did end up playing the organ for the morning interdenomina-

Our darling Japanese maid, Toshiko.

tional services in Yokohama, as well as the afternoon L.D.S. services in Tokyo. That was my first experience with Mormon hymns, but I managed okay. A couple of servicemen asked me to teach them piano. I hadn't had any actual piano lessons since I was twelve and studying with Helena Lewyn, but I relished the chance to try my hand at teaching, and I found it very rewarding. I also took a few lessons myself from Mamasan's voice teacher, Maestro Camelli. A professional accompanist, he had long ago come to Japan with an Italian opera company, then ended up marrying a Japanese woman after he was recruited to teach music lessons to the royal children. He was a friend of the great opera composer, Puccini, since his parents were close friends with that illustrious gentleman. Some background! A similar friend was a Mrs. Fuji, who had been the official doll-maker for the Japanese Royal Family.

I'll never forget the remarkable performance I saw later in the year of *My Old Kentucky Home*. Telling the life of Stephen Foster and featuring his music, the show was produced with an all-Japanese cast, every one of whom wore a Southern-type costume and a bright blond wig!

One of my fondest memories of Japan is of the three young ladies who paid me a weekly visit. No, they didn't arrive by car or even by bicycle, for all such vehicles had been melted down for the War effort. Dressed in kimonos, obis, and tabis, they struck me for all the world as the "Three Little Maids From School" from *The Mikado*. They were just full of giggles and made ample use of the fans all three of them carried. Of course, I struck them as amazingly bold and fearless. Their purpose in walking across town to visit me was to learn "about American women and democracy," for

Mrs. Fuji, eating her first hamburger.

in prewar Japan, women had absolutely no rights, being unable to own property, vote, or even file for divorce. Those three girls were all college graduates and had read Shakespeare in English. I certainly wish that such respect and admiration for America and Americans could have continued to this day.

Tremendous sacrifice was required of the Japanese during World War II. Of course, there were the Kamakazi suicide pilots. On a smaller scale,

Fond memories of 1947 Japan—this old man—

the people were required to turn in any surplus metals. That they did, right down to their wedding rings and the statues from their schools. At the end of the war, there were acres of yet-to-be melted-down metals that the Occupation made available to the American service people and their families. It was great sport searching for treasures through those brass piles—at 5¢ or 10¢ a pound! I brought home several copper planters and the figure of a rhinoceros. I also brought home the severed head of a bronze Nino Miya statue. He was the Abraham Lincoln of Japan, a poor boy who grew up to be a popular mayor, and many school children collected

And these tiny fishermen.

their yen until they had enough money to buy one of those bronze statues for their school. Somehow that decapitated statue head of the child Nino Miya, paid for with children's coins, brought home to me the immense sadness and futility of war.

Of course, the day inevitably came when we had to say "Sayonara" to our home in Yokohama, with all its cultural riches. Since Dick's return from overseas was way overdue, and I had been overseas a year, we were required to come back to the United States.

I was convinced that I would never see that lovely country again, so I was really quite devastated at the thought of leaving Japan. Needless to say, I shed many a tear on our return voyage home.

42 Back to America

I was certainly looking forward to cruising the ocean, this time with my *husband,* rather than rooming with a bunch of civilian employees, the way I had on my way to the Orient. The Army has a way of surprising you, and not always with welcome news. We learned that Dick was to be the Troop Commander aboard our ship, meaning that he was going to have to eat and sleep with the hundreds of soldiers he was in charge of, as they painted the ship and performed other duties. So, I hardly saw him at all on our voyage home!

Our destination was Seattle, Washington, where Dick was to be assigned to Fort Lewis. Not surprisingly, my parents were there on the dock to greet us, when our military ship arrived at the Port. We enjoyed a welcome reunion after a whole year without face-to-face contact or even phone calls. My parents drove us to Utah, where we saw a bunch of relatives. After a full year of separation, my mother and I were as giggly and talkative as a couple of school-girls, as we sat in the back seat and made up for lost time.

While in Japan, we had purchased an innovatively designed Mercury camera that had to have the film fully advanced before shooting could begin, so we could hardly wait to develop the 35mm film that would yield 180 shots of our time there. Alas, we would discover that our weird camera had merely torn the film and not advanced it at all, so that we ended up with totally blank rolls of film!

Like most young people, Dick and I were anxious to buy a car, so that's what we did. I hadn't cashed any of my checks from my work at radio station XMAG in Nanking, where gasoline only cost us 5¢ a gallon and our meals 25¢, so we used the money to purchase a two-tone 1941 Cadillac from the Mayor of Salt Lake City. We bought car insurance from Wendell, an old college buddy of Dick's, then traveled to check out California. Before we got there, Dick entered an intersection at the same time as a motorcycle rider. Both men swerved to avoid an accident, but the motorcycle rider ended up laid out on the street!

"Don't worry; I have insurance!" Dick generously reassured the fellow, and he made a phone call to Wendell, whom we hadn't seen for a week or so.

Wendell told Dick he'd get back to him—and he did—in the form of a terse telegram: "INSURANCE NOT YET IN EFFECT. GET OUT CHEAP!" Welcome to the USA!

Dick's first Army assignment was to take charge of an eight-car Mortuary Train, delivering the remains of World War II servicemen to their families around the country, a grim task to say the least. His next assignment was to engage in winter maneuvers on the top of snow-covered Mt. Rainier, where, like Eskimos, they lived in "snow caves" for weeks at a time. Meanwhile, I was all alone and bored, so I took a job at the personnel office as a clerk-typist. There sat our automobile in its parking spot with no one to drive it. One day, I couldn't stand it any more, so I grabbed the keys and started the engine, but I put it in gear without my foot on the brake, causing the car to lurch violently backwards and scaring me nearly to death. With my legs trembling, I decided that I had to continue *walking* to wherever I needed to go.

By then, Dick had decided—with my encouragement—that he wanted to leave the service and return to college. My parents and I certainly approved, and when he asked for his father's advice, Papasan asked him, "Son, are you trying to get *in* to something or *out* of something?" Dick definitely had college as a goal, so that settled things, as far as our plans were concerned. However, he was Category One, which meant that the Army could hang on to him for just as long as they chose.

When Dick came down from the snow caves of Mount Rainier, we were amazed to read in a bulletin that Category One soldiers could apply to be released from the service. Immediately, Dick put in his application. Good thing, for one month later, that offer was rescinded, since the Korean War had started. Dick received permission to leave the military, so our sights were now set on Stanford University in Palo Alto, California.

Another dose of reality came before we could get on our way. Dick loaned our Cadillac to Doug, the brother of a good friend. Sad to say, said brother (who would die of alcoholism before his thirtieth birthday) wrecked our car! We only had liability, not collision insurance, so our life savings went to fix our automobile.

Chalking up our misfor-

My career as an Army wife was about to come to a halt.

tunes to experience, we traveled to Palo Alto and rented a one-bed-room, one-bath home. It was an ancient dwelling, complete with icebox, a pull-chain toilet, and a floor so slanted that when you placed a marble on the floor, it would roll. However, it did have a sun porch we planned to rent for $50, whereas we were leasing the house for a mere $95 a month.

I had questioned Dick about his eligibility for Stanford, but he assured me that his grades in his two years at the University of Utah were such that he would have no problems. After all, just before his high school graduation, he'd been offered a scholarship to Stanford.

Another dose of harsh reality came in the form of a letter from Stanford. In reply to his application, the answer was "No!" That was no doubt one of the worst days of Dick's life. In the Orient, he had been "Mr. Successful," with a good job, a new wife, and every-thing coming up roses, but things were suddenly looking grim for us. After paying what we needed to on our rental, our money was nearly gone, and we started subsisting on beans and the apricots growing in our backyard.

Stanford did offer Dick a chance to enter summer school. He tried to persuade them to admit him for the fall semester if his grades were excellent, but no dice. However, they did agree that if he got sensational grades during the summer, as well as at San Jose State University, where he'd been admitted for the fall semester, they would admit him in the spring, so was he motivated!

As for our financial condition, fortunately for us, serendipity saved the day. After sprucing up our sun porch a bit, we placed an ad in the newspaper under "Room for Rent," and who should answer that ad but Mr. Herbert, the Assistant Head of Stanford Research Institute, who was looking for a room for his new secretary. Someone else rented our little sleeping porch, but Mr. Herbert did end up offering me a job as a Clerk-Typist at Stanford Research Institute (SRI). Now we just had to wait for my first paycheck from SRI and Dick's GI Bill monthly college education payments to begin. Dick took a temporary job digging ditches for a construction job, and also worked in the Army Reserve one day a month. In the meantime, we ate those apricots!

Just before our year's lease was over, we took a hard look at our situation. We came to the stark conclusion that most of our financial troubles began when we bought our Cadillac, so we made a momentous decision to sell our car and use the proceeds to purchase a home. Our friends all believed in renting, not buying, so they thought we were crazy when we purchased our three bedroom/one bath home on a large corner lot on the border between Menlo Park and East Palo Alto for $11,200 with a 4% GI loan we were able to assume. For the next three years, there we were on either the bus, the train, with friends, or walking. Our lot was so huge, we were able to lot-split and sell the side portion of our land for $7,000, which meant that our home, located in what one day would be high-priced Silicon Valley, only cost us $4,200. That was the total price, not the down payment. What's more, it was an attractive, ivy-covered, comfortable home, complete with a fireplace.

Our furniture consisted of in-law hand-me-downs, and when we finally got brave and sent our hideous green couch to the dump, wouldn't you know it, my frugal father-in-law actually went to the dump and brought it back!

We turned one of the bedrooms into a den for Dick. Another was our bedroom. As for the third, it was covered with adorable pink wall-paper sporting hundreds of rabbits. When we first looked at that wall-paper, we nodded to each other, and said, "Well, maybe someday . . . ."

Meanwhile, there was I, in the typing pool at Stanford Research Institute. When they asked the head of our department how many were in his department, he omitted counting any of the *women* who worked there—my first taste of male chauvinism. (When I was younger, because of my parents, I never felt in any way that my being female limited my options.) I finally got brave and requested a transfer to the Public Relations Department, so that's where I ended up, as the assistant to its Director. I would write my own letters, plus material for both SRI's monthly newsletter and their quarterly journal, *Research For Industry*.

One of my assignments for the latter involved interviewing Dr. Thomas Poulter, who had accompanied Rear Admiral Richard Byrd to Antarctica and ultimately rescued him, when the Admiral was overcome with carbon monoxide poisoning. Another interesting job at Stanford Research Institute was volunteering for the "Smog Chamber," where SRI was trying to determine the root cause of Los Angeles smog. The final answer—automobiles!

Then there was our project for the Pepsi-Cola Company, where they were considering adding vitamins to their popular soda pop. The trouble was that the results were inconsistent. They decided that what they needed was to screen the participants, so everyone at the Institute had to sample three beverages and indicate which of the three had something added. After careful analysis of the results, it was determined that *I* had the most sensitive taste buds in the whole place, and so I was dubbed the "Queen Bee" of SRI, their super taste-tester. Interestingly enough, just as I write this, some fifty-eight years later, the Coca Cola Company announced they were adding vitamins and minerals to their new Coca Cola Plus!

In the early 1930s, my father had received his Doctor of Jurisprudence degree from UC Berkeley and had been the first in his class to open a law office. He had given up his law practice in Oakland in order to further my Hollywood career, surprisingly became a motion picture agent, and then later became an attorney for the government.

In 1948, my father decided to give up his government job and open his own law office. After studying the demographics involved, he decided on Vallejo, California, and with my mother's assistance, began designing his office. Most attorneys in the town dealt exclusively with white clients, but my father seemed to enjoy working with a diverse clientele. I was certainly pleased that he had finally been able to return to his original career of choice. Not only that, a little over a year later, the City of Vallejo made him a Judge. In addition to presiding over hearings, my father had another important duty, performing over a hundred marriages. How amused my mother and I were to see my father, book in hand, going off to perform a marriage ceremony.

43 Motherhood

That pink Peter Rabbit wallpaper in our third bedroom went to waste for several years, while Dick pursued both his BA and MBA degrees at Stanford. His grades were such that he had no trouble getting admitted to their fine Graduate School of Business, and we continued to go everywhere by either bus or on foot.

Then in 1950, I developed a strange case of morning nausea, which our next-door neighbor correctly diagnosed as early pregnancy. I continued to work until shortly before Dick's graduation Cum Laude, at which time they awarded me a special PHT degree, which stands for "Putting Husband Through."

My boss in the Public Relations Department had a monthly column in a West Virginia newspaper. Shortly before I quit work, he published an open letter to the *New York World-Telegram,* publishers of the *World Almanac,* telling them that I was leaving his employ to have a baby! For seventeen years, I'd been listed in the *World Almanac* under "Noted Personalities: Actors, Actresses, Musicians, and Singers," but someone must have forwarded Bill Estler's column to the editors, for 1951 was the last year my name was listed in the *World Almanac*!

I knew little about the skills involved in being a housewife. I knew even less abut the skills involved in being a mother. As a child in my neighborhood, there were few pregnant ladies, babies, or toddlers. Baby and childcare interested me, but I knew precious little about it. For instance, I had never even seen a baby being bathed. My obstetrician, Dr. Thompson, was one of the pioneers in the Read Method of Natural Childbirth based on Dr. Read's book, *Childbirth Without Fear.* Somewhat reluctantly, I signed up for the lectures and exercises classes and faithfully did all the relaxation and other exercises.

My due date was the first week of January. Figuring all the income taxes we would save if our baby was born in 1950 rather than 1951, with my doctor's approval, I swallowed an entire small bottle of castor oil! Sure enough, contractions started, but my journey to the hospital was all for naught—an episode of false labor.

Of course, in the 1950s before the age of ultra-sounds, there was no way of predicting the sex of a baby, so I was super-curious as to what sort of creature would be joining our family. On January 6, I went into labor and had plenty of chance to utilize the slow breathing techniques I'd been practicing. Yes, the "childbirth without fear" did work for me, and at ten o'clock in the evening on January 7, 1951, a seven-pound nine-ounce baby girl was born. Dick had been with me in the labor room, rubbing my back and giving me moral support, but when he left for a short time to get himself a milkshake, that was when our baby decided to arrive, I'm happy to say, by natural childbirth.

As a little trick on my husband, the nurses phoned Dick a few minutes later and calmly told him, "Mr. Goates, you can come back now." Then, they pushed me down the hall on a gurney and covered up our new baby with a sheet. When Dick was close, I threw back the sheet.

"Dick, meet your daughter!" I announced.

Smelling salts were produced, for the poor man came close to fainting!

"Oh," said Dick, "She's beautiful! She looks like a Carolyn!"

So that was the name we gave her.

The time when I gave birth to our beautiful daughter was, without question, the happiest moment of my life, and it made me understand more clearly why my happiness was my mother's hap-

My new precious package, Carolyn

piness. Weddings, appearing on stage, or appearing in the movies were all very exciting, but to my way of thinking, nothing compared to the exhilarating moment of giving birth. I felt just fine afterward. I even said to myself that I could go through the same experience the very next day, if I had to.

My hospital bill came to $35, which certainly didn't break our bank. Dick drove me home in the ancient Mercury car we'd purchased shortly before January. A fine car in sunny weather, but when it was raining, Dick had to lean out the side window, reach to the front of the windshield, and work the wipers *by hand!* More than once, he ended up with an almost frozen left hand.

My first challenge was to bathe my new baby, a procedure I had never observed before. My mother, bless her heart, acted as if she knew nothing about baby care and as if I were the big expert. I had read all kinds of baby care books and was ready, I hoped. Purposely by myself in the kitchen, with my detailed written instructions spread across the room on cabinet doors, I crossed my fingers and began the delicate and scary task of the first bath. Somehow, Carolyn survived my amateurish ways.

I think my new baby gave my mother a wonderful chance to reminisce about her own time as a new mother. She adored Carolyn, and my father was a doting grandfather. Like my mother before me, I often read and sang to my baby. Dick was an adoring Dad, to say the least, and we were a very happy family.

If I were a sparrow, I'd tuck you 'neath my wing,
Keep you warm and safe from every harmful thing.
Since I am your mother, a lullabye I'll sing.

Our new daughter, with my proud parents.

Time to go to sleep, so close your eyes.
Night itself can act like a mother and gently lull us to sleep.
Lullabies have a way of becoming memories that we'll keep!

My pediatrician insisted that I boil all Carolyn's reusable cloth diapers, and that I did, right up to the time that I tripped going down the stairs to our garage carrying the boiling pail of diapers. After that, I wised up: no more boiling! I did still have to put the wet laundry through the ringer, hang them up on the line with clothespins, and in those days before disposable diapers, I still had to carefully fold her nice cloth diapers.

My father-in-law reminded my husband that it was high time that he gave Carolyn a name and a blessing. We took our baby to

With my 8-month-old baby daughter Carolyn.

the Mormon church in Vallejo, where the Bishop of the ward reminded Dick that he could bless his own baby.

Eight-month-old Carolyn melted her Daddy's heart when she looked up and said "Daddy," as he took her in his arms for a blessing. At that moment, Dick regretted the fact that he had been staying away from the Church of Jesus Christ of Latter Day Saints, which was very much a part of his heritage, so after that day, our little family began attending the Mormon Church. Although I wasn't yet a member, they soon had me leading the singing for church services and even playing the organ.

In time, I was able to share with Carolyn some of the special treats my mother had given me, such as her special improvised "makeup stories" that were always with a little girl as the central character and invariably followed by my request to "Please, tell it again!" There were lots of nursery rhymes and fairy tales. In addition to "This little pig went to market. This little pig stayed home," etc., there was my mother's special way of naming toes. Yes, toes! To be exact, there was "Leddy Ped, Paddy Rood, Rudy Whistle, Mary Gozzle, and BIG GOBBLE GOBBLE!"

Our little family.

44 Time Marches On

We had a house, a baby, a car, and soon my husband would have a career as a businessman. Not too many months after Carolyn was born, Dick went to work for the Southern Pacific Railroad as a "Junior Executive," traveling each day to San Francisco on the train. Fortunately for our finances, Southern Pacific operated that train, so Dick's commuting was free. Southern Pacific was a *very* conservative company. Even their Junior Executives were required to wear a conservative suit, long-sleeved shirt with tie, and a felt homburg hat.

To save money, Dick tried taking his lunch to work in a paper sack, but was advised against such a plebian custom. At first, he substituted an attaché case, then was counseled that it was more seemly for a Junior Executive to eat in a restaurant. He discovered "The Alley," where he could purchase a plate of beans or spaghetti for 17¢, plus a hard-boiled egg for a dime. Dick decided he could save even more money by bringing a hard-boiled egg from home. That's what he *thought* he had done one day when fate did not smile on him. The egg that he tapped on the counter to crack open turned out to be as raw as when the hen produced it, which was one embarrassing moment! When the shop owner was anguishing over the thought of a whole jar full of possibly raw eggs, Dick confessed that his frugal ways had caused him to supplement his lunch with an egg from home.

To my surprise, Dick's mother presented me with the gift of a lifetime—a grand piano—my very first to own. Of course, one of her reasons for giving that generous gift was the fact that I could accompany Dick as he played the trumpet. (My in-laws had previously "bought the trumpet from us" when we were about to sell the horn so we could buy some groceries.)

Dick became quite active in our Mormon Church. He also formed a trumpet quartet with some other trumpeters he'd discovered. We heard of a fine trumpet trio that had been written by a nearby composer. When we visited his modest home beneath a freeway and asked if he had any trumpet *quartets* available, that kind man took his trio, and out of the goodness of his heart, wrote in an additional part for the guys. I remember feeling so sorry for that gifted gentleman, who I was sure would probably remain a pauper all his life. I could have saved my sympathy. The composer's name was Henry Mancini, and he would shortly achieve fame and fortune as the composer of "Moon River," "The Pink Panther," and other well-known tunes!

I loved being a mother to Carolyn, but after a while, I did yearn for more of a challenge in the creative department, probably because that part of my psyche had been stimulated at an early age by my time on stage and before a camera. As a result, when Carolyn was about eight months old, I began teaching piano. I parked my tiny tot in her playpen and made it very clear to her that I needed her to be very quiet while I was giving a lesson. Amazingly, the little darling cooperated with me.

Carolyn was slow to walk, but good at everything else, particularly puzzles. I have a movie of her that was taken before she was two years old as she put a 48-piece puzzle map of the United

States together. Carolyn's favorite book involved pictures of animals, including a very stylized owl. One day, she looked at our friend, Gordy, who wore horned-rimmed glasses, pointed at him, and announced proudly and loudly, "Owl, owl!"

Dick had a Pullman pass, as well as a train pass, so we were able to have some fine free trips, traveling in style with our own train bedroom. My husband loved to take his toddler daughter with him places and she liked to go with him, hanging on to the little ring on his attaché case. Dick was a hands-on father and thoroughly enjoyed our baby daughter, as evidenced by the following poem, which he wrote in 1952 while we were living at 2067 Menalto Avenue:

ON COMING HOME

5:20 daily I embark for my home in Menlo Park
With tedious work left well behind and thoughts of happiness I'll find
At my little niche of heaven. Address: Twenty-Sixty-Seven.
I've written verse with no little strife but ne'er conceived one for my wife.
So I'll pen a line or two to let her know I yet wouldst woo
Her favors and her loving smile bestowed on me down chapel aisle.
But life is richer than e'er has been with the joy of Carolyn.
You see why eyes do homeward turn and each day my heart does yearn
For five o'clock to hasten round so once again I'll be homeward bound.

R. B. Goates

Dick and I were both only children, so Carolyn was the first grandchild for both sets of parents, and to say the least, received scads of devoted attention. Dick's parents were stationed at the Pre-

306 Little Girl in Big Pictures

sidio in San Francisco and my parents in Vallejo, so we got together often for wonderful family times.

Another poem from my husband, written in 1953:

ON BEING HOME

Last night while I was on my way home
I decided to try my hand at a poem.
The poor result was so well-received
That another verse have I conceived.

I told of the joys of coming home.
In this abbreviated tome
With due application of the mind
Another subject I shall find.
In search of a theme out the window I stare
Reflecting on home—" on being there."
I shall write of its pleasures, its comforts and joys,
Of this neat little cottage – floors littered with toys.

When I come in the door a small voice will greet me
As two sweet young ladies scoot out to meet me.
"Daddy, bye-bye," the rascal will say
In her own inimitable way.
On such a request I can scarce turn cold shoulder
Particularly when in my arms I do hold her.
I don't believe any dad could do that
Especially when she hands you your hat.

So "bye-bye" we'll go, our girl all excited,
And Mommy and Daddy admit they're delighted
With the sweet little baby riding between them,
Wishing and hoping the whole world has seen them.

R. B. Goates

At Southern Pacific, my husband performed the studies recommending the "Piggyback Service" that is now all too common in America. That involved truck trailers resting aboard a specially designed rail car so that much transportation can go by rail, rather than by highway. He also, with Southern Pacific's blessing, secretly rode in boxcars, installing machinery that would measure the jolts that cattle were receiving. That enabled him to be an expert witness "from the cow's point of view" at special interstate commerce hearings. An attorney in one such case sternly objected, stating, "Mr. Goates was testifying as a goat; now he wants to testify as a cow!"

I was still taking my daughter places on the bus, for my driving lessons had been interrupted all too many times, whether in Shanghai, Yokohama, or in Seattle. I finally decided to sign up for an adult education driving class when I discovered that I was again expecting. What's more, my conservative doctor insisted I not take driving lessons while I was pregnant!

Three years and three months after Carolyn's arrival, I received my best birthday gift ever: on May 12, 1954, I gave birth to a bouncing baby boy. I had had precious little experience with babies and even less with little boys, so I couldn't believe my eyes when I gazed into the clear blue eyes of our little son, Brian Lesley Goates.

Amazing! I gave birth to a son!

If I were a bunny, I'd keep you furry warm;
Sleep with one eye open, to save you from all harm.
Since I'm only human, I'll hug you in my arms.
Time to go to sleep, so close your eyes!

I quickly became aware of the differences between girls and boys. I began nursing Brian, as I had my daughter, but the little tiger kept biting me, and so I had to abandon the whole idea. I'll never forget the nurse's words to me:

"Mrs. Goates, if I were you I'd just give up and move to a cattle ranch!"

A five-day-old baby, and I'm supposed to *give up*? Yes, being the mother of a son was going to be different.

Immediately after Brian arrived, I enrolled in an adult educa-tion driving class and finally got my license—at the age of twenty-eight. What a relief! Dick was doing well at work, so we sold our home and purchased a nice contemporary-styled home in Menlo Park. It had mahogany siding, a cathedral ceiling, and cork floors. It was built in a cul-de-sac off a dead-end street, and its slanted driveway would before long be a perfect place for Brian to drive his foot-powered toy tractor.

In 1956, my father-in-law gave us a Christmas gift that for me was quite unwelcome since I was expecting again, and a new dog and a new baby seemed like a poor combination. That gift was our Siberian Husky-Collie-German Shepherd puppy, Laddy. The fluffy little ball of fur took no time at all to win me over, and little did I know how much that dog would eventually mean to all our family.

Three years and three months after Brian arrived, I gave birth to our third child. Carolyn had high hopes that our baby would be a little girl, but there was no little sister in store for her. On July 11,

1957, while his fa-ther was away on a business trip, Kevin Robert Goates ar-rived, his middle name coming from my father, Robert E. Knowlden.

Marilyn & baby Kevin

Fate smiled on us by sending us a blond, curly-topped baby, who was delightfully easy to care for. In fact, we called him "The Cheerful Cherub." As with my other children, I composed a special lullaby for him:

> *I love little Kevin. He's sweet as can be.*
> *He lights up inside like a Christmas tree*
> *And some day, yes some day, he's going to be*
> *A man who will marry a woman like me.*
>
> *He'll be the kindest, the wisest, the best.*
> *He'll be the king of all the rest.*
> *But for the moment, he's happy here,*
> *Just to be my baby dear!*

So, there I was, the mother of three, and for an only child like me, my family seemed enormous!

Our three wonderful children.

45 Change of Direction

In 1954, Dick accepted an offer to work for Consolidated Freightways. Every time we passed one of their truck-trailers, three-year-old Carolyn would call out, "There's my Daddy's truck!" After just a short time, the powers-that-be made Dick a Vice President and transferred him to Southern California, to head up their subsidiary, Trans-Ocean Van Service.

Dick went on his own to find us a place to live and, to my great distress, rented us a home for what seemed to me to be the astronomical figure of $300 a month. The house overlooked the Pacific Ocean and was just behind the Wayfarer's Chapel. It was designed in the unmistakable style of Frank Lloyd Wright, since both the Glass Chapel and our home were built by his son, Lloyd Wright.

The house was completely furnished with custom-built furniture designed for the unique house, with some drawers cut on the diagonal. The living room was six-sided and had a magnificent view of the Pacific Ocean, while the thirty-foot bathroom had both an indoor and an outdoor fountain. The owner of the home was Ralph Jester, who would be living in Europe in search of antiques for the film *Solomon and Sheba*, for which he was the Art Director. His artistic leanings accounted for the fact that the home was filled with original art objects, including original Picasso etchings, plus the headboard for our bed, an ancient three-sided Altar-Piece. In addition to furniture, the rental included sheets, blankets, silverware, and dishes, together with the services of an exterminator and a gardener. Altogether, not too shabby for $300!

I'll never forget the Christmas we traveled to Santa's Village at nearby Lake Arrowhead. We were late arriving, but the kind owners let us in anyway, and we headed straight to Santa's Cottage. Peeking through the open half of his front door, we discovered Santa Claus not on his throne, but looking very much at home as he used a broom to sweep his cottage. He invited us in and asked each of our children his classic question, "What do you want for Christmas?"

When it was six-year-old Brian's turn, he replied tongue in cheek, "A bicycle."

Santa quickly turned to Brian and pointedly asked him, "So what happened to the one I gave you last year?"

The color drained from Brian's face, for he had taken his shiny bicycle apart and had never put it back together again. At that magical moment, all five of us were absolutely sure that clairvoyant gentleman with his genuine white beard and whiskers was indeed the *real* Santa Claus!

We eventually sold our Menlo Park home and purchased a Palos Verdes Estates home on Paseo del Mar directly overlooking the ocean. As the children got older, Dick had fun teaching our whole family to play the trumpet. Finally, a trumpet quartet was formed, and the group was known as the Four Billy Goates Gruff, with mother Marilyn at the piano. Fortunately, there were a few talent shows where that illustrious group was able to perform, playing songs like "Rock of Ages," where five-year-old Kevin played a

Our kids, the year before we met the *real* Santa Claus.

The Four Billy Goates Gruff performing.

very simple part, to the accompaniment of his Daddy's complicated variations.

> *There's nothing like a family band.*
> *The sound we make is really grand.*
> *It's hard to fully understand*
> *The fun of playing in a family band.*

In 1960, after Dick had been in charge of TransOcean Van
Service for several years, Consolidated Freightways decided it was

time for them to get out of the international freight business. However, Dick did not agree that it was time for *him* to get out of such a business. So, with Consolidated Freightways' blessing, Dick decided to start an international freight forwarding business of his own. Years before, he and Mischa Kluge had talked often of going into the international shipping business. Papasan and Mamasan had sponsored the Kluges' immigration to the United States, so Dick called on his old friend, Mischa, to secure agents in Europe, while he was performing the same task in the Orient.

Meantime, I was given the task of locating operating space for the fledgling company, which was to be named Intercontinental Transport. By the time Dick returned from the Orient, I had leased offices and arranged to purchase fine executive desks and file cabinets formerly used by Trans Ocean. Before long, the new corporation had offices in thirty-six countries, its funding coming from my father, who assured me that the money he was investing was solely for my sake, not in hope of profits. Good thing, for the company was always so cash-hungry that my father never got back a dime on his investment!

46 Drama, Anyone?

I had left the world of Hollywood and the movies far behind me. In that era before the overwhelming impact of television on all our lives, the Mormon Church had a very active speech and drama program going on, each ward having both speech and drama directors. I could have tried out for plays, but I think I felt a change of direction was in order. Like Jackie Cooper and Ron Howard, I was much more interested in writing and directing. At that time, before the appearance of the video recorder, I had no way of assessing my own acting in any of the films from my childhood. I wondered, had I done a credible job, or not? Also I think a part of me was fearful of becoming a pitiful child actor "has-been," for I had seen too many instances where former child actors were snickered at, and I didn't want to be one of them.

It's hard to be a has-been. The future looks mighty cold.
It's awful to be a has-been when you're just fifteen years old!

Little did I realize that I was preparing myself for composing future musicals, when I agreed to write the scripts for an entry in the yearly Roadshow contest for our ward (parish). Each ward had to come up with an original (except for the music) fifteen-minute miniature musical comedy. Most wards wrote original lyrics to familiar tunes, but I chose to write a lot of the music, too.

319

Russia had successfully launched the first artificial satellite, Sputnik, on October 4, 1957, so I wrote a script about strange-looking visitors from the Planet Venus who were looking for romance, for Venus has no moons, and "How Can You Have Romance Without a Moon?"—the title to one of my original songs. At that time, computers filled entire rooms, and it was long before Internet web sites such as eHarmony.com and Match-Mate, yet I wrote a script about computer dating, which included the song, "Mister Computer, Oh, Won't You Play Cupid For Me!"

My favorite script was called *Farewell, Blue Monday*, about the history of laundry methods. In a parody of the Beatles' "I Want To Hold Your Hand," prehistoric women beat clothes on a rock while singing "I'm Wearing Out My_Hands," followed later by "Have Some Clorox, Mr. Bendix," a parody on "Have an Egg-roll, Mr. Goldstone." At the end of that mini-musical, a woman places a dirty shirt into a huge machine, with a *clean,* nicely-ironed shirt emerging at the other end. At that point, the entire front of the machine falls forward and reveals a woman inside with a washboard, a tub, a clothesline, and an ironing board. To my great delight, that particular show won first prize in the Stake's Roadshow contest!

I was soon made Stake Drama Director, and in 1962, I was asked to direct the Mormon Church's ambitious musical, Crawford Gates/Arnold Sundgaard's *Promised Valley*, the story of the Mormon trek to Salt Lake City. That was no minor undertaking, since the script called for a cast of 200, including two large choruses, an orchestra, and a children's chorus. Fortunately, the latter included our own three children, even five-year-old Kevin.

Promised Valley proved so successful that our stake decided to

My big job, as Director of *Promised Valley*.

put on another musical. When my husband and I couldn't seem to find a suitable one to produce, we decided to write one. Necessity is the mother of invention, so without worrying too much about the difficulty of such a project, we wrote a musical comedy in 1962 that was called *Never Put Off Until Tomorrow,* which we produced and I directed at Mira Costa Auditorium in Manhattan Beach. Our accompanist was Karen Lookinland, mother of the Mike Lookinland who would one day be Bobby in televisions's *Brady Bunch.* The facility held 1,600, and we did two performances, so plenty of people saw that production.

On opening night, I confess that Dick and I experienced a case of producer jitters similar to those portrayed in many a B-movie. Our musical got good reviews and, at the request of the City of Redondo Beach, we produced the show at their bandstand as part of that city's celebration for the opening of King Harbor.

The setting for *Never Put Off Until Tomorrow* is an army hospital, where a young lieutenant about to be released from the service has his X-rays mixed up with those of a patient who has just died on the operating table. The lieutenant's change of attitude affects everyone in the hospital, after a nurse helps to ease the young man's distress by suggesting he needs to crowd a whole lifetime into a short time.

Never put off until tomorrow
Things that you can do today.
For life is slipping by,
The minutes seem to fly.
For time is moving on
And soon this moment will be gone!

Is there a trail you yearn to follow?
Is there a lake you long to swim?
Have you a favorite secret hollow
Where daylight grows dim?

Or does the excitement of the city
Beckon to you to come and play?
Never put off until tomorrow
The things that you can do, things that you can do,
Things that you can do today!

Marilyn & Dick Goates 1962

Of course, the philosophy expressed in that song is not unlike the one that pervaded my life. My father often reminded me, "When opportunity knocks, answer the door!" As my own life demonstrates, one thing can certainly lead to another. So when we fail to open a door, we'll never know what wonderful opportunity we have lost!

47 Around the World in Eighty Days

I long ago learned an important lesson about life and creativity: first comes the dream, only followed later by the reality. My father had a dream about his own law office, as well as me being in the movies. I had dreams about composing music, college, and a wonderful family. Dick had dreams about me joining him in China, and later about an overseas business with offices around the world. All those dreams actually turned into reality, but without the dream, nothing much would have happened. On the other hand, it would have been nice if, as maintained in *Snow White* and *Pinocchio*, "wishing can make it so!" In real life, without effort and planning, nothing much is likely to come of that wish or that dream.

> *Dreams can come true, and oftentimes they really do!*
> *Now doesn't it seem clear to you that we have dreamed a dream together.*
> *Now I can see that even for someone like me,*
> *A dream can turn out to be a hint of reality.*
> *If you work and do your darndest and do all that you can do,*
> *It won't take a Genie or a Magic Lamp to make your dreams come true!*

In 1960, Intercontinental Transport was only "a dream, a desk, and a blond," but by 1963, Intercontinental Transport had fifty-six offices around the world that Dick really wanted to visit. We bought a travel agency in Palos Verdes that we renamed "Intercontinental Travel." As owner-operators, we purchased airline tickets at 75 percent off, in preparation for a round-the-world tour. Yes, we did indeed have a dream of going "around the world in eighty days!"

We listed our home for rent for a three-month period, but we hadn't counted on the realtors being so efficient. The very next day they brought around very desirable tenants, whose only requirement was that we'd move out *"the day after tomorrow,"* and they meant that literally, not figuratively. We hadn't begun to pack, and preparing for such a long trip in that amount of time seemed impossible, but the realtor advised us just to shove our clothes to one side in the closet, pack up a few duds, and move! We followed the realtor's advice and moved to a small hotel right on the water in Redondo Beach, which suited our kids just fine.

Amazingly, the prospective tenants had admired our giant dog, Laddy, and inquired "Oh, could we take care of him while you're gone?" So that solved one of our problems. We introduced Laddy to our tenants and dropped by our home frequently so Laddy would understand that he was supposed to stay with the new tenants. *"Laddy, stay!"* we told him.

Eventually, we all traveled to Northern California, where we deposited the boys with Dick's parents in Los Altos Hills and our daughter with my parents in Vallejo. Kevin was about to enter first grade, but we crossed our fingers and hoped the situation would work our all right for him, as well as the other two. Away we flew on Pan American Airways on a voyage that would indeed take us "around the world in eighty days."

Our departure was a happy day! The plane was beautiful, and because we were travel agents, our entire trip was upgraded to first class with deluxe seats, hors d'œuvres, food, treatment, and a VIP clubroom at the airport, unlike today's rough-and-tumble, inconvenient situation. In order to be fair to all the countries we visited in our extraordinary trip around the world, I'd have to write a separate book, so I'll content myself with just a few brief comments.

Our first stop was Honolulu, where I'd never been before. We were amazed by colorful shirts and muumuus, the fragrance of flowers, the ever-present strains of Hawaiian music, the graceful dancers, and by the island's incredible racial diversity.

Then, we journeyed on to Guam, where we were slated to spend a full week. Sadly, the place was just recovering from Typhoon Karen, which had pretty much destroyed the place. As a result of the typhoon, there were absolutely no hotels, rooming houses, or even picture postcards available. Fortunately, we were able to stay with one of Dick's business associates, Jack Atencio and his wife. They lived right on the water in a home filled with twenty-eight—count them—twenty-eight cats! Jack amazed us by strolling out into the very shallow water of the ocean and eating raw clams right on the spot. I was invited to an unusual Guamanian christening party, and I loved the colorful paint jobs on the small shacks that had survived the typhoon. I noticed that the residents spoke of "Karen" as if they were talking about an old, highly respected, but thoroughly disliked acquaintance.

Our next stop was Manila, Philippines, where I was aghast at the extreme poverty. I'll never forget a little beggar girl who carried in her skinny arms her blind baby brother. So tragic! The most shocking sight of all was the National War Memorial Cemetery containing thousands and thousands of United States gravesites.

Taipei, Taiwan, the place to which Chiang Kai-shek and his buddies escaped after the Chinese Revolution. Everything was way behind the times. We were amused by visiting a beauty parlor, where the old style of permanent was being given, the kind that had women's hair hooked to an electrical octopus.

Traveling to Okinawa, our hotel room was right at street level, so I had a fantastic view of the people strolling by. Okinawa was as quaint as Japan must have been some fifty years earlier. Everyone wore kimonos and there was absolutely no American influence. We visited a museum that contained a sad replica of their beloved palace, which had been totally destroyed in the war, except for a few pieces of surviving marble carvings.

Tokyo, Japan. People often talk about bringing home "a ton of stuff" from their trips. In my case, I literally brought home a ton of stuff. I amazed the Intercontinental Transport office people by arriving in the cab of a cement truck that, instead of cement, carried my purchases including authentic stone lanterns that had been actually carved from granite, and tansu chests, those Japanese-style modular chests-of-drawers with large round black locks.

We attended the office Sayonara party with sixty-five in attendance. During the Chinese cuisine dinner, each individual presented himself in turn to us and proposed a toast, to which Dick and I had to respond with impromptu speeches, an interpreter translating our words as we went along. One of the checkers then did a Kabuki-style dance and led the men in some rousing Japanese songs. The next day, nearly the entire office staff was on hand to give us a splendid send-off, as we boarded our plane for Hong Kong.

Hong Kong—a shopper's paradise! I discovered in our hotel's

antique shop some black Coromandel chests, which I had shipped back to our home to adorn our living room.

I was nervous on September 25, 1963, when it was time for us to fly from Hong Kong to Saigon, Vietnam. The Vietnam War was threatening, and I was particularly worried because, when it was coming in for a landing, an American passenger plane had been shot at just the day before. I was concerned, but Dick assured me that Pan American would not fly into the Saigon airport unless it was safe. A while into the flight, the plane seemed to change course and the stewardesses began scurrying about distributing blankets and pillows. Then, they started turning off the cabin lights. Soon, we looked around and even the outdoor running lights for our plane had been turned off! No stewardesses were around, and no announcements were made, so we didn't know what was happening. A heavy silence filled the entire plane. Finally, the captain came on the loudspeaker and announced, "Due to the conditions in Saigon, we have over passed the airport and are about to land in Bangkok!" In effect, that was the start of the Vietnam War, for that airport was never opened again until after the war was over.

Thailand is my choice for the most interesting country we visited in our around-the-world tour. A fantastic gentleman called Bangkok Joe escorted us through that fascinating place. First stop was a courtyard filled with fifty bronze life-size Buddhas, each modeled in a different style. As an "act of merit," the people were pressing thin sheets of gold against the statues to gold-plate them.

We visited a temple with an ancient fourteen-ton Buddha made of solid gold. The statue had been covered with plaster, whose secret had been discovered only five years earlier when workmen chipped off a piece of the plaster and uncovered the shiny metal.

Joe took us on a small motor-powered riverboat to see Bangkok's floating markets. The river was filled with naked children, women washing clothes, and dead dogs! Many homes were built on stilts at the edge of the river, and the whole thing reminded me of Disney's Amazon Riverboat ride.

One of the most impressive of the 300 Bangkok temples was that of the Emerald Buddha, the latter a huge life-sized all-emerald affair dressed by the people in solid gold robes. Dick was able to play ping-pong with some of the orange-robed monks, several of whom spoke English. They claimed that the Buddhists respect all religions, even Christianity, and sometimes invite Christians to lecture to them.

We visited the Thai Boxing Palace, where I first witnessed kick-boxing. Each fight was preceded by a religious ceremony and a dance pantomime. Presents were exchanged, and then the participants fought, to the accompaniment of a six-piece band that was mostly percussion plus flute. Sad to say, we witnessed one fighter receive a broken rib. Nevertheless, their fighting was less ferocious than in the historical past, when pieces of broken glass were embedded in their boxing gloves!

Back on our tour, the next stop was Karachi, and then Istanbul. We were certainly looking forward to soaking in the Hilton bathtub, but, sad to say, there was no room for us at that inn, or even at the tenth best hotel in Istanbul. We ended up at the Ciragan Hotel and faced the crude reality of its bathing facility. It consisted of a showerhead at the height of our eyebrows, with nothing underneath but a small plastic basin—and no hot water. There were no pillow-slips on the pillows, and the hand towels were clearly crudely laundered by hand.

To compensate for all that, the Ciragan was indeed loaded with atmosphere. Our fourth-floor room overlooked the burned-down remains of a Sultan's palace and harem. Still standing were the Sultan's Mosque and Minaret, and I felt almost close enough to touch the Meizen, during his spooky-sounding night-and-morning calls to prayer that came from his tower directly across from our room.

In Athens, Greece, I took my first visit to the Acropolis and its Erechtheum, that astounding ancient structure that looks like a bunch of women are holding up a building. Our man in Europe, Frank Schuster, spoke five languages fluently, and he joined us in Athens for the remainder of our trip. Our Olympic Airlines flight apparently didn't fly high enough, so we were the victims of horrible turbulence. Shortly after we were served dinner, we heard a ghastly noise—the bending of the wings as we dropped I don't-know-how many feet! Our dinner trays ended up on the ceiling, and a butter patty ended up in Frank's ear!

In Italy, I borrowed our rented car and, as the only woman on the road, drove twenty-five kilometers to Pompeii, where I lost all track of the time and sauntered through the remains of ordinary homes thousands of years old. However, on the way back it was dark and raining, and the many round-abouts in the road got me totally confused. No one spoke any English or knew a simple way to our hotel. It took me two hours to make it back, and I totally missed the cocktail party being given in our honor.

In Rome, I visited the Coliseum and the Vatican and threw a coin in the Trevi fountain, which they assured me guaranteed that I would return. (P.S. It worked!)

In Madrid, Spain, we brushed elbows at our Castellena Hilton with film actress Rita Hayworth. Then, we dined the next morning across from John Wayne and his wife, Pilar. We visited a restaurant that was formerly a cave and were serenaded by five "wandering troubadours," who were dressed in black capes and toreador hats, and they were accompanied by guitars and mandolins.

In Frankfurt, Germany, while eating breakfast with our business associate, Former U-Boat Commander Helmut Mohr, he proclaimed, "Ya, if ve had had breakfasts like dese, ve vould have von de var!" So, in both Japan and Germany we had hobnobbed with our former enemies, both of which proved the futility and stupidity of war!

Paris, France, our biggest thrill was when I took a sightseeing tour to the Louvre. I was overwhelmed by seeing the Venus de Milo, Winged Victory of Samothrace, and even the Mona Lisa back from her visit to America. I became so absorbed that the tour bus left without me. I talked my way onto another bus (I suspect from a different company) and made it to Notre Dame Cathedral after all, catching up there with my original bus. My next memorable experience was attending an Yves St. Laurent fashion show that was narrated by the master designer. The show featured the Robin Hood look and the kind of tall boots that are only today becoming common. As for the rest of our trip, let's just say that we had a fantastic drive through Europe with multi-lingual Frank Schuster at the wheel of our rented car.

During our trip, at every stop, Dick began laying the foundation for the Household Goods Forwarders of America. (In 2009, he would be honored as being the founder of that organization, now known as the International Association of Movers.)

When we returned home to California, I wondered if I should feel guilty about being away from our three children for so long. I need not have troubled myself. Carolyn will never forget the glorious time she had with my mother. She tells me that this was the time her Nana taught her what it means to be a lady.

As for the boys, they both maintained that *this* was the time when they acquired their work ethic—under Papasan's excellent tutelage. In Los Altos, there were horses to ride, power tools to use, Mamasan's fabulous cooking to consume, and a creek in which to wade. Kevin adjusted well to his first days in the first grade, while nine-year-old Brian successfully completed a business arrangement with Mr. de Martini's Fruit and Vegetable Stand. Wading out in Adobe Creek in Papasan's hip-length boots, he gathered baskets full of watercress, which he cleaned, bunched, and sold to Mr. de Martini—Brian's first experience with entrepreneurship.

The first two months we were gone, everything went just fine for our Laddy-dog, but when that family moved out and the realtor procured another tenant for our place, our poor canine became disoriented and began roaming the neighborhood, looking for either us or his new masters. Laddy, therefore, had to be put in a kennel for two weeks. When we learned that new tenants had taken over, we were worried about our dog, plus the difficulty of pinning down responsibility for our property in case anything was damaged. We need not have fretted. The new resident of 1604 Paseo del Mar was head of the School Board and a fine gentleman. We returned to a clean house that even had new sheets upon the beds, and Laddy was overjoyed when we were finally all back home together again.

I am so grateful that I had my around-the-world-experience, making me realize how different the world's people are, although, in many ways, so similar. It suited me just fine that in 1963 so many of those countries still remained un-Americanized, with nary a McDonald's in sight.

48 Christmas-Caroling a Murderer?

When we returned home from our around-the-world journey, there was an urgent phone message waiting for me from my
girlhood friend, Maxine Lazlo. Years before, while in the seventh
grade, the two of us had gone Christmas caroling in Beverly Hills,
where we sang Christmas songs at the home of Jack Benny, then
proceeded to the home of the silent screen star Mary Miles Minter.
After we had finished singing, Mary turned to me and said warmly,
"Oh, with your blue eyes and long brown curls, you remind me so
of *my daughter*. Will you please sing that song again?" And so, we
again sang "Silent Night."

Fast-forward some twenty-six years to the day when Maxine
read in the paper that they were probating the huge estate of Mary
Miles Minter. The lady owned scads of property in exclusive areas, but had died without a will. A woman had come forward who
claimed that Mary had secretly gone to Europe to have a baby and
that *she* was her illegitimate daughter! According to the newspaper,
the claim was being dismissed because "everyone knows that Mary
Miles Minter had no children!"—everyone, that is except Maxine
and me, for judging from her "true confession" to the two of us, she
did indeed have a daughter!

My friend, Maxine, had contacted me to back up her story, but I was away on our trip. She went to court anyway, but all to no avail. She was one sole lady with no proof, no one to corroborate her story, and all that in 1963 before the science of DNA could have reinforced her claim. Unfortunately, by the time I returned from our long trip, the Mary Miles Minter estate had already been probated, and it was way too late!

Another little postscript to that tale: in a very famous Hollywood scandal, William Desmond Taylor, who was Mary's director from the time she was seventeen, had long ago been murdered. The man was said to have switched his affections from Mary to actress Mabel Normand. The police had interviewed Mary, but concluded that she was devastated by his death and not his murderer. Many felt that it was Mary' *mother* who had done the deed, although the crime is considered "unsolved" even to this day.

A few years ago, I read in the *National Inquirer* (a reliable source of information if there ever was one) that on her deathbed, Mary had confessed to her housekeeper that *she* was actually the one who had murdered Taylor! Could it possibly be that Taylor had fathered her child and then cheated on her, and could that have led to her shooting him in the back? If that was true, lucky us, for Maxine and I had gone Christmas caroling to the home of a murderer!

49　Suburbia and The Sixties

In Palos Verdes, I gave piano lessons, eventually working up to nineteen students. I also did all the typical suburban mother things, such as attending Little League games when our boys were players and their father was a coach, as well as helping out in Carolyn's Brownie troop. However, I had to resign as a Cub Scout Den Mother after their craft meetings kept giving me migraine headaches. The moment of truth came when one little Cub Scout appraised my pathetic effort at modeling a turtle and not at all tactfully asked me, "Is that *your* turtle?!"

I always played the piano for the monthly birthday party that our Junior Women's Club gave for the young women at Las Palmas School for Girls, Los Angeles County's juvenile detention home. One time, we found the piano locked. That was no problem; one of the girls used a bobby pin to open the piano!

Our pets became increasingly important to us. Our dog, Laddy, was never confined to a fenced yard, but yet he never left our yard. One day when Laddy was out on our front lawn chewing on a particularly large, juicy soup-bone, the police called at our door. With drawn arms, they inquired if we thought that was a *human* bone our dog was chewing on!

Another animal we all dearly loved was our pet white rat, Hubert. He lived in a cage, but would often journey across the floor to visit us. Unfortunately, Hubert eventually developed a large tumor, which the vet said would cost us $30 to remove. We decided that our Hubert was truly a member of the family, so we gave Brian the $30 for Hubert's operation.

As Brian sat at the vet's with Hubert in a small cage on his lap, the lady with a pet cat next to him inquired incredulously, "Is that a *rat?*"

Brian responded, "Is that a *cat?*"

When he was nine years old, Kevin developed a lively business for himself. He wrote the manufacturers of STP gasoline additive and requested they send him decals of the product. His requests, in his childish scrawl, produced an endless free supply of such stickers, and they were in demand among his friends. Kevin did not sell most of the stickers himself; he just set up a distribution system among his friends and made quite a bit of money by his standards of the moment. So he was then taking after his older brother by being a natural-born entrepreneur. Not surprisingly, Kevin would before long become an Eagle Scout, with all kinds of badges to his credit.

In the eighth grade, Brian grew his hair long and at one point ran away from home. We began to suspect that he was living close by when we discovered his dirty clothes in our laundry hamper. Sure enough, he was living up the hill in our garage! (I wish I could have known that he would one day be Vice President of The Pasha Group, a transportation and logistics company!)

While he was on his "adventure," in a renewed bid for independence, Brian took a pair of pliers to his expensive braces, dealing what seemed to be a death blow to the teeth for which we'd expended many an hour and many a dollar. "That's the end of braces for Brian," we exclaimed. "He'll just have to suffer the consequences and live with crooked teeth!" But the joke turned out to be on us, for Brian's teeth ended up looking picture-perfect even without the braces!

Yes, we owned a television set—an impressive seven-inch black and white one that only showed programs a few hours a day, which were all live, of course, since the video recorder had not yet been invented. I was thrilled with the whole idea of television and sometimes contented myself staring at the Indian-head logo that appeared on the screen when no programs were scheduled. Who knew that by the mid-1950s television would steal away over half of the motion picture business!

I'm sometimes asked about any residual payments for my films when they were shown on television. Before August 1, 1948, (and long before anyone's home had a television set) U. S. movie producers, in their infinite wisdom (and with the aid of brilliant attorneys) had a standard provision in all freelance contracts calling for the actors to sign away all such television rights. It was only in 1948 that the Screen Actors Guild was able to stop that practice. By 1948, that ruling was way too late to help me any.

The 1960s were the time of the "flower children," psychedelic art, "free love," and an era when anyone over thirty was considered unworthy of paying attention to. In other words, the 1960s were a hideous time for raising teenagers, and we had three of them! Dick said that raising teenagers reminded him of his first days in combat, when he realized they were using live ammunition.

I'll never forget the day we drove Carolyn and two girlfriends to the Hollywood Bowl to see the very first Los Angeles performance by The Beatles. When a helicopter appeared overhead, they were sure it contained the illustrious four, and our car nearly exploded with the outbursts of three hysterical females!

Brian clearly couldn't wait to grow up, and so he signed up for "work experience" each year he was in high school, working at the Pat Simmons Golf Club Company. When he was seventeen, they made him the Night Foreman and gave him the key to the building. Brian was also the only one in the family who choked back his tears and had the strength to carry our poor ailing Laddy in to be euthanized when that inevitable day came.

With an entrepreneurial instinct like her brothers, Carolyn set up a successful jewelry-making business, though she could not be dissuaded from wearing makeup in the overdone style of Elizabeth Taylor in *Cleopatra*. (One time, she snuck out the window to attend a dance, even though the front door was readily available to her.) She also did lots of marionette shows for children's birthday parties and other events. She was another independent spirit.

The children's middle school was written up in *Time* magazine as a place where, on their way to school, children were accosted by drug-pushers! Kevin solved his situation by sticking closely to his Mormon buddies. I remember when I asked him why he no longer was associating with one of his old nursery school friends. Kevin just looked at me without answering. I eventually learned why, for apparently his friend was one of the "stoners" and eventually became a heroin addict, never recovering until his forties.

I think the only time my kids were reminded that their mother had ever had a Hollywood career was during their days at Palos Verdes High School when either the movies *David Copperfield* or

Les Misérables were shown in their classrooms, with the help of a 16mm projector. I found out years later that my Brian was too embarrassed to let the teacher or his classmates know that they were watching his *mother* up there on the movie screen!

Among the milestones of that time, we wondered if our country would ever recover from the three major assassinations that occurred in the 1960s. Shortly after our 1963 around-the-world tour, President John F. Kennedy ignored warnings for his safety and rode in an open convertible through Dallas, Texas, where he was cruelly gunned down. I stared in disbelief at our kitchen radio, when it was announced that he'd actually passed away! In 1968, Dr. Martin Luther King, Jr., speaking to an inspired crowd and appealing for civil rights, met a similar fate. Then, on the same day that John's brother, Senator Robert Kennedy, took up the torch of freedom as he announced the death of Dr. King, he was also assassinated in the kitchen of the Ambassador Hotel! No, none of us would ever be the same.

In a contrasting mood, I'll never forget the July 20, 1969, when we gathered our children in front of our television and watched astronauts land and Neil Armstrong take his first steps on the moon. Talk about tension—and our relief when they all safely returned to earth!

50 Grab-Bag

Since our kids were in school all day, I decided I wanted to do something useful with my life, so this was the time for my volunteer activities that were mainly concerned with substance abuse. In 1968, I became part of the Alcoholism Task Force of the California Council for Criminal Justice, where I had monthly meetings with people like judges and police chiefs, including Judge Leon Emerson of Downey, the first judge who ordered both alcoholics and drug users to attend A.A. and N.A. meetings. Judge Emerson arranged for me to tour the women's prison at Corona, where nearly every woman blamed her man for her troubles, and the men's prison at Chino, where I dined with an embezzler!

As part of our studies, the Los Angeles Police Department kept detailed records for two weeks of alcohol involvement in crimes and misdemeanors. Our 1970 report showed that 92.3 % of Los Angeles domestic disputes, 67.3% of traffic violations or accidents, 78.5% of all assaults with a deadly weapon, and 71.9% of all arrests were alcohol related!

Dick and I both attended the week-long School on Alcohol Studies at the University of Utah, and I was part of a group that began the very first women's shelter, Haven House in Pasadena. I later ended up as Chairman of the South Bay Drug Abuse Coalition, which started the area's first drug abuse clinic.

You are probably—and appropriately—suspicious of my interest in the field of alcoholism. No, it wasn't a sudden interest, and yes, I developed it the hard way—by being married to an alcoholic! My tee-totaling, apparently non-drinking Mormon husband—whom I dearly loved—was surprisingly a closet alcoholic! He was afflicted with what's known as a periodic form of alcoholism, evidenced mostly by binge drinking when he was away on trips.

For many years, thanks to my protective efforts, I was able to conceal that fact from the world, including my parents and my children. I figured what they didn't know wouldn't hurt them. Yet when she was twelve, Carolyn, who had just seen a movie on television about Martians taking over people's bodies, came upstairs, sobbing to me, "Daddy's turned into a monster!" His problems had spilled over to the inside of our home. I remember my desperation the time I wrote the following song, when my husband had gone to Japan on a trip with his business associates, whose frantic phone call informed me that he'd disappeared!

> *If I should lose you, if ever I should lose you,*
> *Forever I would wander 'till at last I brought you home to me.*
> *Roam the ocean wide, 'till you're by my side,*
> *For without you, life's a cold and angry sea!*

Fortunately, Dick's Japan disappearance was only temporary. Meanwhile, my life was filled with my children and my other activities. I became friends with Patricia Pratt, a gifted young composer, who was head of the music department at Palos Verdes High School, and we wrote a couple of songs together. Eventually, the two of us decided to collaborate in writing a musical for the school's

Summer Show, my job being to write the lyrics to her music. Since I was the Safety Chairman for the PTA, I felt obliged to remind Pat to fasten her safety belt, just before she drove away in her small British convertible. Just two days later, Pat had a horrible accident! Without her seatbelt on, her car overturned and threw her onto her head. She was in a coma for two weeks, and then passed away!

Peggy Pique, a beautiful sixteen-year-old, who was one of her adoring students, took her death particularly hard, stopped eating, and ended up with a supposed case of appendicitis. When she was operated on, she vomited and aspirated, resulting in pneumonia and *her* tragic death!

Just two days before her own death. Peggy had written of her beloved teacher, "She once told me of her definition of immortality. It's when you leave a piece of yourself in others and they will carry you on. I know she has given of herself so much and so generously and so humbly that there are few who have known her who do not possess her immortality in some way."

The youngsters in Pat Pratt's Madrigals class were so incredibly traumatized by those two deaths that they found it nearly impossible to practice for the coming *Messiah* joint concert with other schools. Not only that, their substitute teacher had a limited musical background. So, at the request of the high school's principal, I ended up being in the classroom along with the substitute teacher and directed the singing.

I really needed to do something to honor Pat and Peggy, so when the P.T.A. asked me to produce their 1965 summer show, I agreed to be the producer for Gilbert and Sullivan's *The Mikado*. I hired directors and musical directors, and my mother-in-law supplied us with Japanese kimonos. A Japanese friend created authentic choreography, complete with fans and parasols, and my Makeup Chairman was the woman who would become Joy Glenner, founder of the Alzheimer's Association.

Our production was dedicated to the two special people we'd lost. Below are the strangely prophetic lyrics to "Grab-Bag," a song I wrote to Pat Pratt's music and which her students loved singing

This world's a giant Grab-bag, full of booby prizes and a few million kicks.
It is a mystery package and a hidden time-bomb and a barrel of tricks.
Now if you see a lamp, go on, turn on the light.
And if you see a plum, go on and take a bite.
And if you see a wrong, you better make it right.
A little fight just rounds out the day!

My head is really spinning, each exciting inning of this whole crazy game.
As long as we are in it, every wasted minute is a terrible shame.
So pull out every single organ stop.
So move those dancing feet until you drop,
And then say, "Thanks. Old World, we're mighty, mighty glad we came!

At that time, I'm afraid that my own "grab-bag" was filled with a booby prize or two. My children and I will never forget the time the five of us were looking forward to attending Stanford's summer camp at Fallen Leaf Lake. After our station wagon was packed up with our gear, we sadly discovered that Dick was among the missing, so I had to break the unfortunate news that our trip was off!

However, seeing the expressions on their faces, I reconsidered and announced: "Guess what! We're going on a vacation after all!

Where would you like to go?" The vote was for Mexico, where none of us had ever been, so I grabbed a map, loaded up the kids in our huge station wagon, and off we went!

I'd heard that Tijuana was a rather unsavory place, so I studied the map and decided on the border town of Tecate. Little did I realize that the route to Tecate was a long, scary, almost deserted mountainous road! When we finally completed our treacherous journey and arrived in Tecate in our beautiful, powder-blue De Soto station wagon, the people surrounded our car, their faces full of wonder! Frankly, I was just scared to death, so I turned our car around and headed back to the good old USA.

The kids then voted for visiting Big Bear, and so we headed in that direction. It was getting late, so early on we located a campground. Most of the people were in trailers, but we just spread out our sleeping bags and hunkered down for the night. In the morning, we were so grateful that Big Bear had not lived up to its name, for the folks in the camp ground informed us that a large grizzly bear had recently been seen nearby. We all had an adventure we would never forget!

After the Stanford Camp affair, Dick continued to preside over our weekly family nights as if nothing had happened, but his problems only got worse, for alcoholism is above all a *progressive* illness.

Our Bishop became aware of Dick's problem and told me of a program for family members like me, but I assured him that I was okay without it. He later sent a fine woman named Priscilla to our home, and she dragged me to a meeting in downtown Los Angeles. Before long, Priscilla and I began an anonymous self-help group in our own area.

In the weekly meetings, in addition to learning more about the cunning disease of alcoholism, I learned to work on myself and my own responses. I learned not to let my pride make me cover up the truth and turn me into an *enabler*. I also learned to combine that with the healing power of forgiveness, for I had seen time and time again how toxic resentment could be to a person. Though the focus was not on trying to control another's behavior, at least any reduction in misplaced guilt or anxiety on my part could possibly reduce additional excuses for drinking on his part.

A while later, Carolyn wrote a letter to her father that motivated him to actively seek help and sobriety. Dick told me he figured that he became an alcoholic when he took his very *first* drink way back in Shanghai while waiting for my arrival. Because of his religious background, he didn't believe in drinking and felt much guilt about it, which I guess he tried to eliminate by more drinking. In her letter, Carolyn admonished him, "You say you can't help it. But how many meetings have you been to in your lifetime?" Carolyn's "intervention" worked. He returned to meetings and did recover, and my worst problems seemed to be behind me!

A Raft Called Lehi

In 1969, I took advantage of an opportunity to be the Assistant Director for a documentary movie, *A Raft Called Lehi,* which was the story of Captain DeVere Baker, who made five attempts and spent ten frustrating years before successfully sailing to Hawaii on a raft. I wrote a song score for the 35mm film, and in our den, I tried my hand at editing, synchronizing the music with the action. In July

1969, our full-length documentary, *A Raft Called Lehi,* was shown at a Hollywood theater, and the *Hollywood Reporter* commented on the special significance of the participation of the Southern California Mormon Choir with its "pleasant song score." My music and lyrics, with five songs recorded by the extraordinary Southern California Mormon Choir, included "North Wind, South Wind," "If I Should Lose You," plus the film's theme song:

> *Once a man built a raft he called "Lehi."*
> *In his dreams he sailed over the sea.*
> *But his plans all went wrong.*
> *Folks were sure before long*
> *He'd give up all his plans for his Lehi.*
>
> *Ten years passed. Then at last came the Lehi*
> *To a port that was far 'cross the sea.*
> *At the helm that last mile was a man with a smile*
> *Who'd had faith all that while in his Lehi.*
>
> *So hold on to your dreams. Build your Lehi.*
> *You may fail. But at least you should try.*
> *Sail away, sail away. All your dreams really may*
> *Finally come true some day on your Lehi . . . sail away!*

Unfortunately, I didn't just blissfully sail away, for I had new problems with which to deal. Our children had problems of their own, I believe caused by the discrepancy between the values they'd been taught and what was going on behind closed doors.

Dick was then the "concerned family member," and the two of us began attending a nearby meeting for the "relatives of addicts," the closest thing we could find to our actual needs as concerned parents. We were disappointed that we were the only *parents* attending the meetings. When our local paper decided to print the names of *juvenile* arrests, I just knew how devastated their parents must be. I looked up their names in the directory and phoned them, telling them that "a little bird told me" of their situation, and then I invited them to our local meeting. Responding to an anonymous caller inviting them to a corner of a very dark local church, those parents were so desperate that every one that I called attended the next meeting! Eventually, those very parents became the core of a new program for concerned family members. Happily, their children all recovered!

In 1971, I became a nearly full-time volunteer for that self-help family organization, which ultimately became international. I served on its telephone hotline, where I received many a frantic phone call from worried parents in the middle of the night. In addition, I was a volunteer with the probation department, where I gave several talks, encouraging them to refer people to area self-help programs, including programs for the family, since the local judges were unfamiliar with such local programs. One of my messages was that helping the family could help the offender, which struck them as a rather odd idea in that day before family therapy became common. My own dream of my husband's recovery had indeed come true, and I was reminded of the lyrics I'd written to end "If I Should Lose You."

And when I found you, and when at last I found you,
I'd make a vow that never would I let you far from me.
When at last I found you, wrapped my arms around you,
I would promise from then on to keep you near me,
Close enough for you to hear me
Whisper just how much you mean to me!
So always stay near to me!

Mr. Peacock displaying his feathers to, his plain-Jane wife.

51 New Beginnings

$\mathcal{D}$ick and I bought the Japanese-style home we'd wanted for a long time. It was located on Via Panorama in Palos Verdes Estates and overlooked the white water of the Pacific Ocean. Strolling peacocks, with their plaintive human-like cries, added considerably to its ambience, as did the authentic teahouse that was prominent in the backyard.

The front door was reached by crossing a bridge that spanned a pond full of multi-colored koi. Our swimming pool overlooked a fire pit and the white water of the ocean and had a Bouquet Canyon stone diving wall covered with dripping water. I kept reminding myself to be grateful for all that, considering some of the places we'd lived in the past.

Since our home was not fenced and on the side of a hill, nearby peacocks loved visiting us and truly

Proud Mr. Peacock, on his favorite tree-limb.

acted as if they owned the place. I often studied the antics of those peacock families and ended up writing the following song about one of the coy females:

The Peacock's Lady; (Song of the Peahen)

(The female peafowl is all gray except for a faint band of green around her neck.)

I'm a drab, gray-feathered bird; that's me.
Dumpy and plain, not much to see.
I just peck at my food and nibble at the grass
And pretend not to notice when I see him pass.
He---lp! I'm in love, but I don't want to show it.
He---lp! I'm in love, but I don't want him to know it!
So I peck at my food and nibble at the grass
And pretend not to notice when I see him pass!
When he spreads his tail and his feathers quiver,
Something inside me starts to shiver,
And my whole body turns to liver!
So I peck at my food and nibble at the grass
And pretend not to notice when he waves his . . . tail feathers!
Peacock, you are beautiful! Peacock, wild and beautiful!

Now some may say, "Poor peahen! An ugly bird is she!"
They can save their sympathy for someone else, for you see,
Someone very handsome is in love with me!
And to him . . .
I'm not a drab, plain, gray-feathered bird who only knows how to peck -
But a dainty, pearly-hued princess—
With a strand of emeralds round my neck!

Serendipity (finding something nice when you're not looking for it) once again came my way in 1974. We had hosted a large open house at our home in support of the new Torrance office for the National Council on Alcoholism. The next day, I received a phone call from a doctor who had attended. He was working with a very depressed teenager who had been orphaned at age ten. He told me she really needed a friend and asked me to visit her. When I did, I was shocked to realize I was visiting someone who had twice been a student in the Sunday School class I taught. Unfortunately, Liz concluded that it was her aunt and uncle who had put me up to that visit to get her more interested in the Mormon Church. It was hard for her to believe that was all just a coincidence, but that's exactly what it was—like so many in my life!

Eighteen-year-old Liz eventually became our foster daughter and joined our weekly family night meetings. By that time, Carolyn was back from a church mission to France and had left for Brigham Young University, and Brian was off working, so a spare bedroom was readily available to her. My husband also arranged for her to have a car so that she could attend college.

Kevin was still living at home and did a wonderful job of befriending that extremely depressed young girl. I recently found out that he'd told her, "Don't worry. We have plenty of love to go around!" Such compassion from a sixteen-year-old boy. Not surprisingly, Kevin would later serve three times as a Mormon Bishop, plus eventually become a Stake (Regional) President.

Liz' aunt and uncle offered to pay us as her foster parents, an offer that we declined. I believe it meant a lot to her that we wanted her for herself and not for any monetary reimbursement.

**Sons Brian and Kevin and daughter Carolyn
finally get that sister, Liz—front row.**

Liz' sad appearance was gradually replaced by a smile and she allowed us to hug her. Before long, she actually tried out for a play at Harbor College and, of all things, received the lead in *The Diary of Anne Frank!* Unaware of Liz' past emotional fragility, the director said he was uninterested in a person's resume; he just wanted to hear them read the part! Her role was demanding, to say the least, for the director had her recite all the letters from Anne Frank's diary from *memory* during a series of blackouts, while she changed costumes on stage as needed, all the while keeping the dates straight. I'm happy to report that she did a wonderful job. Richard Boleslawski would have been proud of her, for she undoubtedly drew on the experiences and emotions of her own sad childhood. Of course, I was delighted to have another daughter to love, and Carolyn was thrilled to have that younger sister she'd always wanted.

One gift that Liz was able to give me was my precious cock-a-poo puppy, Muffin. She was a stray that one of Liz' boyfriends presented to her. Of course, you can guess who ended up feeding her and to whom she gave her loyalty.

52 My Heritage

In 1962, my father's recurring backaches drove him to the doctor, where it was determined that he had a serious abdominal aneurism, which is a ballooning of the main artery. The operation to repair such a defect involved opening up the chest and replacing part of the aorta with a piece of Dacron. The procedure was brand new and highly dangerous. My father consulted with his nephew, Dr. John Dixon, seeking his advice. My cousin said, "Uncle Bob, I'd have the operation all right, but only with the best and most experienced doctor I could find! I recommend Dr. Denton Cooley in Houston, Texas."

My parents decided to take his advice, which necessitated the three of us flying to Houston. My father was convinced that he would not survive the operation, but said he'd be content no matter how it turned out. To his great surprise, he pulled through just fine, giving him ten additional years of life! (Incidentally, his doctor was the same Dr. Cooley who became US Vice President Dick Cheney's personal physician forty-seven years later.)

Once I was out of the nest, my mother was free to pursue some of her own interests. She took up tailoring and hat-making, (more formally known as millinery), enjoyed a weekly game of bridge, and was an occasional model in fashion shows. She also became quite a skilled interior decorator, helping her friends with their homes. She refused to take any money for her efforts; my mother just liked to make people happy. I was so pleased that she was at last interested in her own projects, instead if focusing all of her attention on her one-and-only child. No matter what, my mother always managed to remain cheerful. With her giving, unselfish ways, I think she had discovered the secret of happiness.

My dear Mother—my true collaborator on this book—and on my life.

Happiness is a little like a butterfly.
If you chase it and struggle to find it night and day,
That butterfly will only fly away!
Do you know how to find the Happiness Butterfly?
Well, there isn't a really correct way.
At least, there is not a direct way.
But if you keep your mind on other things,
Like helping folks in need and mending birds with broken wings,
One day, to your great surprise, you just may find,
Resting gently there upon your shoulder,
What else but that missing Butterfly!

After many years as an attorney, and later as a Judge in Vallejo, California, my father decided to retire. My parents were always in fear of being a nuisance, so in 1967, they spoke of moving to Santa Monica, but I pleaded with them to move closer to Palos Verdes. They finally settled on a wonderful condominium complex in Torrance. Before moving there, so I would inherit items I'd really like, my mother sold all her beloved French provincial furniture and switched to Oriental modern, including many Chinese antiques.

My father served on the first Board of Directors for New Horizons, and both my parents were very happy there, especially since I was able to spend lots of time with them. In 1972, my father made his third trip to Houston for an aneurism operation by Dr. Cooley. That time, there had been too much damage to his arteries, so my dear Daddy did not pull through!

My father's casket ended up on the same airplane on which my mother and I traveled home. Shortly after we were airborne, an emergency occurred such as you never expect to happen. Our plane

My mother, in her new Oriental style living room.

I admit it—I was Daddy's girl.

lost pressure, and those famous oxygen masks automatically lowered into place! The pilot told us not to be concerned if it looked like the wings were on fire. Our plane had a full load of high-octane fuel on board, and our pilot had to ditch most of it over the ocean—and yes, it did indeed look like the wings were on fire!

I was busy helping my mother use the face-mask, as well as

instructing her how to hold a pillow over her face. It was pretty clear to me that a crash landing was scheduled for us, but I tried to reassure her as best I could. We finally—and surprisingly—did land successfully and were transferred to another plane, but I believe my mother suffered a small heart attack during the scary part of our trip home!

True to form, my mother was a trouper during my daddy's memorial service. A childhood friend of my father, James Blaine, gave the eulogy, so that was a real treat. He recalled how my father included Blacks among his clients in a day when his fellow white attorneys excluded them. He also reminisced about some of the amusing times in my father's life, such as when, as a youngster, he charged admission for a rabbit slide he'd rigged up, similar to the horse-slides he'd seen at the county fair.

He also recalled the time when Daddy procured a bunch of stadium cushions that he rented to people, with a request that they return them when the game was over, but at the end of the game, the entire crowd had great sport repeatedly tossing those pillows high in the air to an unfortunate fate, which destroyed any profits for my father!

My parents' marriage had begun when my father proposed to my mother by having a dozen roses delivered to her with a fine diamond engagement ring on one of the stems. I could only be grateful that for the more than fifty years during which my mother and father had had such a beautiful relationship and that they had been my loving parents. The day of my Daddy's funeral my mother was forcing a smile as she walked across the bridge in our back yard—and, indeed, walked to a new life.

My mother soon broke her hip, then developed a case of Parkinson's disease, and sadly ended up in a wheelchair, but a wonderful black woman named Irene Strong was sent her way. She stayed in my mother's condo with her full-time, and my mother said she felt as if she was her sister. Irene promised to stay with my mother, Bretta McKenzie Knowlden, all her days.

The Mayflower Society

One day, my mother received some genealogy information from her cousin Helen Jackson. The material talked about two brothers, but we couldn't figure out which of the two was our ancestor, so we laid the papers aside. It was only many years later that my daughter, Carolyn, and I would make sense of the material. After considerable effort and research by Carolyn, we figured out that those two brothers, Samuel and Edward Fuller, plus Edward's wife and son, were actually all passengers aboard the Mayflower, which arrived in Plymouth in 1620. Since cousins down the line intermarried, we were actually descended from *both* brothers. So my ancestors were not only Mormon pioneers, they were also Pilgrim pioneers!

Dr. Samuel Fuller was the physician aboard the Mayflower who assisted the Pilgrims during the horrible epidemics of 1629 and 1633. He was an organizer of the small band of Pilgrims that fled from England to Leyden, Holland, in 1609, and then later sailed to America. He was also an original signer of the Mayflower Compact, America's very first constitution. A church deacon in both Holland and Plymouth, my ancestor may very well have given the prayer at the first Thanksgiving.

His third wife, Bridget Lee, also our ancestor, sailed with her little son, Samuel, to America in 1623 on the *Anne.* When her husband passed away during the smallpox epidemic of 1633, the town of Rehoboth requested that she dwell among them and be their midwife. Also at that time, she started a small private school that was probably the *very first school* in America. Bridget Lee Fuller was one of the few educated females in America and arrived in this country only thirteen years after the arrival of the Mayflower. I would say that, for the seventeenth century, that ancestor of mine was certainly one independent woman.

A product of the nineteenth century, my great-grandmother, Elizabeth Wood, was also one independent woman, serving as an Indian language interpreter for the US Government, as her father, Gideon Durphy Wood, the first Mayor of Springville, Utah, had adopted two little Indian boys who had taught my great-grandmother their language.

With considerable effort, Carolyn and I obtained proof of birth, marriage, and death dates for the ten generations following Dr. Fuller, proving our connection to him and his wife, Bridget Lee, and even correcting a bit of the historical record with the fastidiously precise Mayflower Society. However, I'm sorry to say that the Mayflower Society Certificate arrived too late for my mother to see during her lifetime. My schoolteacher mother, who had always longed for more of a connection to her family, would have been so proud!

53 Lots of Surprises

In 1971, Dick was flying to Hawaii on a business trip and invited me to go along. It was only when we were airborne that he revealed that this was not really a business trip after all. It was a trip to celebrate our twenty-five years of being married. What a thrill for me.

We flew to the island of Kauai, where we stayed in the same cabin-on-the-beach that Liz and Richard Burton had stayed in some years before. A special feature of the room was its washbasin adorned with hand-painted flowers. Our almost private beach was the same one where *South Pacific* had been filmed, and our dining room was adjacent to the ocean-view, top-of-the-world veranda where Mitzi Gaynor had sung "Cockeyed Optimist" in that film.

Even though Dick headed up five corporations, during the next few years I felt a sense of his uneasiness. He had to have the very snazziest car to drive, and he made quite a few unsuccessful efforts to purchase a steamship line. He did join with three other men and purchased a small airline, McCulloch International Airlines, which owned luxury airplanes used by rock stars. The planes were complete with king-size beds, piano bars, and even an occasional "fireplace." To my great distress, purchasing the airline required us to place all of our assets on the line. Fortunately, we eventually managed to sell the airline without any monetary loss, to my great relief.

Then in 1976, Dick made another business trip to Hawaii, but without me. However the reservationists did seat him next to an attractive single woman from Chicago, who was nineteen years his junior. You've guessed the next chapter in the scenario: Dick had numerous trips to Chicago from then on, and our marriage was clearly crumbling. Finally, after thirty years of marriage and three biological children, none of whom lived at home, Dick broke the sad news to me. Since I was still crazy about the guy, it was indeed sad news. My first response was to suggest marital counseling. Then after Dick had moved out of our lovely home, my second response was to enroll fulltime at California State University at Dominguez Hills.

Unfortunately, the conflicts that the dilemma of "the other woman" presented to Dick drove him back to the periodic form of alcoholism from which he'd recovered ten years earlier. Consequently, our marital counseling sessions were rather a joke, and not a particularly funny one.

I had received plenty of help for myself from attending family meetings. However, it had been Carolyn's heart-felt letter to her father many years earlier that was the intervention he needed to drive him back to his own meetings and previous recovery.

I decided to bide my time, and so I spent the next three years in college, taking every music class I could get my hands on, including, of course that important counterpoint class, where you learn to pit one melody against another. By then, Mills College's famous composer, Darius Milhaud, had passed away, but my private composition class from Marshall Bialosky, a talented published composer, was the next best thing.

When fate steps in and hands you a lemon, don't just stand there dismayed.
When life plays tricks and hands you a lemon, better make some lemonade!
We try so hard to write our own story, but we don't have the final say.
Just when our script calls for endless glory, things turn out another way!

When fate steps in and hands you a lemon, there's a choice to be made.
So now that life has tossed you a lemon,
Measure the sugar and squeeze that lemon.
Maybe it's time to make some lemonade!

After having completed a church mission in France, Carolyn graduated from Brigham Young University. Finished with student teaching, she then went to work for Western Airlines. Liz was really upset about all the family problems, and the next thing I knew, she had eloped to Las Vegas. Brian had graduated from Trucking School and was busy driving his refrigerated semi-truck on icy roads back East. He phoned me almost daily, which was great because I really needed his support, for I was by myself, with only my little dog, Muffin, to keep me company.

Muffin.

There I was, alone in our beautiful home, with its beamed ceiling, sliding walls, authentic Japanese teahouse, and spectacular view of the ocean, but I would have gladly traded it all for that little one-room cabin in Nanking, or the $95 home with the apricots we'd lived in long ago.

Our teahouse.

I wrote this song in 1977:

How could I have known
His favorite chair would look so bare,
Its vacant stare reminding me its occupant had flown!
How could I know how slowly each silent hour goes by
When someone you have loved has said goodbye,
Or that I'd have this empty feeling now that we're apart!
I would have listened closer with my heart if I'd only known.
When the lights are dim,
Late at night across the room,
I see his chair, and I could swear that I am seeing him!
Sometimes until dawn, I lie in bed,
Imagining each little thing I love about that someone who is gone.
How could I know
I'd miss him so.

I never knew I'd feel this way.
And I wouldn't be alone today,
If I'd only known!

Right in the midst of all my marital problems, the Mormon Church called Kevin on a two-year mission to Bolivia. He had been preparing for his mission for many years, and gave a beautiful talk at his missionary farewell. Dick showed up for the ceremony at the back of the chapel, but he had been drinking, and it was all very sad.

Dick's abuse of alcohol led to many crises, including an urgent trip to Harbor General Hospital, following a bout that nearly killed him. I finally realized that my husband's solution to his dilemma was to drink himself into oblivion. After years of biding my time and keeping busy with my studies, *my* eventual decision was to file for divorce.

Like thousands of similar family members before me, I had been busy for years concealing the truth about his drinking from the world, including both my children and my parents. Unfortunately, such protective behavior only turned me into an "enabler!" Suddenly, I had to explain everything to my mother, but she was wonderful and understood. Of course, my children had found out the truth a few years before.

To maintain harmony, I used our family attorney, and even though we didn't share a residence, Dick and I actually drove together to his office, but then the courts insisted we have separate attorneys. Soon, the adversarial approach prevailed, so that the attorneys ended up with most of the money.

54 Backstage Visits

There were a few bright spots in my life at that time. Some friends accompanied me to see Claudette Colbert perform on-stage in *The Four-Poster*. To the amazement of those friends, she permitted me to come backstage and visit her. She had never raised any children, and our *Imitation of Life* was almost the only time she had played a film mother, so I believe Miss Colbert felt a special kinship with me.

She wanted to know all about my life, and was relieved when I told her that I'd had a happy one. She was especially curious about my mother. "Oh, goody!" she said, when I told her that my mother, who was in her eighties, was still alive. Miss Colbert told me that she was living on the island of Barbados and that she was also happy. Fortunately, she got her wish to live to a ripe old age, for she was ninety-two when she finally passed on.

Another time, my concert-pianist friend, Leonard Pennario, who many consider to be "America's greatest pianist," was performing locally. A musician friend was with me, as I went to pay my respects after his fabulous concert. My friend almost fainted, as Leonard not only remembered me, but gave me a hug, along with the comment, "Oh. Marilyn, you were always so talented!"

In October 1976, I attended a performance of *A Matter of Gravity* starring Katharine Hepburn, who had since been named by the American Film Institute as its greatest actress. Having stepped in a hole in her garden and broken her ankle in three places, she had to perform in a wheelchair, but, of course, the show must go on. I wrote a note reminding her that I'd acted in three of her films, but I had a hard time convincing the Ahmanson Theater usher to deliver that note backstage to her. He assured me that it wouldn't do any good, but I told him in no uncertain terms "Just deliver it!" He was rather chagrined when he came back and told me and my friends that I should wait by the stage door following the conclusion of the play.

There were dozens of people waiting by that door, but when an assistant read from his clipboard, it was only my name that was mentioned. I'm sure everyone wondered who in the world I was, as I was ushered in to her private dressing room. She greeted me standing up, rather than in her wheelchair, and gave me a warm hug. Like Claudette Colbert, Miss Hepburn seemed anxious to reassure herself that my early acting experiences had not interfered with my future happiness.

That was a very special moment for me, revisiting a pleasant period of my childhood. Since at that time I was the only one who had ever played her daughter, I suspect it felt to her like a glimpse at her child who might have been.

55   The Show Must Go On!

When I took any kind of a tumble, my mother always taught me to "Pick yourself up; dust yourself off; and start all over again." As someone who was an only child, I did not look forward to being alone. I'd spent my adult life being a wife and mother, and I felt the rug pulled out from under me. After three years of biding my time, I decided that what I really needed was a whole new life, and I made up my mind to achieve that goal! Of course, to get myself to that point, I had to go through a whole heart-wrenching exercise in forgiveness.

Eventually I decided that the program "Parents Without Partners" might well be my answer. As required by their program, I attended three of the introductory PWP meetings, deliberately not having any expectations at all about anyone I would meet there, but just doing what was required. I then joined their program, paid my measly dues, and went to my first regular meeting, a Mexican dinner-dance held at someone's home. While there, I met a widower gentleman three years my senior, a tool-and-die maker named Eliseo. His wife had died of a heart attack, and I guess he felt as lonely as I did. We began dating, and I met his two children and five siblings. We eventually became engaged, and in 1978, we married, just three months after Dick had tied the knot. In other

The day of our wedding.

words, I did indeed find that new life, for I was following Davy Crockett's motto: "Be always sure you are right—then go ahead!"

Eliseo sold his home, and our beautiful home at Via Panorama was put on the market, but not before Eliseo and I had been married there with all of our families in attendance. His son, Rick, served as his Best Man, my daughter, Carolyn, served as my Maid of Honor, and my son, Brian, escorted me from the tea house over our backyard bridge into the ceremony, conducted by our Bishop.

I always thought our Via Panorama home would be a perfect place for a wedding, but I didn't dream that the wedding would be mine. When it was time to sell our home, I actually spoke to the peacocks and told them, "You were right all along. This really is *your* property!"

My new husband and I bought another Palos Verdes home that we planned to live in for five years and then sell. To take advantage of its ocean view, our new home was built above its garage. My wheel chair-bound mother wondered how she would ever visit us, but Eliseo chopped down a huge palm tree and painstakingly built a fifty-foot-long brick pathway up to the main floor. My mother, who was so happy I'd found Eliseo, said, "When I look at that brick pathway, it just means love to me!"

Sadly, after a few years, my mother's caretaker, Irene, lost her daughter and had to resign as a caretaker in order to take care of her own grandchildren. As a result, we moved my mother in with us, where she loved sitting in her wheelchair and looking out at the ocean and other scenery. In her eighty-ninth year, I used the video recorder my mother had given us as a wedding gift to make a half-hour-long video of my interview with that special lady. What a fabulous memory she had.

"For everything there is a season" was the inscription we had engraved on the brass plaque on my father's grave, and the truth of that phrase was brought home to me again in 1982. My mother developed a stroke and ended up in the hospital in a coma. It was at that time before her death in her ninetieth year that I did most of my grieving for her. However, I had to be grateful that she'd been my mother and that she'd had the unique experience of living through an era of the greatest contrasts of all times. She was born in kerosene lamp/horse-and-buggy days, was twenty-eight years old when American women received the right to vote, then lived to witness a man walk on the moon, as well as a world dominated by television and computers.

Although she was in a coma, I visited my mother every day and would talk to her, telling her how much I needed her. One day, I was amazed to hear her mumble "Mimi," her pet name for me. She did indeed wake from her coma for a few weeks, but then the inevitable happened, and I lost that dear person, though, of course, I never really lost her. She would always be with me!

Every night my mother a lullaby would sing.
Like a tiny sparrow, I'd cuddle 'neath her wing,
Feel all snug and safe, far from every harmful thing.
Time to go to sleep, so close your eyes.

Like a tiny bunny, I'd snuggle up to her,
Feel all warm and toasty, as if we both wore fur.
I was like a kitten whose mother makes her purr.
Time to go to sleep, so close your eyes.

Now it's time for sleep, only peaceful rest will do.
Like most any mother, I want what's best for you.
Soon it will be morning, and there'll be much to do.

I sing to you, my love.
Sleep and dream, my love.
Time to drift to sleep with tight-closed eyes.
No more time for mother's lullabies!

Kevin's darling family—with Jessica, Maureen,
Shelisa, Jason, and wife Dianne.

What fun seeing my grandchildren perform
on stage—perhaps taking after their grandmother!

56 Transitions

My daughter, Carolyn, gave a beautiful eulogy, with special written input from my ex-husband, as had been requested by my mother. My two sons served as pallbearers at their "Nana's" funeral. According to plan, we moved away from Palos Verdes and settled on a fine place we'd heard about, Fallbrook, California, where we bought six and a half acres that were filled with 300 avocado trees. Eliseo built us a wonderful home, and I became an avocado farmer's wife, even at times, garbed in overalls, turning on water spigots, clipping stems, and scattering fertilizer!

In search for that new life, I joined all kinds of organizations. I became a regular Direct Patient Care volunteer at Fallbrook Hospital, joined the Newcomers Club, the Angel Society, as well as a local exercise club. I wrote drama reviews for the local newspaper, accompanied weekly lessons for a local voice teacher, played the piano monthly for an Alzheimer's center, and eventually joined the Fallbrook Woman's Club, for whom I wrote many songs. I was a busy country housewife. My biggest treat was any time I could do overnight babysitting of my four grandchildren, who arrived one by one to Kevin and his wife Dianne.

Eliseo had actually been born in Italy, where his parents had gone on a trip "to the old country." Eliseo's grandfather had been taken care of in his older years by his daughter, but when the gentlemen died, in accordance with old-world customs, he left all his money to his *sons* and none to Stephanie, who had been taking care of him for years. Eliseo's father felt so bad about this that he turned over his entire inheritance to his sister! Out of gratitude, when Aunt Stephanie passed away, she left all her money to my husband and his five siblings.

So it was that in 1988, we traveled to Italy to collect everyone's inheritance. We returned to the home where Eliseo's father had been born, a three-story converted red barn that they told us they'd been remodeling "since the War," and we learned that the war they were talking about was World War I! Lydia went to the bank and brought home stacks of Lira that she divided among the family. Each person's share was about $1,600, but it was enough to pay for our airfare, plus most of our hotels and our railroad pass throughout fascinating Italy. Neither Dick nor I had ever had brothers or sisters, but Eliseo had five of them, and I truly enjoyed being part of this large Italian family.

57 New Opportunities and New Musicals

My daughter, Carolyn, worked for a while at a Congressman's office in Washington DC, then took a job at a computer store in Boston—one of the first of its kind. Since she sold far more computers than anyone else, and showed great leadership skills, they chose her to design, stock, and staff a new computer store. In a remarkable promotion, Carolyn succeeded in having the Governor of Massachusetts at the store's opening. With that achievement, she got written up in an *Apple* magazine, and soon the Apple Computer folks ended up hiring her. She loved being part of the Apple II and then the Macintosh Computer development and launch teams, and she was part of the group that developed the QuickTime technology for multimedia playback. Carolyn stayed with Apple for thirteen years until she decided to move closer to her parents and settled into the place she had purchased in Southern California.

One day, Carolyn told me that I had let too much get in the way of my writing, telling me, "Mother, you have too much talent to not write music any more." With a daughter's pride, she said, "You know you are depriving the world of your talents" With newfound resolve, in 1990, I contacted a Fallbrook resident, a former editor of the Palos Verdes News, and suggested that she write a script to which I could write the music and lyrics.

My friend responded, "You want to write music? Two ladies in Orange County wrote a musical version of *The Pied Piper of Hamelin*, but they lost the music. Would you like to write some music for their play? The Fallbrook Players would like to produce the show."

With permission from the Orange County ladies, I wrote new music, plus altered the lyrics as needed, and talented pianist Pat Stinton was signed on to perform the piano score I'd composed. The musical was indeed produced in the Mission Theatre, which was in the process of being converted from a movie theater into a setting for live performances. There were fifty youngsters in the cast, and a good time was had by all, particularly me.

The King's New Clothes

Buoyed up by the success of The Pied Piper of Hamelin, and since I'd always loved the story of The Emperor's New Clothes, I wrote a musical called *The King's New Clothes*, including fourteen original songs. In my version of the tale, the king has a family, whose four royal children are feeling neglected by their clothes-conscious parents:

> *What good are diamond rings and other fancy things*
> *Like clothes of every possible description,*
> *Without the thing I hesitate to mention:*
> *We sure could use a little more attention!*

The charlatans who promise to make the "invisible" clothes for the king are two wandering gypsies:

We're weaving, weaving, weaving,
For we have the king believing
That we'll soon turn out the finest clothing ever worn by man...
But nobody will dare
Point out it's just thin air
We're planning for the king to wear!

**Cast of *King's New Clothes*, including "Queen" Erin Crouch
and "King" Mike Shumaker.**

The King has a wife obsessed with shoes. I'm happy to report that my Queen in this production was Erin Crouch, who would later move to New York and appear on Broadway in *Forty-Second Street*, as well as become the Dance Captain for the 2007 motion picture, *The Producers*. In my show, she sang:

> *When I'm feeling kind of low and kind of down,*
> *My forehead wrinkling up into a frown,*
> *There's one activity I always choose:*
> *I just buy myself a brand new pair of shoes!*

After the King's humiliation as he marches in the Tri-Centennial Parade in his long red underwear, his children, together with some of the youngsters from the village, try to persuade him not to redecorate the palace, but rather to use his wealth for the benefit of the:

Children of the World

> *The Children of the World, they call to you.*
> *Their voices, although small, can be heard.*
> *As citizens of earth, they say to you,*
> *"Please remember the Children of the World!"*

> *Let's make a world where no child goes hungry,*
> *Where fish jump high as clear water flows,*
> *Where air is clean and fruit trees grow heavy,*
> *Where peace is all that anyone knows!*

> *We'd like to say a word to the leaders*
> *Of every nation, large or just small:*
> *Please take especial care of the children,*
> *Their moms and daddies too, help us all!*
> *Their young lives have just barely begun.*
> *With the Children of the World we are one.*
> *Can't you hear what the children say:*

"There just must be a better way!"
Help the world bring a bright new day!

Up to that time, I had written all my compositions painstakingly by hand, and how I longed for the day when I could finally have some of my songs professionally printed. Carolyn had previously introduced me to the world of computers, and then she invited me to attend the Mac Music Festival with her, held on a sound stage at Paramount Studios. Revisiting the studio where I'd made my very first movie, I felt like the aging actress of Andrew Lloyd Webber's *Sunset Boulevard,* when that lady herself returns to Paramount through that famous gate, spots the fake trees and painted scenes and feels "as if we never said goodbye."

I entered the world of computer music and would shortly buy my first MIDI keyboard. Soon after, Carolyn was able to take me to the National Association of Music Merchants convention, where the people were amazed that it was Carolyn's *mother* who was the potential customer. They even recorded my keyboard-playing as a sample to use on one of their instruments. I ended up procuring Finale, the high-tech software program, and at last, I fulfilled my dream of professional-looking printed sheet music.

They say to write about what you know, so not surprisingly, I next decided to write a musical about child actors in the Golden Age of Hollywood. With the help of my Macintosh computer, my computer guru Carolyn, and an inter-connected musical keyboard, I wrote a full-length show complete with seventeen original songs. Many of those lyrics have been scattered throughout this book.

I'm Gonna Get You in the Movies

The Fallbrook Players again agreed to produce my musical in the newly restored Mission Theatre. Most exciting of all, they hired two professionals to direct, costume, choreograph, set-design and light the production. I can't say enough about Randall Hickman and Douglas Davis, who have won numerous acting, directing, choreography and set design awards, including the National Youth Theater and Robbi. Today they own Vista's Broadway Theater—in 2008 and 2009 voted the Best Theater in San Diego County on ABC's A-list. Indeed, my show was in excellent hands.

All of the many children in the forty-five-member cast were scheduled to have both a singing and a speaking part. Teenage girls can perform believably as 1930's mothers, and there were plenty of parts for them.

The Fallbrook Players decided to give the show an old-fashioned type "Hollywood Premiere," complete with red carpet, gala buffet in the lobby, searchlights in the sky, and celebrity attendees. My husband and I, together with Broadway's John Schuck (Daddy Warbucks in *Annie*), and Robert Hays (star of *Airplane*) were driven to the theater in antique cars, while searchlights fanned the sky, letting everyone know that something exciting was about to take place! That was surely a glorious evening, one of the high points of my life!

The story for *I'm Gonna Get You in the Movies* involves a Midwestern young widow, mother of four, who gives money to a so-called agent, who promises her teenage daughter a Hollywood career. With considerable difficulty, the five of them arrive in Hollywood, only to learn that they've been scammed. However, they

Curtain calls for *I'm Gonna Get You in the Movies.*

do win the prize in an amateur hour, winning scholarships to a Hollywood professional school. The rest of the plot involves the successful career of the youngest girl in the family, who is *not* the one interested in acting and who only reluctantly signs a seven-year contract. At one point, she also is forced to wear some custom-made shoes that don't really fit her—an echo of my 1931 experience in *The Conquerors.*

The show was a success. Just as important, Randall Hickman and Douglas Davis really liked my music and asked me to write songs for Hickman's version of *Aladdin.* Indeed, I did create fifteen songs for that show, produced with a large cast at the Mission Theatre. I ended up composing music and lyrics for six of Randall Hickman's shows, including *Charlotte's Web* and *Pinocchio,* every one of which were produced with a full cast, sets, and costumes.

I repeatedly took a Choral Music Class from Palomar College, and when the college finally cancelled that class, a bunch of us decided we would not let our group die. We organized a non-profit corporate entity called the Fallbrook Chorale, for which I was the group's second President and continuing publicity chairman. Conductor Geoff Lutz agreed to have the Chorale perform my setting to the Eighth Psalm. Later, at his urging, I composed many original compositions that were performed by the Chorale: the music for Elizabeth Barrett Browning's sonnet, "How Do I Love Thee;" for Christmas, music and lyrics: "A Star Looked Down;" for Easter, "Beginnings;" and for an April Fool's Day concert, "April Surprise." Our Spring 2001 concert was entitled *Face of America* and featured my song for young people with that title: At the risk of overusing my song lyrics, here are my words to that song:

I saw the Face of America, and I found it included me.
I found my place in America. I can play a part in how things will be,
And I saw that the current Establishment were only kids not very long ago.
And I saw that the future Establishment will depend on
what we learn as we grow.

I saw college halls and shopping malls and singers at the Met;
Fire-fighters and news-writers and miles of Internet.
I saw country towns and circus clowns and marvelous inventions;
Saxophones and telephones and political conventions.
I like the pace of America; living here in a land that's free,
And in the broad space of America, there is room for all faces,
All ideas and races!
I saw the Face of America.
And I saw the quest for truth
Blended with the zest of youth

Plus a little bit of you – and you – and me!
And a sign of hope, a look of hope,
A broad smile of hope on the Face of America!

When 2001 brought us the horrible tragedy of 9/11, I wrote words and music for the following song; a special tribute that our Fallbrook Chorale sang at a Community Memorial:

Climbing Into the Fire

The day the twin towers came down in New York City town,
Hundreds were killed in an instant, then thousands later on,
And some their families would never be sure that they were really gone.
We can't forget all those who died that sad September day –
Police and emergency workers who refused to run away!
And yet it's our fire-fighters we especially admire.
Three-hundred-forty-three gave up their lives
When they climbed into the fire!

Hundreds of miles away, that same 2001 day,
More terror was taking control;
More heroes announcing, "Let's roll!"
And since that September day came,
Our country's never been the same!

With new respect for courage, we honor and admire
All those who push their fears aside and climb into the fire;
All those who push their fears aside
And seize the moment, cross the threshold,
Calm their fears and climb into the fire!

392 Little Girl in Big Pictures

No, none of my musicals or songs have ever been published. It seems like I've always been so absorbed with my next project that I never took the time to submit any to a publisher. Also, perhaps I needed that agent I got used to as a child in Hollywood! However, I think I'm about to change my ways, for vocalist-guitarist Robert Hardaway has just recorded my song, "Children of the World;" Matt and Jasmine Commerce will soon record it; and I'm about to publish this book.

58   On Stage

When Randall Hickman asked me to write songs for his version of *Alice in Wonderland,* he produced a flute and saxophone player and asked me to score the music for them, as well as the usual piano part, to be played by talented accompanist Pat Stinton. I wrote so many new songs that Randy and Doug had trouble learning them all, so at Randy's request, I sat and recorded the songs while both singing and playing the piano. I didn't like the fact that expert song-sters would be listening to my singing, but I made the recording anyway, never even bothering to play it back. What I didn't realize was that the recording would turn out to be my "audition" for a coming production.

At the end of one of the *Alice* performances, Randy said, "I have a part for you—a singing role in *One Hundred Years of Broadway.*"

"In a group?" I responded.

"No, a solo."

"One solo?" I asked.

"No, two solos!"

One Hundred Years of Broadway

I actually ended up singing three solos, even though my adult sing-ing had been pretty much confined to my singing alto with the

Fallbrook Chorale. Amazingly, after a fifty-year absence and at the age of sixty-nine, there I was, returning to the world of acting.

Dressed in a short black flapper dress, long pearls, headband, and feather boa, I found myself reclining on a grand piano at the side of the Mission Theatre, as I sang "Cabaret." I was joined by good-looking, thirty-two-year-old Randall Hickman, singing "Welkommen" from the same show. Then, as friends my age looked on enviously, he proceeded to lift me off the piano and carry me across the theater, as I dragged my feather boa across the laps of the audience! I also sang a solo on "Broadway Baby" and "Everything's Coming Up Roses," and indeed, for me, everything *was* coming up roses!

Randy chose the five women in the cast with an eye to spanning a wide spectrum of ages, from sixteen-year-old Erin Crouch (shortly to appear on Broadway in *Forty-Second Street*) to sixty-nine-year-old me. We were joined by three young men, Randy, his partner Doug Davis, and Sean Tamburrino (later on the star of Disney's Diamond Horseshoe in Tokyo). Particularly fun was the closing number, where, topped by gold derbies, our entire cast did the high-kicking closing number of *Chorus Line.*

My ex-husband, accompanied by his wife, attended opening night and amazed everyone by bounding up the stairs center stage and handing me a narrow glass vase full of carnations!

"Who was that?" Randy muttered incredulously.

"That was my Ex!" I said.

Randy replied—too loudly—"I bet he wishes you were still married!"

On opening night, the cast was as nervous as could be, every-

An advance performance at the Fallbrook Woman's Club—Marilyn singing "Cabaret," followed by Randall Hickman's "Welkommen."

Our cast for *100 Years of Broadway:* Randall Hickman, Jolinda Crocker, Douglas Davis, Sharon Hyma, and Sean Tamburrino. I'm just to the right of Erin Crouch, on the stool.

one except yours truly. With my acting genes and experience serving me well, I was as calm as a cucumber.

My Fair Lady

CAST Productions were about to stage *My Fair Lady* at the Mission Theatre. Having gotten out of my non-acting rut, I auditioned and got the part as Professor Higgins' mother, using the upper-class British accent I'd learned sixty-three years earlier at MGM for *David Copperfield* and hadn't used since. (Thank you, George Cukor!)

My seventieth birthday took place following one of the matinees, when the cast gave me a surprise party in the lobby. My daughter, Carolyn, presented me with videos of a dozen of my

Playing Mrs. Higging. center, in *My Fair Lady* **at Fallbrook's Mission Theatre.**

movies (all amazingly now available on DVD and VHS), plus a large framed collage of photos from my movies. Later, at an awards dinner, I received a nice acting award for my part in the show.

Vista's Moonlight Amphitheatre was also planning to produce *My Fair Lady*. With my fellow actors' encouragement, I screwed up my courage and tried out for that show. Again, the dialect coaching I'd received at age seven paid off, for I was once again cast as Professor Higgins' mother. In the audience were all my children, as well as my four grandchildren.

What a thrill, at the start of the second act, listening for a sound cue from the large orchestra before I walked on stage, all alone before 2,000 people, as a twenty-foot-high set sailed past my ear!

When Premiere Productions produced a second *Hundred Years of Broadway*, my senior-citizen friends were most impressed by the fact that I was able to instantly stand, after kneeling on the floor during a performance of a *Sweeney Todd* sequence. During a subse-

Playing Mrs. Higgins at the huge Moonlight Ampitheatre.

quent performance of *Hollywood's Greatest Hits,* since I was the only woman able to change costumes in one minute, I was the one on stage with five young men as they sang "I Only Have Eyes For You!"

Cinemagic

When Randy cast me as Dale Evans opposite young Greg Bailey as Roy Rogers in a song/dance duet on "Happy Trails to You," I'm afraid that nineteen-year-old Greg was anything but happy at being paired with a seventy-year old woman, even if I would be wearing cowboy boots and a large cowboy hat! But then Greg discovered that my strong alto would free him to take the high tenor lead. He later said to me, "Marilyn, I'll be happy to sing a duet with you any time!"

Arsenic and Old Lace

Some months later, talented director Randall Hickman pre-cast me as Aunt Abby in *Arsenic and Old Lace.* I checked with Randy

Seventy-year-old me, with my nineteen-year-old
singing-dancing partner, Greg Bailey.

before I began memorizing the part, for I wanted to be absolutely sure which aunt he wanted me to portray. "Aunt Abby. You know, the ditsy one," responded my director, and I began memorizing the very large part. Imagine my horror at an Awards Dinner, when a young man addressed my friend, Kate Hewitt, as "Aunt Abby!"

"What part did Randy ask you to learn?" I queried Kate.

"Why, Aunt Abby," she replied.

Houston, we had a real problem!

A scene from *Arsenic and Old Lace* at the Avo Theater, with Jim Fahnstock and Larry Parker joining Kate Hewitt as Aunt Martha and myself as Aunt Abby.

Our director told us we girls would have to "work it out somehow." However, we said, "Oh no, Randy. We have to have auditions!" And we did—as Randy sat on the concrete steps in the back alley behind the Mission Theatre. I was so relieved when I received the part because I'd already memorized most of the lines, though somewhat difficult to memorize because Aunt Abby tends to talk off the wall, rather than relating to the previous cues.

Randall Hickman himself portrayed cousin Teddy, and Douglas Davis played the romantic lead. I'll never forget the moment when Doug and his leading lady waltzed quickly by the table where I was sitting. Incredibly, his foot caught the leg of my chair and caused me to land straight down on my fanny, while the chair noisily cart-wheeled across the Avo Theatre stage!

The show must go on, so I exclaimed, "Oh, *deah*!" while still maintaining my Aunt Abby persona.

Doug helped me up, and then exited backstage, where Randy asked him, "What was that crash? What happened?"

Upon hearing the story, Randy exclaimed, "Well, is Marilyn all right?"

Doug responded, "Well, she's talking!"

Quilters

In the show *Quilters*, I felt like I was playing my own grandmother, when I played the role of a pioneer woman not unlike my grandmother, Sarah McKenzie—similarly-named Sarah McKendrie Bonham. Often that role is treated strictly as a speaking part, but I sang the alto part and also received two nice solos.

Randall Hickman as Scrooge, with Marilyn as a perennial Christmas Past.

Christmas Carol

In 1967, Randy cast me as the "Ghost of Christmas Past" in Premiere Productions' *A Christmas Carol.* I figured my ghost costume would be a somber gray, but, oh no! My costume, made by an expert seamstress, was long red velvet trimmed with white ostrich feathers. It was good that I loved doing the part, for I ended up doing the show for five different Christmases, and I ended up receiving a Best Character Actress award for two of those Christmases. Randy told me, "Don't worry, Marilyn. If you get too old, we can always prop you up!"

You Can't Take It With You, Fiddler on the Roof, and Oliver

As a "mature actress," I ended up appearing on stage in over twenty plays or musicals, including *You Can't Take It With You, Fiddler on the Roof,* and *Oliver!* I was an omnipresent judge in area talent shows, and newspaper reporter/producer Tom Morrow gave me the leading role in the radio drama, *Sorry, Wrong Number,* a juicy part previously portrayed by both Agnes Moorehead and Barbara Stanwyck.

My mother always taught me that when one door closes, another door may well open, and that is certainly what happened to me. The door to my latter-day composing, singing, and acting adventures opened wide only after the door to my first marriage had closed.

Indeed, for me there has been considerable life after Hollywood, not to mention after divorce! I've learned that you surely don't have to be in front of a Hollywood camera or on a Broadway stage to have a wonderful acting experience. While I may not have

**Carolyn and I admire my new star in the
courtyard of Fallbrook's Mission Theatre.**

At Brian and Terie's ranch, their wedding—on horseback!

a star on the Hollywood Walk of Fame, my dear children arranged for me to have a similar star in front of Fallbrook's Mission Theatre.

Carolyn is a consultant living in Newport Beach. Liz is one of the country's few female morticians. Brian is a Vice President of The Pasha Group, a transportation and logistics company.

Kevin, today one of Northrop Grumman's directors, is a fine exemplar of the Goates family motto: "The rougher it gets, the better we like it!" In 1968, he would leave Garden Grove to work in Redondo Beach, attend classes at USC in downtown Los Angeles, study, and then go home to his wife and two children. By the time he received his MBA, he miraculously was the father of four!

It's now been many years since I made my last motion picture, and nearly all the people I worked with are gone. Occasionally, I receive a small reminder that once upon a time a little girl named Marilyn Knowlden was "in the movies." Perhaps it will be one of the many items about me in the Ohio *Harrisburg Press* by movie-buff columnist Bill Baird, who claims he's President of my fan club. (He says that he fell in love with me—someone he's never met—when he was twelve years old.) Or perhaps something like my daughter's discovery that a "Marilyn Knowlden Doll" was available on eBay and our dismay when we learned that Carolyn and I were bidding against each other.

I can't forget being invited to a 2005 charity party in Beverly Hills that was hosted by Sharon Stone and *People* Magazine and attended by many previous Oscar nominees. That evening, it was certainly a thrill for me when I was one of "five special people" including Margaret O'Brien (who hugged me warmly) presented to the group by Sharon Stone. Later, I was introduced to the noted actor, James Woods, as "the child Cosette in the 1935 version of *Les Misérables*." I caught my breath when he said, "But I know you! In preparation for a part I'm about to do, I've been watching some of the classic movies, and just last night I saw you in *Les Misérables*!"

Incidentally, the invitation to that gala, red-carpet party came to me courtesy of the Mutti-Mewse twins of London, England. They became acquainted with my movies as young boys when they sat on either side of their blind grandmother and described to her the on-screen action, as she listened to classic films like *David Copperfield* and *Les Misérables*. They learned my name when they were forced to pay attention to the credits after she would ask them, "Whose voice is that?"

59 Slight Change of Plans

*A*t the end of 2005, I had a routine tooth-cleaning, without the aid of antibiotics, and that procedure changed all my plans. As a result of that tooth-cleaning, I awoke in the middle of the night with a 104° fever, and I ended up in the hospital for a full month.

Believe me, I have no recollection at all of that month in the hospital. I ended up with a severe case of blood poisoning, and the doctors actually didn't know whether I'd make it or not! The doctors explained to my family that two strains of streptococcus bacteria (Virens and Merrilee) had infected my body, attacking both my brain and spinal cord, and that they could not predict the outcome for me, or even say if I would survive! (As evidence of the effect of this sepsis condition on my brain, my son Kevin says that while I was in the hospital, I confided to him that I was pregnant!)

I had to be on round-the-clock intravenous injections of antibiotics for two months, necessitating my being moved to a care center for one of the months. Then, instead of my *ever* returning to our home, my stepson moved us into a retirement community, with nursing care available, where I was flat on my back in bed, or being pushed by Eliseo in a wheelchair. I couldn't even roll over in bed, and life did not look too promising.

I thought I would be the happiest person in the world if only I could walk, even using a walker. As for finishing my autobiography, that seemed largely out of the question, but I did not give up, and I decided to put first things first. With the aid of two therapists, I exercised while in bed, and then later, while hanging onto the sink, and after several months, I recovered the use of my legs. I'll never forget the déjà vu moment ("You can do it, Mother. You can do it!"), when Carolyn held out her arms to me—as I had to her, some fifty or so years before when she took her first baby steps—as I walked to her, then collapsed in her arms!

Miracles do happen, for I completely recovered. I did not need a wheelchair, a walker, or a cane. My recovery was no doubt assisted by the entire Fallbrook Chorale visiting my care center and giving me a private performance

As proof of my total recovery, I recently portrayed Mrs. Chauvenet in *Harvey* at the Avo Theater, and in 2009, I received a Best Character Actress award! Once again, I felt that special kinship that trapeze artists or soldiers on the battlefield must experience with their comrades. It meant so much to me to be able to do the part without ever forgetting my lines or tripping backstage. Happy day! As a woman in her eighties, I was back!

Rather symbolic of all this, my son, Brian, on a recent trip to New York, spotting the little girl logo of the musical, *Les Misérables,* with the caption "She's back!" dominating the heart of Times Square, found what seemed to him to be the face of his own *mother*—as an eight-year-old Little Cosette!

At a recent family reunion, I thoroughly enjoyed getting together with my children, grandchildren, and great-grandchildren. What else could replace the happiness these wonderful creatures have brought me!

The "Les Mis" poster, in the bright lights of Times Square. Brian sent it to me from his cell-phone, and we both agreed it was meant for me!

I'm sad to report that after nearly thirty-two years of marriage, my Eliseo finally passed away, from natural causes. Thirty-two years is a long time, and with him I had indeed received a "whole new life." He had brought me security, stability, and companionship, and I will miss him. Coming from a close Italian family, there were a large number of people at his funeral, but once again, I was reminded that "the show must go on!"

My link to the future—my children.

Grandchildren

And great-grandchildren!

The four of us at Boston's
Paul Revere monument.

Dick phoned me his con-
dolences. The thing that had
most devastated me about
our divorce was that I had so
looked forward in our old age
to chats with him about our
family, so it's good that we can
have friendly discussions.

I received a small taste of
Heaven in 2010, when my
three children invited me to
join them on a trip to Plymouth, Massachusetts, com-
memorating our Pilgrim ancestors.

"Mother, to celebrate the
heritage you've given us and to
discover it as never before, we
are giving you the gift of a trip
with all three of us to the Plimoth Plantation. We will travel
at a mutually convenient time
close to your birthday and
share the discovery together."

After our flight to Boston, we stayed together in a delightful
bed-and-breakfast in Plymouth. In the town we discovered a monument with huge statues portraying the principles on which our
country was founded.

The eighty-one-foot-tall Forefathers Monument, the largest granite monument in the U. S. The central figure, Faith, is thirty-five feet tall and weighs 180 tons. At left is Freedom (breaking chains); at right Morality. Education, and Law are also portrayed.

I had just discovered our ancestors' names on the Mayflower passenger list, plus a carved panel of the signing of America's first constitution, the Mayflower Compact—which both brothers signed.

In Plymouth, many of our childhood history lessons seemed to come to life before our eyes. We were thrilled to find the names of our ancestors, Dr. Samuel Fuller, his brother Edward Fuller and his son Samuel Fuller as part of the Forefathers Monument, dedicated by the Pilgrim Society in 1889.

The weather was gorgeous as we hiked around Plimoth Plantation's reproduction of an English village, ("Plimoth" is the original spelling.) its twenty-some houses filled with actors posing as pilgrims, taking on their names, appearance, viewpoints, and life histories. One thatched-roof home was a recreation of that of our own ancestor, Samuel Fuller, where the woman portraying his wife Bridget greeted us.

We then toured Mayflower II, an authentic reproduction of the original. A gift of England, it had sailed to Plymouth in 1957. Climbing down the stairs into the bowels of the ship, we were aghast at the living conditions that our pilgrim ancestors must have endured during those sixty-six days at sea.

Our guide explained to us about the ship and all about how the pilgrims had fled to

Holland. Then, 102 of them had boarded the ship for America, most of them for religious freedom, though, sadly, half of them did not survive that first winter.

When I finally asked our costumed guide his name, imagine our amazement when he replied, "Why I'm the Deacon—Deacon *Samuel Fuller!*"

Carolyn and I prepare to board the Mayflower II.

60   Return to Hollywood

There is one advantage to being a child movie actor that is not usually mentioned: if you take care of yourself, if the film you have a part in has extraordinary longevity, and if luck comes your way, you can perhaps have value in your old age as a "survivor" of one of those movies. That happened to me on January 22 of 2010, when I was invited to the Academy of Motion Picture Arts and Sciences for a private showing of their four-month-long exhibition of Posters of the Ten Best Picture Nominees of 1936-1943, for I was in two of those films.

To meet my daughter, I took the train to Irvine. Wouldn't you know it, the weather was full of wind and rain, and some called it "the worst storm in a century." But the show must go on! Arriving in Irvine, I found the electricity was off in the station elevator, so in the pouring rain, I had to walk up *four* flights, across the bridge, and then down *five* flights, while carrying my suitcase for the trip! (This was a far cry from my previous near-death condition, just four years earlier!) On the drive north, I thought that hailstones would surely break the windshield of Carolyn's car, but it was all worth it when we finally arrived at the Academy!

At the entrance to the basement garage, two attendants checked off our names on a clipboard and directed us to the fourth floor. When the elevator door opened, Marvin Paige, a man I'd never met before, announced, "Oh, Marilyn, you made it! Stay right there. There's someone dying to meet you!" Soon, author Miles Krueger appeared, hugging me and saying, "Oh, Marilyn, you're the reason I'm here tonight!" From his book *Show Boat*, he had two pictures of Alan Jones and me that he wanted me to autograph, along with a treasured copy of his comprehensive book on *Show Boat*, filled with dozens of signatures of actors from all the various productions. What a thrill I had, as I signed my name right next to that of Irene Dunne, who had played my mother in the movie version of *Show Boat* some seventy-five years previous!

Since ninety-three-year-old Olivia de Havilland was in Paris, I was the *only* one from *Anthony Adverse* available to be photographed with its 1936 poster. Ann Rutherford was there for *Gone With the Wind,* along with, for *Boys' Town,* champion "survivor" Mickey Rooney, with whom I'd filmed *The World Changes* and *Slave Ship.* When I was introduced to film star Marsha Hunt, she was amazed when I informed her that we'd appeared together in an obscure film called *Easy To Take.*

I learned that my "mystery man," Marvin Paige, was not only the mainstay Research Archivist for the Motion Picture Academy but also a noted casting director *(Star Trek,* etc.) Following a gorgeous buffet supper, how wonderful it was—after some seventy years— to meet and be photographed with fellow actors Cora Sue Collins and June Lockhart, next to an original 1940 poster of *All This and Heaven Too!* Cora Sue and I enjoyed chatting about our devoted mothers, both of whom we each remembered. I also received a hug from *Mash* Producer/Director Gene Reynolds, who, the last time I'd seen him, had been a teenage boy! Meeting friends

Casting Director Marvin Paige introducing two old friends to each other:
"Cora Sue Collins, meet Marilyn Knowlden!"

from a distant past— the whole evening was what I like to think arriving in Heaven will be like!

Having made my last movie in 1940, I had long ago resigned myself to being totally cut off from Hollywood. Then, that lovely invitation came to the Motion Picture Academy Poster Exhibit.

So how did I become reconnected with Hollywood after all those years? Mark Carlson, the blind son-in-law of a friend, asked if he could write an article about me, came to my home with his guide-dog and tape recorder and wrote an article which, when published, enabled the Motion Picture Academy's Marvin Paige to trace me. Once again opportunity knocked, and I answered the door. Once again in my life, one thing led to another!

A few months after the Poster Exhibition, there were more adventures: Marvin Paige phoned and invited me to the Cinecon Classic Movie Festival where, on Hollywood Boulevard, they would be screening *Easy To Take*, a film I made in 1936 when I was nine years old! Cinecon is an international Society of Cinephiles—ardent movie-lovers intent on resurrecting, restoring, and viewing silent or obscure movies, and *Easy To Take* certainly qualifies as one of those obscure movies. I was particularly looking forward to seeing it, since it had been seventy-four years since I'd seen the original, and it was the only film in which I got to sing.

Remarkably, the Cinecon Film Festival features the screening of silent, old, and often obscure movies, shown for five days from early morning to late at night. People attend from all over the United States, not to mention other countries. Friday, September 3, 2010, Grauman's nearly 700-seat Egyptian Theatre was almost full as *Easy To Take* was screened. I was pleasantly surprised by the fact that I not only got to sing an *entire* song, but also had a pretty nice little role to play that I hadn't quite remembered.

At the time of filming *Easy To Take*, Marsha Hunt was eighteen and I was nine. Following the movie, Marsha Hunt and I were given a standing ovation, as hand-in-hand, we walked down the aisle to the front of the theater! We were seated on tall stools, where for twenty-two minutes, Stan Taffel interviewed us—followed by questions from the audience.

"What was the name of your last film?" one man asked.

I replied, "*The Way of All Flesh.*"

Remarkably, he asked, "You mean with Gladys George and Akim Tamiroff?"

Ninety-two-year-old film star Marsha Hunt and eighty-four-year-old Marilyn Knowlden, following a screening of *Easy To Take*.

Yes, those Cinecon people are true Cinephiles (movie-buffs)! Sunday evening called for the formal Career Achievement Banquet in the Grand Ballroom of the Renaissance Hotel. Leaving our beautiful 19th floor hotel room, with its view of the city and the Hollywood sign, Carolyn and I headed for the cocktail party preceding the banquet.

As we entered, Bob Birchard, President of Cinecon, stopped

Holding my new Film Career Achievement Award from Cinecon.

me and said, "Now Marilyn, you'll be receiving an award tonight, but you'll have to return it to us so we can get it engraved!"

Big shock! (My Carolyn knew I was to receive a once-in-a-life-time Film Career Achievement Award, but had managed to keep it a secret from me. (She did pay particular attention to me looking my Hollywood best that night, but it certainly was a surprise!)

Nearly 200 movie-business folks were in attendance at the fancy Career Achievement Banquet, otherwise known as the Celebrity Banquet. On the raised dais at one end of the huge ballroom, Carolyn and I joined the two others receiving awards, actor-producer-director Don Murray and actor-dancer-director Bobby Scheerer, together with their presenters, actress Michele Lee and dancer-choreographer Miriam Nelson. On my right sat film star Marsha Hunt. During dinner, we chatted about our past lives and enjoyed spotting famous actors in the audience, such as Richard Chamberlain, Ann Jeffries, Joan Van Ark, and Ann Rutherford. I guess Marsha Hunt was plumbing me for additional information for, unbeknownst to me, she was also scheduled to be my Presenter!

Master of Ceremonies and film historian Stan Taffel mentioned the many classic films in which I'd appeared: "Marilyn Knowlden is the only person in the whole world who in the 1930s appeared in six films nominated by the Motion Picture Academy as Best Picture of the Year: *Imitation of Life, Little Women, David Copperfield, Les Misérables, Anthony Adverse,* and *All this and Heaven Too.*"

Marsha Hunt had lovely things to say about me. Said she was impressed with my depth, being an "actress, author, playwright, composer and lyricist." She particularly liked the fact that I'd written the words and music for ten musicals that were actually *pro-*

duced, including three for which I also wrote the script.

In my acceptance speech, I told how pleased my father would have been with my award, since his goal was for me to be in high-class films. I recalled how in making the film *Les Misérables,* whenever Director Richard Boleslawski was particularly happy with my work as Little Cosette, he would say, "Marilyn, that deserves a Big Black Cigar!" Then when the film was completed, he announced that it was time for me to receive my cigars and presented me with a long floral box filled with a dozen skewer-reinforced chocolate cigars with hand-painted cigar-bands. I told the banquet crowd of movie buffs and film industry folks, "Tonight I feel like I just received another box of Big Black Cigars!" And that is surely the way I felt!

Back home, just when I was pinching myself as to the year's good fortune, I learned that Turner Classic Movies wanted to schedule me for an on-screen interview! On November 3, 2010, I truly felt like "Queen For a Day," as a Lincoln limousine took me and my daughter on a three-hour ride to Century City.

After a half-hour spent on my makeup, I was interviewed on film for over an hour—and I do mean filmed, not videotaped —on expensive 35mm film. For me, the fourteenth floor of the Intercontinental Hotel felt like an old-time movie studio, complete with all kinds of microphones, lights, cameras, and technicians. I was told that film clips from the interview would be shown from time to time, in conjunction with relevant films shown on Turner Classic Movies. Marvin Paige also showed up in person to deliver my newly engraved Cinecon "Film Career Achievement Award." He informed me that my interview was considered "oral history" that would be archived at the Academy of Motion Picture Arts and Sciences. No one could take it out, but it could be viewed at the Academy. What a wonderful way to celebrate my "return to Hollywood!"

Then, there was soon another event making it indeed pleasant to be eighty-four years old: in January 2011, the seventy-fifth anniversary of the 1936 *Show Boat* was being celebrated at the Egyptian Theatre by American Cinematheque, and author Miles Kreuger and I had been invited to introduce it. I was only nine years old when I played Alan Jones and Irene Dunne's daughter, Kim, and I hadn't seen that film on a giant movie screen since 1936, so it was quite surreal, giving a ten-minute introduction of the movie to a large audience at a theater I'd often gone to as a child!

I thank God for the full life I've lived. I've been a busy little girl and an equally busy old woman, without brothers or sisters, but with the best family in the world. I've been a little poor and a little rich, a world traveler, and a stay-at-home mom. I've been surrounded by lights and cameras, and I've lived the life of an ordinary person. I've been healthy and very sick, extremely happy, and near despair!

As to wealth or lack of it, I prefer the middle ground, where the neighbors are friendlier. It's clear to me that fame and fortune are no substitute for family and successful relationships, although the creative process comes close. Certainly, there's nothing more desirable than good health, but losing it for a while keeps you grateful for whatever good health you have.

Concerning years on the calendar, I've discovered that each time of life has its advantages, even old age, for folks at my advanced age seem more willing to help each other, the competitiveness of the past being replaced by a certain kind of serenity.

I think I shall end this book the same way I ended my musical, *I'm Gonna Get You in the Movies*. The tiny star of that show announces, "Maybe instead of *being* in a movie—maybe we could just *go* to a movie!" followed by the entire cast singing:

Let's go to the Movies; see a Saturday matinee.
Let's go to the Movies.
Gee, I wonder what picture's playing
At our favorite theater down the way.
Let's go to the Movies; take me to the Movies!
Let's go to the Movies today!

Feature Films of Marilyn Knowlden 1931-1940

1931

Women Love Once
Studio: Paramount
(Director: Edward Goodman)
Played Janet Fields, as the 4 year daughter of Paul Lukas and Eleanor Boardman.

Cisco Kid
From unpublished story: *"The Silver City"*
Studio: Fox
(Director: Irving Cummings, also former director of silent version)
With Warner Baxter & Edmund Lowe. Played Annie, daughter of Nora Lane.

Husband's Holiday
Studio: Paramount
(Director: Robert Milton)
Played Anne, daughter of Vivian Osborne & Clive Brook.

Susan Lenox
Studio: MGM
(Director: Robert Z. Leonard)
With Clark Gable & Greta Garbo. who played Susan Lenox, as her Governess, taught Marilyn geography lessons. (Scene cut in later releases.)

Wicked
Studio: Fox
(Director: Allan Dwan)
With Elissa Landi, Victor McLaglen & Una Merkel. (In uncredited role.)

Once a Lady
Studio: Paramount
(Director: Guthrie McClintic)
With Ruth Chatterton, Ivor Novello and Jill Esmond

1932

The Conquerors
Studio: RKO
(Director: William A. Wellman)
(Producer: David O. Selznick)
Played young Frances, one of the twins and daughter of Richard Dix & Ann Harding.

Young Bride
aka: *Love Starved,* and also *Veneer*
Studio: RKO
(Director: William Seiter)
(Exec Producer: David O. Selznick)
With Helen Twelvetrees, Eric Linden & Arline Judge.

Call Her Savage
Studio: Fox
(Director: John Francis Dillon)
With Clara Bow & Thelma Todd. Played Clara Bow's mother, Ruth, as a young pioneer crossing the plains in a covered wagon. One of the few "talkies" that Clara Bow was in and her next to last film.)

Handle With Care
Studio: Fox
(Director: David Butler)
With James Dunn, Boots Mallory & El Brendel.

Life Begins
Studio: Warner Bros.
(Exec Producer: Darryl F. Zanuck)
With Loretta Young, Eric Linden & Aline MacManon.

1933

Best Of Enemies
Formerly: *Five Cents a Glass*
Studio: Fox
(Director & Screenplay: Rian James)
With Charles "Buddy" Rogers, Marian Nixon & Frank Morgan.

Humanity
aka: *The Road To Heaven*, and also *I Am Guilty of Love*
Studio: Fox
(Director: John Francis Dillon)
With Ralph Morgan & Boots Mallory.

The Mind Reader
Studio: 1st National Pictures/Warner Bros.
(Director: Roy Del Ruth)
With Warren William, Allen Jenkins & Constance Cummings.

Little Women
Studio: RKO
(Director: George Cukor)
(Original Music: Max Steiner)
1 Oscar Won: Best Writing, Adaptation
2 Oscar Nominations: Best Picture
        Also Best Director
With Katharine Hepburn, Frances Dee & Joan Bennett. Played one of King
    children and Amy's classmate, taught by Frances Dee.

Morning Glory
Studio: RKO
(Director: Lowell Sherman)
1 Oscar Won: Best Actress
With Katherine Hepburn & Douglas Fairbanks, Jr.
Played child actress in Prologue. (Entire Prologue, with Katharine Hepburn
    and Douglas Fairbanks, Jr., omitted in later release.)

The World Changes
Studio: 1st National Pictures/Warner Bros.
(Director: Mervin LeRoy)
With Mickey Rooney, Paul Muni, Aline MacMahon, Guy Kibbee, & Mary
    Astor. Played Selma, as a child. (uncredited)

My Bridge Experiences
aka: *Culbertson Featurettes*
Studio: RKO
With Ely Culbertson, bridge expert.

1934

As The Earth Turns
Studio: Warner Bros.
(Director: Alfred E. Green)
With Jean Muir, Donald Woods, Russell Hardie, David Durand, & Wally
    Albright. Played Esther and sweetheart of David Durand.

Imitation Of Life
Studio: Universal
(Director: John Stahl)
(Sound Director: Theodore Soderberg)
3 Oscar Nominations: Best Picture
    Also Best Asst Director, & Best Sound, Recording
2005 Award: Natl. Film Preservation Board
With Claudette Colbert, Warren William, & Rochelle Hudson. Played Jessie
    Pullman, at age 8, Claudette Colbert's daughter. (Baby Jane Quigley
    played Jessie as a baby, and Rochelle Hudson played her as an adult.)

1935

David Copperfield

aka: *The Personal History, Adventures, Experience, & Observation of David Copperfield the Younger*
Studio: MGM
(Director: George Cukor)
(Screenplay: Hugh Walpole)
3 Oscar Nominations: Best Picture
  Also Best Asst Director & Best Film Editing
With W. C. Fields, Freddie Bartholemew, Frank Lawton, Edna May Oliver, Basil Rathbone, Lionel Barrymore, Maureen O'Sullivan & Hugh Walpole. Played Agnes, daughter of Mr. Wickfield (Lewis Stone) who is the girl David eventually marries. Also played theme song on the piano.

Les Misérables

Studio: 20th Century Fox/United Artists
(Director: Richard Boleslawski)
(Producer: Darryl Zanuck)
(Original Music: Alfred Newman)
4 Oscar Nominations: Best Picture
Also Best Asst. Director, Best Cinematography & Best Film Editing
With Fredric March, Charles Laughton, Rochelle Hudson, John Carradine & Cedric Hardwicke. Played Little Cosette opposite Fredric March (Jean Valjean.) Screenwriter Hugh Walpole adapted script to an 8-year-old, rather than 13-year-old Cosette.

Pepper

aka: *Public Nuisance No. 1*
Studio: 20th Century Fox
With Irvin S. Cobb, Slim Summerville Dean Jagger & Jane Withers as Pepper Jolly.

Metropolitan

Studio: 20th Century Fox
(Director: Richard Boleslawski)
With Lawrence Tibbett, Virginia Bruce, Cesar Romero, Christian Rub, Walter Brennan & Alice Brady. Played little girl in tea room.

Condemned To Live
Studio: Invincible
(Director: Frank Strayer)
With Ralph Morgan. Played Maria, the Young Girl.

1936

A Woman Rebels
Formerly: *Portrait of a Rebel*
Studio: RKO
(Director: Mark Sandrich)
With Katherine Hepburn, Van Heflin, & Herbert Marshall, Played Katharine
Hepburn's daughter, Flora, age 9.

Easy To Take
aka: *Right in Your Lap*
Studio: Paramount
(Director: Glenn Tryon)
(Producer: Adolph Zukor)
With Marsha Hunt & Carl Sweitzer (aka Alfalfa)
Played Gwen Ferry, a "radio entertainer," and sang solo "Cross Patch."

Show Boat
Studio: Universal
(Director: James Whale)
1996 Award: Natl. Film Preservation Board
With Paul Robeson, Helen Morgan and played Irene Dunne & Alan Jones'
daughter Kim, as a child.

Anthony Adverse

Studio: Warner Bros.

(Director: Mervyn LeRoy & Michael Curtiz - uncredited)

4 Oscars Won: Best Actress in Supporting Role, Best Film Editing, Best Cinematography, Best Music & Score

3 Oscar Nominations: Best Picture.

Best Art Direction, Best Asst Director

With Fredric March, Olivia de Havilland Billy Mauch, Claude Rains, Akim Tamiroff & Scotty Beckett.Played Florence Udney, who would become Anthony's eventual bride.

Rainbow On The River

Later released as *Down In New Orleans*

Studio: RKO

(Director: Kurt Neumann)

With Charles Butterworth,, May Robson, Alan Mowbray, the Hall Johnson Choir & Louise Beavers. Played Lucille Layton, Bonita Hume's daughter, opposite Bobby Breen, and played the piano.

1937

Slave Ship

Studio: 20th Century Fox

(Director: Tay Garnett)

(Producer: Darryl F. Zanuck)

With Warner Baxter, Wallace Beery, Elizabeth Allan & Mickey Rooney, Played girl who christened the ship.

1938

Marie Antoinette
Studio: MGM
(Director: W.S. VanDyke II)
3 Oscar Nominations: Best Actress in Leading Role, Best Actor in Supporting
   Role, Best Art Direction & Best Music, Original Score
With Tyrone Power & Robert Morley and played Norma Shearer's daughter,
   Princess Thérèsè.

Angels With Dirty Faces
Studio: Warner Bros.
(Director: Michael Curtiz)
3 Oscar Nominations: Best Actor in Leading Role, Best Director & Best
   Writing, Original Story
With James Cagney, Pat O'Brien & Humphrey Bogart. Played Laury (Anne
   Sheridan later was the adult) as a child.

Barefoot Boy
Studio: Monogram
(Director: Karl Brown)
Played girlfriend of Jackie Moran, Julia Blaine.

Just Around The Corner
aka: *Lucky Penny*
Studio: 20th Century Fox
(Director: Irving Cummings)
With Shirley Temple, Joan Davis, Charles Farrell. Played Gwendolyn.

Men With Wings
Studio: Paramount
(Director: William A. Wellman)
With Fred MacMurray, Ray Milland & Louise Campbell. Played Patricia
   Falconer, age 18 (uncredited)

1939

Hidden Power

Studio: Columbia
(Director: Lew Collins)
(Producer: Larry Darmour - uncredited)
With Jack Holt, Dickie Moore. Played Imogene.

1940

All This And Heaven Too

Studio: Warner Bros.
(Director: Anatole Litvak)
3 Oscar Nominations: Best Picture
      Best Actress in Supporting Role & Best Cinematography/B&W
With Bette Davis and Charles Boyer. Played one of Bette's students, Marianna
    Van Horn.

Way Of All Flesh

Studio: Paramount
(Director: Louis King)
At age 14, played Julie Kriza, 19-year old daughter of Gladys George & Akim
    Tamiroff.

1942

Son of Fury

Studio: 20th Century Fox
(Director: John Cromwell)
With Tyrone Power, Gene Tierney & George Sanders. Played Isabel as a Girl in
    Prologue. (Prologue cut in later releases.)

1944

Broadway Rhythm
Studio: MGM
(Director: Roy Del Ruth)
With George Murphy, Lena Horne, Eddie "Rochester" Anderson, Tommy Dorsey & Gloria DeHaven. Played co-ed in drugstore (uncredited & cut from current release.)

Other Films Of Marilyn Knowlden

1932

Vitana Mix - Short Subject
Studio: Independent

1934

White King - 3 Short Subjects
Studio: E.B. Taylor
(Writer & Producer: Photoplay)
Played the official "White King Girl"

1939

An Evening With Edgar Guest
Studio: Jam Handy
Filmed in Detroit.

John Deere Short Subject
Studio: Independent

Snickerty-Nick And The Giant
Studio: Independent
(Writer & Producer: Julia Ellsworth Ford)
A pioneering color film.
Played Spring.

Goldilocks And The Three Bears
Studio: Independent
(Writer & Producer: Julia Ellsworth Ford)
A pioneering color film.
Played Goldilocks.

Queen of Hearts
Studio: Independent
(Writer & Producer: Julia Ellsworth Ford)
Played the queen.

I'll Tell The World
Studio: Independent
(Director: Lynn Shores)
With Billy & Bobby Mauch.
Shown at Liberty Hall Exhibit at N.Y. World's Fair.

Index

CPSIA information can be obtained at www.ICGtesting.com

264007BV00005B/5/P